AFRIKA-STUDIEN Nr. 47

Publication series "Afrika-Studien" edited by Ifo-Institut für Wirtschafts-forschung e. V., München, in connexion with

Prof. Dr. PETER VON BLANCKENBURG, Berlin
Prof. Dr. HEINRICH KRAUT, Dortmund
Prof. Dr. OTTO NEULOH, Saarbrücken
Prof. Dr. Dr. h. c. RUDOLF STUCKEN, Erlangen
Prof. Dr. HANS WILBRANDT, Göttingen
Prof. Dr. EMIL WOERMANN, Göttingen

Editors in Chief:

Dr. phil. WILHELM MARQUARDT, München
Afrika-Studienstelle im Ifo-Institut
Prof. Dr. HANS RUTHENBERG, Stuttgart-Hohenheim,
Institut für Ausländische Landwirtschaft

This volume is edited jointly with the
Economic Research Bureau, University College
Dar es Salaam

ECONOMIC RESEARCH BUREAU, UNIVERSITY COLLEGE
DAR ES SALAAM
IFO-INSTITUT FÜR WIRTSCHAFTSFORSCHUNG MÜNCHEN
AFRIKA-STUDIENSTELLE

Balance of Payments Problems
of a Developing Country:
Tanzania

by

M. J. H. YAFFEY

WELTFORUM VERLAG · MÜNCHEN
HUMANITIES PRESS INC. · NEW YORK

SPONSORED BY THE FRITZ THYSSEN-STIFTUNG, KÖLN

Review of Published and Forthcoming Studies within the African Research Programme

The entire research programme being conducted up to January 1970 by the African Studies Centre of the Ifo Institute – partly by the Centre itself, partly in conjunction with other institutes and researchers – covers the studies listed below (see also introductory remarks in vols. 1 and 2 of "Afrika-Studien").

For readers' information on changes, supplements, and forthcoming publications, each volume of "Afrika-Studien" will contain a review of the programme as a whole.

Vols. 1–18 have been issued by Springer Publishing House, Berlin–Heidelberg–New York, subsequent volumes by Weltforum Publishing House, Munich, in co-operation with publishing houses in the United Kingdom and the United States. The studies published as mimeographs (African Research Reports) can be obtained through the African Studies Centre of the Ifo Institute for Economic Research (early editions only); the more recent editions (from 1968 onwards) are available through the Weltforum Publishing House, Munich.

A chronological list of published and forthcoming studies is attached at the end of this book.

General Economic Studies

a) Tropical Africa

N. AHMAD / E. BECHER, Development Banks and Companies in Tropical Africa (printed as volume 1), in German

R. GÜSTEN / H. HELMSCHROTT, National Accounting Systems in Tropical Africa (printed as volume 3), in German

N. AHMAD / E. BECHER / E. HARDER, Economic Planning and Development Policy in Tropical Africa (mimeograph), in German

H.-G. GEIS, The Monetary and Banking Systems of the Countries of West Africa (printed as volume 20), in German

Africa-Vademecum (Basic Data on the Economic Structure and Development of Africa), prepared by F. BETZ (series Information and Documentation, vol. 1), in German, with additional headings in English and French

5

H. HARLANDER / D. MEZGER, Development Banks and Institutions in Africa (Series Information and Documentation, volume 2), in German

H. AMANN, Operational Concepts of the Infrastructure in the Economic Development Process (mimeograph), in German

K. ERDMANN, Development Aid to Africa – with Special Reference to the Countries of East Africa (mimeograph), in German

b) East Africa

L. SCHNITTGER, Taxation and Economic Development in East Africa (printed as volume 8), in German

R. GÜSTEN, Problems of Economic Growth and Planning: The Sudan Example (printed as volume 9), in English

P. v. MARLIN, The Impact of External Economic Relations on the Economic Development of East Africa (mimeograph), in English

R. VENTE, Planning Processes: The East African Case (printed as volume 52), in English

F. GOLL, Israeli Aid to Developing Countries with Special Reference to East Africa (mimeograph), in German

W. FISCHER, Problems of Land-Locked Countries: Uganda (printed as volume 41), in German

H. HIEBER, Economic Statistics in Developing Countries: The Example of Uganda (printed as volume 40), in German

G. HÜBNER, Importance, Volume, Forms and Development Possibilities of Private Saving in East Africa (mimeograph), in German

M. YAFFEY, Balance of Payments Problems in a Developing Country: Tanzania (printed as volume 47), in English

E.-J. PAUW, Money and Banking in East Africa (Kenya, Tanzania, Uganda) (printed as volume 35), in German

D. BALD, Administration and Economic Exploitation of German East Africa before 1914 (being printed as volume 54), in German

M. BOHNET / H. REICHELT, Applied Research in East Africa and Its Influence on Economic Development (in preparation), in English

P. v. MARLIN and Contributors, Financial Aspects of Development in East Africa (being printed as volume 53), in English

Agricultural Studies

a) Tropical Africa

H. KLEMM / P. v. MARLIN, The EEC Market Regulations for Agricultural Products and Their Implications for Developing Countries (mimeograph), in German

H. PÖSSINGER, Agricultural Development in Angola and Moçambique (printed as volume 31), in German

J. O. Müller, The Attitude of Various Tribes of the Republic of Togo, Especially the Ewe on the Plateau de Dayes, towards the Problem of Commissioned Cattle Herding by the Fulbe (Peulh) of West Africa (printed as volume 14 in German, mimeographed in French)

E.-S. El-Shagi, Reorganization of Land Use in Egypt (printed as volume 36), in German

H. Thorwart, Methods and Problems of Farm Management Surveys in Africa South of the Sahara (in preparation)

B. Mohr, Rice Cultivation in West Africa – A Presentation of the Economic and Geographical Differences of Cultivation Methods (printed as volume 44)

R. Bartha, Fodder Plants in the Sahel Zone of Africa (in German, English and French), (printed as volume 48)

b) East Africa

1. Basic Studies

H. Ruthenberg, Agricultural Development in Tanganyika (printed as volume 2), in English

H. Ruthenberg, African Agricultural Production Development Policy in Kenya 1952–1965 (printed as volume 10), in English

H. Dequin, Agricultural Development in Malawi (mimeograph), in English

H. Kraut/H.-D. Cremer (ed.), Investigations into Health and Nutrition in East Africa (printed as volume 42), in English

H. Blume, Autonomous Institutions in East African Agricultural Production (completed), in English

2. Studies Concerning Grassland Use and Husbandry in East Africa

H. Leippert, Botanical Investigations in the Masai Country/Tanzania (an Example from the Semi-Arid Areas of East Africa), (mimeograph), in German

H. Klemm, The Organization of Milk Markets in East Africa (mimeograph), in German

K. Meyn, Beef Production in East Africa with Special Reference to Semi-Arid Areas (completed), in English

H. Späth, Development Possibilities of the Pig and Poultry Industry in East Africa (in preparation)

Walter/Dennig, Comparative Investigations into the Efficiency of Utilizable Ruminants in Kenya (in preparation)

3. Studies in the Organization of Smallholder Farming in East Africa

D. v. ROTENHAN, Land Use and Animal Husbandry in Sukumaland/Tanzania (printed as volume 11), in German

H. PÖSSINGER, Investigations into the Productivity and Profitabilility of Smallholder Sisal in East Africa (printed as volume 13), in German

S. GROENEVELD, Problems of Agricultural Development in the Coastal Region of East Africa (printed as volume 19), in German

V. JANSSEN, Agrarian Patterns in Ethiopia and their Implications for Economic Growth (in preparation), in German

H. RUTHENBERG (ed.), Smallholder Farming and Smallholder Development in Tanzania – Ten Case Studies (printed as volume 24), in English

M. ATTEMS, Smallholders in the Tropical Highlands of East Africa. The Usambara Mts. in the Transition Period from Subsistence to Market Production (printed as volume 25), in German

F. SCHERER, Vegetable Cultivation in Tropical Highlands: The Kigezi Example (Uganda) (mimeograph), in English

v. HAUGWITZ/THORWART, Farm Management Systems in Kenya (in preparation)

W. SCHEFFLER, Smallholder Production under Close Supervision: Tobacco Growing in Tanzania. A Socio-Economic Study (printed as volume 27), in German

H. RABE, Crop Cultivation on the Island of Madagascar with Special Reference to Rice Growing (mimeograph)

E. BAUM, Traditional Farming and Land Development in the Kilombero Valley/Tanzania (mimeograph), in German

R. GOLKOWSKY, Irrigation in Kenya's Agriculture with Special Reference to the Mwea-Tebere Project (printed as volume 39), in German

4. Other Studies Concerning Agricultural Development

M. PAULUS, The Role of Co-operatives in the Economic Development of East Africa, and Especially of Tanzania and Uganda (printed as volume 15), in German

N. NEWIGER, Co-operative Farming in Kenya and Tanzania (mimeograph), in English

J. VASTHOFF, Small Farm Credit and Development – Some Experiences in East Africa with Special Reference to Kenya (printed as volume 33), in English

F. DIETERLEN / P. KUNKEL, Zoological Studies in the Kivu Region (Congo-Kinshasa) (mimeograph), in German

W. ERZ, Game Protection and Game Utilization in Rhodesia and in South Africa (mimeograph), in German

M. Bardeleben, Co-operatives in the Sudan: Their Characteristics, Functions and Suitability in the Socio-Economic Development Process (in preparation)

Studies in Commerce, Trade and Transport

H. Helmschrott, Structure and Growth of the East African Textile and Garments Industry (printed as volume 45), in German

H. Kainzbauer, Trade in Tanzania (printed as volume 18), in German

K. Schädler, Crafts and Small-Scale Industries in Tanzania (printed as volume 34), in English

K. Schädler, Manufacturing and Processing Industries in Tanzania (mimeograph), in English

H. Reichelt, The Chemical and Allied Industries in Kenya (mimeograph), in English

R. Güsten, Studies in the Staple Food Economy of Western Nigeria (printed as volume 30), in English

G. W. Heinze, The Role of the Transport Sector in Development Policy – with Special Reference to African Countries – (printed as volume 21), in German

A. Amann, Energy Supply and Economic Development in East Africa (printed as volume 37)

R. Hofmeier, Problems of the Transport Economy in Tanzania with Special Reference to Road Transport (in preparation), in English

P. Zajadacz and Contributors, Studies in Production and Trade in East Africa (being printed as volume 51), in English

T. Möller, Mining and Regional Development in East Africa (in preparation)

H. Milbers, The Requirements for the Means of Transport in East Africa with a View to the Economic Expansion of these Countries (in preparation)

Sociological and Demographic Studies

A. Molnos, Attitudes towards Family Planning in East Africa (printed as volume 26), in English

O. Raum, The Human Factor in the Development of the Kilombero Valley (mimeograph), in English

O. Neuloh a. o., The African as Industrial Worker in East Africa (printed as volume 43)

H. W. Jürgens, Contributions to Internal Migration and Population Development in Liberia (printed as volume 4), in German

I. Rothermund, The Political and Economic Role of the Asian Minority in East Africa (printed as volume 6), in German

J. Jensen, Continuity and Change in the Division of Labour among the Baganda (Uganda) (printed as volume 17), in German

W. Clement, Applied Economics of Education – The Example of Senegal – (printed as volume 23), in German

H. W. Jürgens, Examination of the Physical Development of Tanzanian Youth (mimeograph), in English

H. W. Jürgens, Investigations into Internal Migration in Tanzania (printed as volume 29), in German

A. v. Gagern, The African Settlers and How They Organize Their Life in the Urambo-Scheme (Tanzania) (printed as volume 38), in German

Gerken / Schubert / Brandt, The Influence of Urbanization upon the Development of Rural Areas – with Special Reference to Jinja (Uganda) and Its Surroundings (in preparation)

E. C. Klein, Social Change in Kiteezi (Buganda), a Village within the Sphere of Influence of the Township of Kampala (Uganda) (printed as volume 46), in German

U. Weyl, Population Trends and Migration in Malawi with Special Reference to the Central Region of Lake Malawi (in preparation)

M. Meck, Population Trends in Kenya and Their Implications for Social Services in Rural and Urban Areas (in preparation)

Staewen/Schönberg, Cultural Change and Anxiety Reaction among the Yoruba of Nigeria (printed as volume 50), in German with English Summary

J. Muriuki, The Mau-Mau Movement: Its Socio-Economic and Political Causes and Implications upon British Colonial Policy in Kenya and Africa (in preparation), in English

H. Desselberger, Education's Contribution to Economic Development of a Tropical Agrarian Country – the Example of Tanzania (in preparation)

Legal Studies

H. Fliedner, Land Tenure Reform in Kenya (printed as volume 7), in German

H. Krauss, Land Legislation in the Cameroons 1884–1964 (printed as volume 12), in German

G. Spreen, The Present State of Legislation in East Africa (in preparation)

K. v. Sperber, The Implications of Tanzania's Administrative System for Her Economic Development (completed), in English

F. v. Benda-Beckmann, Development of Law in Malawi (completed), in German

10

Studies in Economic Geography

W. MARQUARDT, The Interrelationship between Man, Nature and Economy: the Example of Madagascar (in preparation)

H.-O. NEUHOFF, Gabun: History, Structure and Problems of the Export Trade of a Developing Country (printed as volume 16), in German

H. D. LUDWIG, Ukara: A Special Case of Land Use in the Tropics (printed as volume 22), in German

R. JÄTZOLD/E. BAUM, The Kilombero Valley/Tanzania: Characteristic Features of the Economic Geography of a Semihumid East African Flood Plain and Its Margins (printed as volume 28), in English

A. J. HALBACH, The Economy of South West Africa (a Study in Economic Geography) (mimeograph), in German

J. A. HELLEN, Rural Economic Development in Zambia 1890–1964 (printed as volume 32), in English

K. ENGELHARD, The Economico-Geographical Pattern of East Africa (in preparation)

J. SCHULTZ, Iraqw Highland/Tanzania: Resource Analysis of an East African Highland and its Margins (in preparation)

K. GERRESHEIM, Evaluation of Aerial Photography in East Africa (an Inventory) (mimeograph), in German

Bibliographies and Others

D. MEZGER / E. LITTICH, Recent English Economic Research in East Africa. A Selected Bibliography (mimeograph), in German

A. MOLNOS, Annotated Bibliography of Social Research in East Africa 1954–1963 (printed as volume 5), in German

B. HEINE, Status and Use of African Lingua Francas (being printed as volume 49), in English

M. BOHNET, Science and Development Policy: The Problem of Applying Research Results (mimeograph), in German

Preface

In an earlier volume of this series of Africa-Studies, the words of L. J. LEBRET were approvingly quoted:
"As soon as we start speaking (of development) in *global* quantities, we are no longer speaking about anything at all."
This is certainly true of balance of payments analysis. There is, for example, no such thing as "Tanzania's marginal propensity to import", as vain attempts to calculate it have showed. Different commodities, different entrepreneurs, different inventory situations and changing Government policies all play their part from year to year, and the economy is not large enough to permit the general application of stochastic methodology. For the reader who insists on examining the balance of payments of Tanzania within the framework of an econometric model, reference is made to other studies (CLARK, VAN DE LAAR, DAHL) but I myself have preferred not to follow in their footsteps. It is more in the tradition of the Africa-Studies to assemble the facts concretely and in detail, having due regard to geographical, historical and other "non-economic" factors, leaving theoretical generalizations or policy implications to emerge (if at all) at the end.

In this volume, therefore, description outweighs analysis; predictive model-building is avoided. There is, however, one conclusion of a general nature which is not kept to the end, and that is the crucial importance of *institutional change*. In every chapter, the rôle of institutions is brought out; not deliberately, but because it inevitably emerges.

The study on which this volume is based was limited in time to two years (June, 1966 to June, 1968). On the other hand the balance of payments is materially affected by all major developments in agriculture, industry, transport and communications, incomes policies and so forth within the country, not to mention world trends. Consequently there are inevitable omissions in this present study. My policy has been to confine the omissions as far as possible to areas in which previous writers have already specialised, and in which a cursory non-specialist survey or a plagiaristic recapitulation would not be a useful contribution. The largest omission made for this reason concerns the determinants of agricultural productivity, very important for exports. A considerable volume of literature on this already exists. On the other hand a relatively detailed study is offered of some quantitatively less important topics because it is of a pioneering nature; examples of this are the sections on confirming house and shipping agency commissions. To the reader who is unacquainted with the previous literature, therefore, this volume may seem in some respects to be oddly proportioned; this was, however, a deliberate choice.

During these two years I worked as a Fellow of the Economic Research Bureau at the University College, Dar es Salaam, with financial support by the IFO-Institut, Munich and the Fritz Thyssen Foundation, Cologne. I wish to thank both of these institutions for their respective rôles, without which this work would have been impossible. I also wish to thank the Government of Tanzania for creating an environment in which economic research work is a pleasure and a privilege.

Dar es Salaam, September 1968   Michael Yaffey

Contents

List of Tables

16

I. INTRODUCTORY SURVEY OF THE BALANCE OF PAYMENTS

1. Principal Features of the Balance of Payments

Tanzania is engaged in an intense struggle for economic growth; consequently, imports of producers' goods are rising rapidly. At the same time,
urban incomes have risen and consumer goods imports have also risen;
measures taken in 1967 (nationalisations, a severe Budget, introduction of a
restrictive incomes policy) should, however, succeed in containing this. On
the export side, energetic measures by the Government have achieved considerable increases in volume, offset to some extent by falls in prices due to
the constraints of demand and of marketing ability frequently associated
with tropical produce. Efforts are being made toward greater invisible
earnings, especially tourism. In all these activities Tanzania is faced by competition from other developing countries, notably Kenya, and seeks to substitute co-operation wherever possible, particularly through the Treaty for
East African Co-operation and through international commodity-control
agreements (coffee, sisal). A considerable amount of external finance is forthcoming despite Tanzania's selective approach to overseas aid (and her policy
of "socialism and self-reliance"). The reserves, which had been built up by the
Currency Board system before independence, have risen in recent years and
are at an adequate level given the present rate of development. The danger
that the reserves will be inadequate when the development accelerates,
particularly if the terms of trade continue to deteriorate, is known to the
Government, and strenuous attempts are being made to improve the balance
of payments position *structurally* in every possible way. Some of these
attempts will be described in the following chapters.

a) Exports — General Situation

Tanzania has a population of 12,231,000 people[1], and a GNP of Shs. 5,575
million or Shs. 456 per head, per year[2]. Agriculture is responsible for 52%

---

1 *Monthly Bulletin of Statistics*, January, 1968. Data are from 1967 Census, con-
  firmed as satisfactory by post-enumeration checks. Includes Zanzibar.
2 *Background to the Budget, 1968–69*, provisional 1967 figures. Excludes Zanzibar,
  which makes an error of around 3% in the per capita product.

of the GDP (Table 1) and agricultural products, raw or semi-processed, account for about 70% of the exports[3].

Table 1. *GDP by Origin, 1965–1967*

Industry	1965 Shs. mn.	1966 Shs. mn.	1967 Shs. mn.	Annual Growth Rate 1960—1967 %
Agriculture	2,651	2,905	2,944	+ 3.9
Mining	121	141	154	+ 5.8
Manufacturing	234	283	314	+16.1
Construction	151	172	215	+13.1
Public Utilities	37	48	51	+10.8
Commerce	658	766	781	+ 9.2
Rent	246	267	304	+ 9.6
Transport	216	247	280	+ 6.9
Services	580	615	649	+ 8.6
Total	4,894	5,444	5,692	+ 6.4
(Index 1960 = 100)	132.2	147.1	153.8	

Source: Background to the Budget 1968–1969, provisional 1967 figures. Excludes Zanzibar.

Merchandise exports account for 43% of monetary GDP[4] (or about 31% of total GDP).

Table 2. *Exports as % of Monetary GDP, 1963–1967*

Year	Merchandise Export Shs. mn. (1)	Monetary GDP Shs. mn. (2)	(1) as % of (2) % (3)
1963	1,419	3,011	47.1
1964	1,597	3,424	46.6
1965	1,465	3,527	41.5
1966	1,878	3,929	47.8
1967	1,760	4,116	42.8

Source: Background to the Budget 1968–1969. The trade data come from East African Customs and Excise originally.

1965 was a bad-weather year which adversely affected agriculture, and as exports contain a larger proportion of agricultural products than does GDP, the percentage fell to an abnormally low level (41.5%) in that year, but despite that, a falling trend is visible, reflecting the growing independence

3 Taken from Table 11 *Background to the Budget, 1968–69,* giving near to Shs. 523 mn. non-agricultural exports, from a total of Shs. 1,760 mn.
4 About 40% in 1967 if an allowance is made for the Zanzibar GDP.

of the economy and the development of manufacturing and service sectors — a change which is related to the attainment of political independence in 1961 and to the operation of the first Five Year Plan (1964/65–1969/70).

The principal exports are coffee, cotton, sisal, diamonds, cloves and cashewnuts, which together amount to Shs. 1,093 mn. or 62.1% of the total (1967 figures). Coffee is in difficulties with quota limitations and the threat of coffee-berry disease; cotton is at present on a firm market (subject to USA policy), but is unirrigated and so susceptible to bad weather; sisal is depressed below a price level which can cover the average cost of production; cashews are liable to fluctuations and there is a marketing difficulty here in that the principal producer, Mozambique, is a country with which Tanzania has no diplomatic relations. This means that, in coffee, sisal and cashewnuts at least, priority must be given to cutting costs, improving quality, local processing, and above all diversification into other crops or into manufactured (or service) exports; nevertheless the presence of large numbers of farmers producing coffee, sisal and cashewnuts, who are tied to those crops because of heavy investments, because of soil conditions and climate, or because social circumstances are not sufficiently conducive to innovation, makes it likely that sizeable increases in output of those crops will continue to come forth, unless prices are driven down very harshly as has happened with sisal.

Manufacturing for export is developing mainly along the lines of the processing of agricultural produce — though some metal manufactures are exported, some petroleum, paper, plastics, cement, footwear, simple pharmaceuticals and clothing; and a diamond-cutting establishment is growing up. The chief processing lines are in sisal, cotton, meat, tobacco, cloves, coffee, and dairy products. The exports of manufactured goods are chiefly to countries which are also at a low stage of economic development and are favourably placed geographically or politically to buy from Tanzania rather than elsewhere: Kenya, Uganda, Zambia, Somalia and Burundi, in particular. These may be described as Tanzania's "softest" markets.

The bulk of the exports, however, still go to developed countries overseas (Table 3).

Thus the U.K. with about Shs. 480 mn. takes 27.4% of total merchandise exports. In 1961–63 (average) the proportion was 31.4%; the proportion is falling following independence. Tanzania is turning more to cheaper sources of supply (India, Hong Kong, Japan, China) for her imports and is attempting to send exports there; new markets in the advanced countries (Holland, Scandinavia, North America) and in the socialist countries (for non-quota coffee, for instance) are being sought out. The existence of trade agreements also plays a rôle here.

The export of agricultural produce is fraught with the usual difficulties. Produce may be sold through overseas brokers (e.g. sisal, cashewnuts); by auction (e.g. coffee, cotton); through foreign-controlled distribution networks (e.g.

Table 3. *Destination of Exports*[a], *1962–1967*
(Shs. mn.)

Area	1962	1963	1964	1965	1966	1967	1967 %of total
U.K.	373	418	436	382	486	473	27
East Africa	65	72	107	121	98	83	5
E.E.C.	239	258	312	241	224	250	14
North America	113	138	167	117	169	117	7
Japan	43	41	56	35	97	67	4
Others	308	450	485	538	692	738	43
Total	1,141	1,377	1,563	1,434	1,766	1,728	100

[a] Excluding re-exports.
Source: See Table 2. Exports include re-exports. Zanzibar is included.

meat products, pyrethrum) or to the socialist countries' state marketing agencies. In no case does the producer have control over the price structure of the goods through the stages of manufacturing and distribution right down to the consumer price, as is frequently the case with imports. The efforts of the Government to influence marketing strategy (and hence, proceeds) through marketing boards are limited by (a) the small share of Tanzania in the world market in most cases; (b) special organisation problems in the few cases (sisal, cashewnuts, pyrethrum) where the Tanzanian share is significant; (c) the political problems which arise when, through the agency of a Government body, the world market inflicts a fall in grower price, and (d) shortage of competent manpower or marketing know-how.

In recent years the export price index has been falling while that of imports has been rising (Table 4).

Table 4. *External Trade Indices, 1961–1967*
(1960 = 100)

	1961	1962	1963	1964	1965	1966	1967 est
Export price	97	98	112	113	103	99	95
Import price	96	91	100	109	114	113	117
Terms of Trade	101	108	112	104	90	88	82

Source: See Table 1.

b) Imports — General Situation

The seasonal pattern of imports closely follows that of exports; importers stock up in the third quarter of the year against peak retail sales in the fourth quarter, when the proceeds of crop sales are at their maximum. There are, of course, fluctuations in inventory policy, owing to shifts in business confidence, and also owing to structural changes in the distributive sector.

In addition to the sales of consumer goods, which fluctuate with exports, there are components with less marked seasonal characteristics, associated with the growing urban sector, the fixed capital investment programme, and items in "Government Stores".

"Government Stores" are one of the biggest importers of all; in 1967, Government imports[5] were Shs. 151 mn. or 10% of total imports. These are goods for which Government Departments place "indents", or requisition orders; Government Stores may buy them from any source, but frequently the purchases are financed by overseas aid and are therefore directed to a particular source by tying provisions. It should also be noted that reliance is placed on a small number of overseas purchasing agents, the biggest of which was formerly the Crown Agent for Overseas Administrations in London, but is now (since 1968) Intrata Overseas, N.V., Amsterdam, in which the Government has a controlling interest. Purchases from London in 1966 and 1967 amounted to 71% and 61% respectively of the total Government imports.

Commercial imports include imports by parastatal and private organisations. Consumer goods are the chief component of private imports, and outstandingly important are temperate-zone foodstuffs and textiles. The market for consumer goods is distinguished by the presence of different groups. In addition to the mass market based on agriculture and industrial employment there are civil servants and a small but affluent group of expatriates including diplomatic staff; and there is a community of business men, who tend to be mostly Asians by origin and are subjected to special social pressures which discourage ostentatious consumption.

According to the annual survey of wage employment, there were in 1967 346,000 wage-earners in Tanzania with average cash wages of Shs. 285 per month each, giving a total cash income (before tax) of Shs. 1.2 billion, an increase of some $5^{1}/_{2}$% over 1966 figures.

On the cash income of the self-employed sector, which is the largest sector, no useable data is available.

The chief imports for the rural market are textiles and clothing, rice, soap, kerosene, tea, tinned milk, cooking oils, patent medicines, enamelware and crockery, biscuits, mirrors and ornaments, and cotton thread; in small towns

---

5 Source: East African Customs & Excise. This is not a wholly accurate guide to "Government Stores" buying since it includes, besides all Central Government imports, imports by East African Airways and other institutions of the East African Community. Zanzibar is excluded from the calculation of 10% share. In 1966 this figure was 7.3%. For the work of "Government Stores" proper, see *The Appropriation Accounts*, 1966/67, p. XXII.

one finds also primitive agricultural implements[6], bicycles and spare parts, radios, watches, paraffin-fired lamps, stoves and irons. The Asians are believed to have a higher average income than the Africans but are believed to spend more on education and insurance, and to save more, avoiding ostentatious consumption, as do expatriate farmers. Expatriate managerial personnel enjoy a standard of living comparable to that of top African civil servants and a few Asians; then at the most lavish end of the scale are the diplomats, of whom there are a remarkably large number in Dar es Salaam. The high-income market takes meat and dairy products from Kenya and tinned foods from Europe in large quantities, as well as consumer durables.

A category of imports which has been rising rapidly in value in recent years is transport equipment (Table 5). This is partly due to the fashion, now probably ended, for Mercedes-Benz cars; but even without ostentation, it is inadvisable to buy the cheapest vehicles for use on the rough roads of Tanzania. Peugeot, Land-Rover and Volkswagen are the most popular. Even so the life-time of a vehicle is shorter than in more developed countries[7].

Table 5. *Imports by Category*[a], *1961–1967*
(Shs. mn.)

Class of Item	1961	1962	1963	1964	1965	1966	1967	Average compound growth rate 1961—1967
Consumer goods	455	493	488	528	543	660	536	2.7
Intermediate	136	149	156	185	205	254	293	13.6
Transport equipment	80	93	106	112	129	197	212	17.6
Capital goods	308	269	281	340	427	455	507	8.7
Miscellaneous	26	26	25	29	31	47	30	2.4
Total	1,005	1,030	1,056	1,194	1,335	1,613	1,578	7.8

[a] Excluding Zanzibar.

Source: Background to the Budget 1967–1968 and *1968–1969*. The primary source is East African Customs and Excise. Imports from Kenya and Uganda, and transfers from Zanzibar are included. In interpeting this table it should be borne in mind that much of the transport equipment is of a capital goods nature. It was considered better to have a separate item of transport equipment than to break it down arbitrarily. In any case the classifications are inevitably somewhat arbitrary.

6 Pangas (large knives) and jembes (hoes suited to hard soil) are commonly marketed at a few shillings each.
7 A study in Zambia, Rhodesia and Malawi showed the mean depreciation costs to be 38% higher on unimproved roads than on bituminous roads for freight vehicles, and 127% higher for buses. *Road Research Technical Paper, No. 76*, Ministry of Transport, London, 1967. As at 1st July, 1968, Tanzania had (central government roads only) 1,052 miles of bitumen, 671 miles of engineered gravel, and 8,654 miles of earth roads. Source: *Background to the Budget, 1968–69*.

Most expatriate families own or use cars. This has a powerful demonstration effect upon others who also wish to own cars, particularly as public transport is subject to long delays. Finally there has been a sharp increase in the number of lorries — including expensive, powerful 24-ton lorries — operating the route to Zambia, following the attempts of that country to reduce its trade dependence on Rhodesia and South Africa.

Among the import commodities which are inputs to production in Tanzania, the most important is oil. In 1966 a refinery commenced operations in Dar es Salaam, which serves parts of Tanzania not adjacent to Kenya, thus reducing unit costs by importing crude oil instead of refined oil, but total demand for oil products continues to rise, especially since exports to Zambia have begun; the maximum effort (including all available planes and lorries, and the rapid building of a pipe-line) is being put into the delivery of oil to Zambia.

Refined oil continues to be imported into northern Tanzania as does cement despite the existence of a cement factory near Dar es Salaam, for geographical reasons.

Table 6. *Categories of Imports as Percentage of Total, 1961–1967*

	1961	1962	1963	1964	1965	1966	1967
Consumer goods	45	48	42	44	41	41	34
Intermediate	14	14	15	15	15	16	19
Transport equipment	8	9	10	9	10	12	13
Capital goods	31	26	26	28	32	28	32
Miscellaneous	2	3	7	4	2	3	2
Total	100	100	100	100	100	100	100

Source: See Table 5.

Capital goods imports appear to be rising relatively slowly though faster than consumer goods (Tables 5 and 6). In the rural sector the capacity to borrow for investment is still very limited for various reasons; in the private manufacturing sector business confidence (with reference to long-term expectations) is affected by the rapid political and economic changes through which Tanzania has passed; in the public sector, capital formation has fallen seriously short of Plan targets (with only 74% fulfilment over 1964–1967), partly because of lack of finance (British aid was cut off in 1965 following the rupture of diplomatic relations) and partly because of lack of skilled manpower needed to plan and supervise the disbursements. There is also an important parastatal sector, headed by the National Development Corporation, which has developed vigorously but is still of very recent origin; and a special group of services shared in common with Kenya and Uganda, but the investments of these in Tanzania have been considered unsatisfactory.

Some improvement in the rate of capital formation is expected to result from the Treaty for East African Co-operation which came into operation on 1st December, 1967, and which aims both at faster economic development in East Africa and at more equitable distribution of that development among the three member countries.

The chief sources of imports in 1967 were the U.K., Kenya, Italy, U.S.A., West Germany and China, in that order; U.K. supplied 24% of the total, Kenya 14% and Italy 8.5%. The whole Sterling Area accounted for Shs. 776 mn. or 48%; in 1966 it had been 52% (Table 7).

Table 7. *Sources of Imports, 1961–1967*
(Shs. mn.)

Area	1961	1962	1963	1964	1965	1966	1967
United Kingdom	323	296	300	304	337	412	382
India	58	61	59	55	72	70	43
Hong Kong	16	17	21	18	20	36	26
Kenya	184	207	216	271	285	269	231
Uganda	35	35	42	49	52	63	49
Other Sterling Area	83	75	57	53	39	31	45
European Economic Community	137	126	147	163	257	292	344
North America	47	58	38	60	63	96	137
Japan	98	111	133	151	100	93	69
Comecon	4	11	9	20	26	39	45
China	–		2	6	40	80	72
Other	122	130	129	109	114	210	182
Total	1,107	1,127	1,153	1,259	1,405	1,691	1,625

Source: East African Customs & Excise, and *Background to the Budget* 1967–1968, and 1968–1969. These figures are for the United Republic including Zanzibar, which explains why the totals are higher than those of Table 5.

The U.K. share, prior to the devaluation of the pound in November, 1967, appeared to be declining for a number of reasons, the chief of which probably was that following independence in 1961 several new sources of external aid have opened up. Moreover, a new factor is Tanzania's State Trading Corporation, set up in February, 1967 by nationalising a number of import/ export businesses, mostly British. Efforts are being made by the S.T.C. to find cheaper, non-traditional sources of supply; of the 654 inherited suppliers, 223 were British.

The restrictive system relies partly on tariffs. Until the operation of the Treaty for East African Co-operation there was a free trade area in East Africa with a common external tariff; protection given to East African manufacturers is high[8], particularly for beer, cigarettes and oil refining. Internal tariffs introduced under the Treaty, euphemistically known as transfer taxes, are at a maximum of 50% of the external tariff rates.

Zanzibar, before the operation of the Treaty, was outside the Customs Union and had, generally, much lower import duties.

In addition to the tariffs, certain goods are subject to import licensing; in terms of the value of goods covered, textiles is certainly the largest, but in terms of protecting domestic industry by the *refusal* of licences, a number of smaller lines (radios, bottles, plastic goods, etc.) are more significant.

There is no particular discrimination against imports from the non-Sterling Area (except for certain countries where an effort is made to balance the trade) other than through the working of the banking arrangement whereby the costs of working with East African banks are frequently lower than with other banks.

A large quantity of goods — probably the majority — are imported under exclusive agency agreements[9]. The overseas manufacturer typically pays a fixed commission and guarantees exclusivity. The agent stocks the goods at his own expense and distributes them. The manufacturer normally controls quantities, prices and advertising. The agent undertakes not to handle similar (competing) lines. This system enables manufacturers to exploit the Tanzanian market with a thoroughness which cannot as yet be achieved by Tanzania's export market men.

The growth of imports (in value terms) is expected to be more rapid than that of exports. GDP rose by 6.4% per annum[10] between 1960 and 1967, and accelerated to 7.8% growth between 1965 and 1967[11]. Personal incomes are pushed up by the entry of producers into the monetary sector, by the urgent programme of technical and general education, and possibly by excessive tariff protection. Population growth is between 2.5% and 3% per annum[12]. At the same time the Government's development programme is gradually widening its bottleneck constraints (finance and manpower) and importing more equipment each year. To some extent this growing demand is offset by the import substitution programme, but this has considerable limitations: it is limited by the small market size, it requires its own imports of capital and intermediate goods, it generates additional incomes and hence further imports, and it requires usually foreign technology and capital with

---

8 See Dudley Kessel, "Effective Protection of Industry in Tanzania, E.R.B. Paper 67.8, Dar es Salaam, 1967.

9 An example of such an agreement will be found in Appendix III.

10 At current factor cost. *Background to the Budget, 1967–68.* See Table 1.

11 *Background to the Budget, 1967–68.* 1967 figures are provisional. Between 1965 and 1966 the rise was 11.8%; between 1966 and 1967 it was 4.5%. In constant prices the 1960/62–1967 growth rate was 4.3% and the 1966–1967 growth was 2%. 1965 and 1967 were bad weather years.

12 Census results, August, 1967.

Table 8. *Effective Rates of Import Duty on the Tanzania Mainland: 1954 to 1966*
(Percentages)

Code	S.I.T.C. Section	1954	1955	1956	1957	1958	1959	1960	1961	1962	1963	1964	1965	1966
0.	Food	15.8	17.3	16.2	15.6	18.6	19.0	20.0	25.4	32.6	26.4	27.5	22.5	18.5
1.	Beverages and Tobacco	216.7	220.1	324.3	281.9	254.1	245.5	241.2	233.5	249.3	203.9	263.3	216.6	185.8
2.	Crude Materials	29.3	24.8	19.9	27.3	26.8	15.7	17.0	27.3	17.1	24.7	23.9	14.2	12.5
3.	Mineral Fuels, Lubricants, etc.	35.2	34.9	37.5	40.8	49.9	53.5	36.3	66.2	86.9	125.9	145.5	185.0	245.0
4.	Animal and Vegetable Oils and Fats	19.8	15.4	18.3	18.3	16.2	28.8	31.6	30.0	30.5	31.3	33.2	–[a]	–
5.	Chemicals	21.8	22.1	18.7	22.0	24.9	26.2	28.5	24.1	41.5	22.1	24.6	11.9	13.1
6.	Manufactured Goods (classified)	15.7	14.8	19.4	18.4	33.8	41.8	38.9	40.4	43.0	43.5	45.8	30.6	28.0
7.	Machinery and Transport Equipment	18.3	16.2	16.1	17.2	17.9	20.6	16.6	17.2	17.4	21.1	24.2	13.5	15.0
8.	Miscellaneous Manufactured Articles	31.8	25.5	24.8	28.2	35.1	35.8	35.6	37.2	36.8	35.4	37.9	25.9	26.5
9.	Miscellaneous Transactions and Commodities	17.5	23.2	24.6	26.8	31.6	39.4	37.7	38.1	50.4	50.3	53.6	46.4	32.5

[a] Negligible Imports.

Source: Background to the Budget 1967–1968.

corresponding foreign exchange outflows for patent rights, interest, profits, managerial services, travel expenses and sometimes exorbitant machinery costs.

Table 9. *Comparison of Exports and Imports, 1961–1967*

	1961	1962	1963	1964	1965	1966	1967	Growth Rates 1961–1964 %	1964–1967 %
Exports and re-exports Shs. mn.	1,131	1,193	1,459	1,597	1,465	1,878	1,760	*12.2*	*3.3*
Imports Shs. mn.	1,107	1,127	1,153	1,259	1,405	1,691	1,625	*4.4*	*8.9*

Source: As previous Tables.

It may be said that the post-independence development programme did not get under way until 1964. The import bill associated with it is reflected in the above table.
A "deterioration" in the balance of merchandise trade is therefore expected.

c) Invisibles and Transfers — General Situation

Until recently Tanzania had virtually no earnings on invisible account except:

- port earnings, especially in Zanzibar;
- receipts from Congolese transit traffic on the Kigoma-Dar es Salaam railway, and associated harbour earnings;
- interest on Government Sinking Funds held in London;
- share of profits of the East African Currency Board.

Even now the chief outflow, i.e. income from investments on private account, is virtually without any corresponding credit entry, since the ownership by Tanzanians of property abroad is negligible (or at any rate, receipts in Tanzania of earnings from it are negligible). The outflow does not, however, amount to a heavy burden on the economy — at present [13].
There is, however, an improvement on travel and transportation account. This has been fundamentally strongly negative: virtually all external sea trade is carried in foreign-owned ships (though this is not accounted for in the statistics, as imports are valued c.i.f. and exports f.o.b.) and moreover a good deal of the trade goes through Kenya to or from the great port of

13 The outflow will be reduced by the recent nationalisations. The value of compensation has been officially estimated (Budget Speech, 1968–69) at Shs. 220 mn.; most of this is external. This suggests a reduction of Shs. 30–40 mn. per year in the private profit outflow, partly offset by increased official payments.

Mombasa, thus losing foreign exchange on the handling charges incurred in Kenya. On the credit side we now have:

- some Kenya and Uganda trade passing through Tanzania;
- substantial earnings from Zambia transit traffic, combined with expansion of Dar es Salaam harbour facilities;
- a share in the expanding East African airways, which up to the present have been profitable;
- a share in the East African National Shipping Line, and in the Tanzania-China shipping line;
- a rapidly developing tourist industry (based on wild-life, coast, mountain and climatic attractions);
- profits of some shipping agencies, retained by nationalisation.

Probably the greatest obstacle to more rapid development of tourism and profitable transit traffic (Zambia, Congo, Ruanda, Burundi) is lack of good roads and railways. The roads are narrow, largely unmetalled, potholed, subject to flooding and degeneration into mud; accidents are numerous; carrier and insurance costs are high. Moreover, the packing is often not adequate to prevent damage to the cargo. The railways, naturally, are superior in respect of the few areas they serve. It is a single-track, narrow-gauge, low-speed system laid out according to a tactical pattern half a century old. There is no rail link to Zambia, but one is planned with Chinese assistance. Airport expansion is under way.

Banking and insurance were until recently almost entirely foreign-owned, and the profits therefrom were accordingly remitted outside Tanzania. The nationalisation of these activities in February, 1967, should bring the credits on these activities more into line with the debits — though still falling short of a zero balance for various technical reasons.

Considerable outflows without corresponding earnings of the same nature continue to be debited to managerial and consultancy services, directors' fees, "general head office expenses" and the services of confirming houses. In some cases these outflows do not represent genuine services at market value, but rather, a means of taking money out of the country in circumvention of the Exchange Control. There is in fact no prohibition on the remittance of profits earned by foreign investors, but many perhaps prefer to establish a hidden escape route — whether out of fear that such a prohibition might be introduced, or whether out of preference for paying profits taxes to their home Government instead of to Tanzania, depending on circumstances.

Transfer payments are approximately balanced. On the debit side are private remittances (mostly by expatriates): personal savings, educational, family maintenance, emigration and medical; and Government transfers out, for the upkeep of representatives abroad and contributions to international organisations. On the credit side are governmental grants received, including grants for the upkeep of students undergoing education abroad[14], private donations received by missions, churches, libraries, etc., and donations from Ford, Rockefeller, Tyssen, and other private foundations for developmental projects (such as University work) in Tanzania.

d) Capital Movements – General Situation

The Government capital account is, of course, positive; external finance is received from a wide variety of national and international sources. Tables 10 and 10a) show loans plus grants broken down by source.

Table 10. *Tanzania Government – Sources of External Loans and Grants*
(Shs. thousands)

Item	1963/64	1964/65	1965/66	1966/67 est.	1967/68 est.
a) Government					
United Kingdom	22,680	23,900	17,520	5,500	3,653
U.S.A.	5,440	19,960	29,960	29,140	23,518
Federal Republic of Germany	16,400	7,220	4,320	3,980	41,280
Israel	700	8,460	6,340	–	–
Sweden	–	–	1,600	17,900	25,551
Netherlands	–	–	–	5,780	3,663
China	–	5,980	–	16,680	40,458
Canada	–	–	–	700	10,202
Denmark	–	–	–	5,000	450
U.S.S.R.	–	–	–	–	5,082
Austria	–	–	–	–	386
Zambia	–	–	–	–	2,958
Miscellaneous	–	–	–	–	3,234
b) Private Trusts or Funds					
British	880	800	420	580	1,146
American	1,940	760	480	–	394
c) Multilateral Sources					
I.D.A.	3,260	12,980	18,700	51,920	45,844
U.N.E.S.C.O.	–	–	4,020	460	–
Refugee Services	180	–	120	–	–
Nordic Council	–	–	–	1,200	11
U.N.D.P.	–	–	–	–	10,086
Total	51,480	78,540	83,480	138,840	217,916

Source: Background to the Budget 1967–1968.

14 Offsetting a debit entry in the travel column of the balance of payments account.

Table 10a. *External Sources of Development Funds 1964/65–1966/67: Zanzibar*
(Shs. thousands)

Item	1964/65	1965/66 est.	1966/67 est.
Grants:			
People's Republic of China	1,600	–	–
United States	748	253	–
German Democratic Republic	–	10,000	3,901
Unicef	–	–	11
Miscellaneous	344	–	100
Loans:			
Soviet Union	–	–	222
German Democratic Republic	–	2,931	13,524
People's Republic of China	–	17,270	994
Total	2,692	30,454	18,752

Source: Background to the Budget 1967–1968.

Prior to independence (1961 in Tanganyika, 1964 in Zanzibar) the U.K. was the main source of capital, both public and private. The desire to find other sources of aid was made urgent in 1965 by the breakoff of diplomatic relations with the U.K. at which time £7½ million of earmarked aid funds were frozen [15]. Owing to the manpower constraint on disbursement the actual aid requirement was rather less than this and the shortfall was largely made good from new sources, of which China was (and is) the most important. Tables 9 and 10 show how the other donors then came in.
Most of the aid on Government account has been loans as distinct from grants, and the proportion has risen.

Table 11. *Sources of External Funds for Capital Budgets, 1964/65–1966/67*
(Shs. mn.)

	1964/65	1965/66 est.	1966/67 est.
Loans:			
Tanganyika	59.06	75.74	134.72
Zanzibar	–	20.20	14.74
Tanzania	59.06	95.94	149.46
Grants:			
Tanganyika	19.48	7.76	4.10
Zanzibar	2.69	10.25	4.01
Tanzania	22.17	18.01	8.11
Total Tanzania	81.23	113.95	157.57
Loans as % of total	*72.7%*	*84.2%*	*94.85%*

Source: Background to the Budget 1967–1968.

15 To be finally cancelled in 1968, when a decision was taken to withdraw all British aid to Tanzania.

For 1967/68 it is likely to be over 85%. At the same time the terms of IBRD loans are hardening as is known to be the case on the world scale. Tanzania is not, however, in the position of having to accept loans irrespective of the terms in order to overcome an immediate crisis in the balance of payments, since the foreign exchange reserves are at a satisfactory level. Moreover, the level of grants is expected to increase in absolute terms.

In addition to the governmental long-term capital account there are short-term movements on the accounts with the Crown Agent in London and other agents abroad; these, however, fluctuate around zero with a limited swing possibility. There are also external assets maintained by other official bodies such as the Post Office Savings Bank, of minor importance. In addition the Tanzanian share of the external position of the East African Airways and other common services, and the Currency Board (the accounts of which are not yet wound up) represent contingent assets and liabilities for Tanzania.

The private long-term capital account is not officially published, but fragmentary information is available. There was a net outflow before June, 1965, when capital outflows within the Sterling Area were brought under exchange control in the same way as outflows to the rest of the world. This measure greatly reduced the gross outflow and converted the net outflow into a net inflow. In 1966 there was a net inflow of around Shs. 90 million[16]. This wavered towards the end of this year and the beginning of 1967 when the Arusha Declaration announced a strengthened programme of socialist measures, and a series of important nationalisations were introduced. This coincided with unusually bad weather (affecting crop prospects) and some deportations which also affected business confidence. It seems likely, therefore, that the private capital account for 1967 will prove to have been roughly in balance or even negative.

The influence of socialist measures on foreign investors is not so marked as might be expected since "full and fair compensation" is promised to them both in general under the Foreign Investment Protection Act and in particular under the terms of the nationalisation Acts. Such compensation is usually given on the basis of audited accounts, i.e. book values, without regard to goodwill or discounted future profits or losses. Apart from some special cases where these factors have proved particularly contentious, investors have received satisfactory treatment and in several cases have come forward asking to be nationalised. This compensation, while it strengthens the private capital account, naturally weakens the Government capital account when it comes to be paid over.

Within the private capital account the major operations of the parastatal bodies are included. Of major importance is the National Development

---

16 *Background to the Budget, 1967–1968.*

Corporation, which generally invites foreign participation on a minority basis; and Industrial Promotion Services Ltd., an international organisation with Ismaili connections. These organisations, entrusted with the main aim of industrial development, are probably less concerned with the balance of payments effects of their activities than with the generation of additional GDP and so the effective yield of foreign capital probably varies widely. Details are not released.

Table 12. *Long-Term Private Capital Movements*
(£'000)

	1961	1962	1963	1964	1965	1966
Change in assets:						
Private Sector	—3,700	—4,300	—4,861	— 9,183	+ 28	— 380
Parastatal (EA)	— 242	— 307	— 175	— 660	— 599	+ 335
Sub-total	—3,942	—4,607	—5,036	— 9,843	— 531	— 45
Change in liabilities:						
Private Sector	+2,477	+2,906	+7,759	+ 3,926	— 284	+ 6,800
Parastatal (EA)	+2,244	— 195	— 234	+ 392	— 661	+ 3,955
Sub-total	+4,721	+2,711	+7,525	+ 4,318	— 945	+10,755
Net credit:						
Private Sector	—1,223	—1,394	+2,898	— 5,257	— 256	+ 6,420
Parastatal (EA)	+2,002	— 502	— 409	— 268	—1,220	+ 4,290
Sub-total	+ 779	—1,896	+2,489	— 5,525	—1,476	+11,710
Add:						
Net errors and omissions, *plus* 10⁰/₀ of imports; if negative:	–	–	—1,309	— 6,573	–	–
Total (estimated)	+ 779	—1,896	+1,180	—12,098	—1,476	+11,710

Source: East African Statistical Dept., Nairobi.

As can be seen from the estimates presented in Table 12, the net private long-term capital account showed an outflow after independence, followed by a heavy capital flight with its peak in 1964 (the year of the army mutiny, the Zanzibar Revolution, and the Union of Tanganyika with Zanzibar). There was some reversal of positions in 1965 with new tightening of Exchange Control, and in 1966, as already mentioned, the net flow was inwards.

Short-term private capital movements are not known except for a single component, namely, international inter-bank balances. These fluctuated, prior to nationalisation, in a manner which combined:

a) a seasonal pattern reflecting crop finance;
b) an element of offset to the basic balance of payments;
c) a random element (hour to hour fluctuations).

Since nationalisation the fluctuations are no longer around the zero mark; the National Bank of Commerce regularly has resources abroad which are substantially in excess of foreign deposits in Tanzania. The seasonal pattern (a) will probably disappear, as will (b) because of new arrangements with the Bank of Tanzania, but (c) will of course be inevitable.

Movements of short-term private capital of which little is known occur in the following forms:

- entries to inter-companies accounts;
- merchandise dispatched on credit, especially from Kenya to Tanzania, and other changes in the terms of payments.

e) Monetary Movements and Reserves — General Situation

Besides the movements of commercial banks' foreign exchange reserves and the swing of the Government Agents' accounts, which have been described above as short-term capital flows but could equally well be regarded as monetary movements[17], changes in Central Bank foreign assets are the only remaining significant item in the balance of payments accounts. Foreign exchange is bought from, or sold to, the National Bank of Commerce and the People's Bank of Zanzibar, the only commercial banks in Tanzania doing foreign business since the nationalisations of February, 1967. Even before that date, such transactions were infrequent by European standards, and an entire week might pass without any such business being done.

The Bank of Tanzania (central bank) was founded in June, 1966 and its external assets have moved as shown in Table 13.

In 1964–66 the average value of Tanzania's total imports was Shs. 1,452 million, and in the first 6 months of 1967 the average reserve holding was Shs. 428 million, so that reserves could be regarded as being worth 29.5% of annual imports, or $3^{1}/_{2}$ months' worth, which is relatively high for a developing country, the more so as the "float" of foreign exchange which the commercial banks have been allowed to retain has traditionally been one of the highest in the world in proportion to the central authorities' own holdings; this was an East African phenomenon, connected with the workings of the old East African Currency Board and the special character of the commercial banks.

Taking central bank foreign assets (liabilities are negligible) and commercial banks' *net* foreign assets together, we have:

---

17 See Chapter IX.

35

Table 13. *Foreign Exchange Liquid Reserves*

	Bank of Tanzania Foreign Assets Shs. mn.	Commercial Banks' Net Foreign Assets Shs. mn.	Total Shs. mn.
1967			
End of			
January	420.4	13.8	434.2
February	434.6	39.2	473.8
March	437.4	48.3	485.7
April	427.8	110.3	538.1
May	428.0	144.3	572.3
June	420.8	118.2	539.0

Sources: Bank of Tanzania, *Economic Reports;* and *Background to the Budget 1967–1968.* At the end of 1967 the central bank's external assets had fallen to Shs. 397.7 mn.; Shs. 35.8 mn. had been lost by the sterling devaluation.

The rise in commercial reserves abroad in early 1967 was due to the aftermath of bank nationalisations, which affected bank operations in an abnormal fashion, together with a short but sharp recession (associated with run-down of inventories) which favourably influenced the fundamental balance of payments in the first three quarters of 1967.

2. Some Fundamental Features of Tanzania's Economic Relations with the Developed Countries

Tanzania is a poor, developing country. This implies a certain relationship to the developed countries, especially (since the First World War) to the U.K. This relationship has undergone significant modifications, and can be divided into (I) the inter-war relationship, (II) the 1939–1961 relationship, (III) the post-independence relationship. Each relationship is expressed in the *structure* and *development* of the balance of payments.

Such relationships are generally considered to be biased against the developing countries. The *result* of this bias is the noticeably growing gap between rich and poor nations. The *nature* of the bias is that notwithstanding the access to the latest techniques which are made available to developing countries at a cost lower than the cost of research and development in the advanced countries, *the already developed character* of the developed countries appears to be, on balance, *a hindrance in itself* to the development of backward countries; in most cases this built-in bias is offset by donations, but such donations are not as a rule sufficient to offset the negative bias completely except in selected cases where the transfer is particularly lavish for political or military reasons.

The *mechanism* of this built-in bias has been the subject of a vast literature. For the Tanzanian case, the following specific features may be mentioned.

36

1. The minimum return required if capital investment is to take place appears to be higher in Tanzania (by return is meant profit and interest together). Even where savings arise in Tanzania there is therefore a preference to deposit or invest them in a more developed country.

This preference appears to be on grounds of risk differential. The least risky 3-month commercial bills in the U.K. can usually be discounted there at rates between 4 and 6 per cent; in Tanzania the minimum rate is 7%. The drawees with the highest credit rating in Tanzania are clearly less substantial — their "own funds" are smaller — than their U.K. counterparts. Since the same criteria have been applied to both, i.e. British banking criteria, the difference emerges clearly; the rentier expects a higher reward in Tanzania. What of the profit element? Here we must distinguish between indigenous entrepreneurs and foreign, mostly European, entrepreneurs. For the European entrepreneur it is clear that an investment project in his own country will be more attractive than an investment project in Tanzania yielding an identical expected return. This is not only because of climatic and language differences, travel expenditure, etc. In his own country, with which he is familiar, he can be nearer to certainty that he has taken into consideration all factors bearing on the yield and on the security of the principal. Nothing approaching this degree of certainty can be found in Tanzania: the institutions of independence are still a novelty, and still changing rapidly; prior to 1961, the effects of independence could not be predicted with confidence; prior to 1940, the possibility of a return to German rule still seemed to be alive; and in German times, especially during the rebellions, the existence of German rule was precarious. The mutiny of 1964, the nationalisations of 1967 and the alterations of Exchange Control of 1966 and 1967 may also be cited. Perhaps even more important are the vagaries of the Tanzanian weather, which affects almost all aspects of the economy; whereas in Europe it is possible to find many types of investment which are not significantly affected by weather conditions. The point need not be laboured; there is a massive borrower's risk facing the foreign entrepreneur. As regards the Tanzanian entrepreneur the position is different. He has little experience of manufacturing management. His accumulated entrepreneurial capital is smaller and since social institutions militate against participation in joint-stock companies, he has difficulty in amassing capital sufficient to undertake manufacturing operations without foreign participation. His activities therefore tend to be in the commercial sector, and for similar reasons tend to be confined, moreover, to internal commerce or to *importing* from familiar foreign sources of supply. It goes without saying that these circumstances tend to perpetuate themselves. The contribution to the balance of payments made by diverting domestic savings towards an unbalanced growth of activities the end-product of which is mostly *domestic sales* is clearly negative.

We may sum up the effect of all this on the rate of investment in terms of
the Keynesian inducement to invest.

The marginal efficiency of capital schedule is shown in its "normal" position
(f) which is that of an imaginary country more advanced than Tanzania,
and again in its "Tanzanian" position (f'). The latter is lower because the

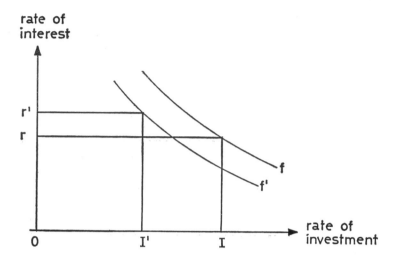

factors discussed above are regarded as an entrepreneurial risk premium
which is deducted from the anticipated net yield of any investment project in
Tanzania. The effective interest rate in Tanzania (r') is shown above its
"normal" level (r) because the lenders' risk premium is added. Borrower's risk
and lender risk combine to depress the inducement to invest.

2. The above analysis takes no account of technical influences on the marginal
efficiency of capital (m.e.c.) which might raise or lower the Tanzanian m.e.c.
relative to that of the more developed country in which capital could alternatively be invested. The smallness of the Tanzanian market, the high costs of
transportation and communications, the shortage of skills, the scarcity of
Hirschman-type linkages, the lack of adequate demand for joint products to
support demand for any given product, are evident. So far as the competi-
tiveness of exports (and hence the attraction for capital in export-processing)
are concerned these disadvantages may theoretically be offset by an
appropriately low wage level [18], with or without a low rate of exchange.
But neither of these offsets can diminish the I' — I gap as it applies to investment in manufacturing for the domestic market. A low exchange rate will

18 A limit to this possibility is set by the effect on productivity, which makes investment again less attractive.

up-value the local purchasing power of foreign capital; but it will equally reduce the foreign value of dividends and profit. Low per capita income probably does not reduce labour costs (because of the effect on productivity) and of course does reduce market demand.

3. The factors mentioned in 2. above reduce the number of apparently profitable projects. The factors mentioned in 1. above tend to make foreign participation in manufacturing necessary, and reduce further the number of projects actually undertaken by confining them to those which appear to offer a higher return than would be considered necessary in a more developed country, the differential being in the nature of a risk premium. If, for any given investment, the risks do not materialise, the remittable profits will be high. The interest charge, which also contains a risk premium, will also be high; and since, until recently, all the banks and a substantial part of the other credit institutions were foreign-owned, this too is remittable. It may or may not be remitted; but it is in a similar position to that of fresh capital, i.e. the factors outlined above militate against its reinvestment in Tanzania.
If the risks do materialise, Tanzania may or may not benefit. On any individual project, which fails, we have initially:

	Cr.	Dr.	
Imports (capital goods and stock)		Shs. x	
Profits to be remitted		zero	
Long-term private capital	Shs. x–y		where
			y = local
			participation
Fall in foreign reserves	Shs. y		

The balance of payments effect is negative and the equipment is a failure. If it is then written off by the foreign investor we have:

	Cr.	Dr.
Long-term private capital (adjustment)		Shs. x–y
Transfer	Shs. x–y	

There is no further effect on foreign reserves; foreign liabilities are back to their initial level; there is no profit liability. Tanzania has an asset of doubtful value (αx) in exchange for a foreign exchange fall of y. If the asset is completely written off its re-export sale value is probably near zero and $y \rangle \alpha x$. Moreover there will be a deterrent effect on fresh investment.
However, if the capital has been invested in agricultural improvements or other irreversible changes which bring benefits to others besides the investor but which are not saleable, the Tanzanian economy benefits. The prime

example of this, not on private account, however, was the famous groundnut scheme, which left behind it ground clearance, transport facilities and harbour works. Examples on private account — since 1918 — are more difficult to find.

It also happens that foreign investment might take the form of investment in stock-building by importers. If these importers then go bankrupt, the stock being sold off cheaply and the investment written down *though the stock is perfectly saleable,* there would be a foreign exchange windfall. Bankruptcies certainly happen from time to time to small-scale importers and although in some of these cases the reason will be unwise purchasing, it seems likely than an enforced sale will cause the assets to be written down even below their actual market value. However, it should be borne in mind that goods which appear slow-moving can be, and frequently are, transferred to Kenya or Uganda for sale there, a fact which operates to reduce the value of such windfalls for Tanzania's balance of payments to negligible proportions.

The fact that occasionally risks do materialise does not, therefore, offset the foreign exchange loss of the risk premium which is successfully remitted from those investments in which the risks do not materialise.

4. Owing to the I' — I gap, the projects most readily undertaken will be those in which the expected return is relatively high because of an element of quasi-rent (scarcity value) and in which the capital outlay is small. Banking is an example. The scarce manpower was provided by importing clerks from India and managers (often very junior) from Europe; Africans were not trained in bank management until after independence (at the time of nationalisation there was one African sub-manager). Initial capital was small; the depositors provided the rest. As the economy grew, bank revenues would grow, analagous to an impost upon all domestic and external trade. Shipping agencies also require practically no capital, and depend on scarce skills. The same is true of insurance agencies, general superintendence agencies, and auditing firms. These are all services which assist trade, and it will be argued below that this group is the most profitable group to nationalise, as soon as the problem of scarce skill can be overcome. These self-perpetuating institutions, innovators initially but in the long run parasitic, have remitted abroad a constant stream of funds which ideally would have been directed into domestic capital formation instead, so as to develop the economy and ultimately narrow the I' — I gap. Thus the I' — I gap encourages parasitic forms of investment which tend to widen the gap further. In trade among advanced countries, this mechanism is not seen because the parasitism is largely reciprocated and in any case the facilities for education and training are such as to reduce the quasi-rent in this special group of institutions to the level of normal profit elsewhere, so that one can scarcely speak of parasitism (except in a more general sense). In Tanzania, however, this has been a feature, and

there has been a notable lack of investments in manufacturing except where the financial arrangements have in effect given the foreign investor a Government guarantee.

5. The misallocation of resources between industrial and service enterprises is further accompanied by the nondevelopment, or slow development, of the domestic economy. Investment tends to be for the export market. The railways run inland from the ports. The reasons for this are in general well known and only one point will be added here, which is characteristic of a highly dependent colonial economy.

The central Government will spend abroad the full amount of what it receives as aid (aided local costs are a very recent innovation of very small amount) and, in addition, a considerable part of what it receives in revenue, i.e. domestically. Assuming (a) a balanced budget and (b) no change in foreign exchange reserves, this means that the Government's foreign exchange transactions show a deficit balance, while the private sector must be equally in surplus, and also it means that taxes exceed Government expenditure inside the country. In terms of domestic currency there is a budget surplus which has a depressing effect on the whole economy; in the private sector there is an export surplus which has an expansionary effect *but* this is confined to the export sector. Thus the exporting sector thrives while the domestic economy (domestic production for domestic consumption) is held back.

Since independence a number of new *export taxes* have been imposed, and other measures taken, to stimulate the domestic economy; the Currency Board has been replaced by a monetary system capable of controlled selective credit creation.

II. INTERNATIONAL TRANSACTIONS BY TANZANIA
IN HISTORICAL PERSPECTIVE

A balance of payments study of Tanzania would be pointless without a time-horizon. This time-horizon is provided by a historical survey, however brief, so that the data of the present time can be judged against their past evolution, and they can be seen as the products of relatively fast or slow moving historical forces, as the case may be, or perhaps the products of fixed geographical endowments. The present rather limited range of exports can best be appraised, for example, not only against the performance of other countries, but against the exports of slaves, ivory, gum copal and sesame seeds of only a few decades ago. Likewise the present direction of trade is considerably illuminated by what history has to show concerning the extent to which this was successfully moulded by official policies, using the more primitive commercial institutions of the pre-independence years.

1. International Transactions before the British Mandate

International trade from the East African coast as distinct from coast-wise shipping is believed to have been very small until the 18th century, apart from the sporadic plunderings by the Portuguese following their landing in 1500.

In the first three-quarters of the eighteenth century, coastal East Africa was part of the Omani Arab empire, and Zanzibar was its commercial and administrative centre. Slaves were exported from Zanzibar itself, from Bagamoyo via Zanzibar, and from Kilwa; ivory and ships' provisions were the main commodity exports. The prosperity and further prospects of Zanzibar caused the Omani Sultan, Sayyid Said, to make it the Omani capital from 1840 onwards. Cloves, introduced in Zanzibar around 1818, were developed by the Sultan using slave labour and ultimately became the island's chief export.

During this period, British and German interests competed for dominance, until in 1889/90 Germany formally took over what is now mainland Tanzania, and the British effectively took control of Zanzibar in 1896. Until the Act of Union of Tanganyika and Zanzibar in 1964, the two territories then pursued separate paths of political and economic development.

In German East Africa, considerable *injections of capital* from Germany commenced; there was a steep rise in the volume of external trade, with *changes in its geographical pattern and commodity composition;* and there was a period of *railway building.*

In 1891–92 the first public accounts were produced, showing a revenue of Mk.1,458,000 and an expenditure of Mk.3,409,000; the balance (nearly £100,000 in sterling equivalent) was met by a subsidy from Germany. In addition to this transfer, there was presumably a capital inflow in the form of an increase of inventories by importers and plantations as they expanded their operations. As the colony developed and tax and customs revenues expanded, the imperial subsidy stagnated. A development budget relying substantially on local revenue emerged. Sir Charles ELIOT commented in 1905:[1]

"The differences in the administration of German and British East Africa are mainly due to the fact that, whereas we (the British) have devoted all our time and attention chiefly to the construction of the Uganda Railway (through Uganda and Kenya), and shown extreme parsimony and indifference in other respects, the Germans have done little in the way of railway construction, but have devoted themselves to the methodical development of the colony with a systematic throughness ... and a lavishness due to the determination to establish a colonial empire at any price ... Five lighthouses have been erected on the coast, and a dock constructed at Dar es Salaam. Carriage roads of considerable length have been made ... The revenue has for some years been about £150,000, whereas that of the British East African Protectorate has in the last five years advanced from under £70,000 to about £110,000."

Between 1897 and 1912 exports ranged from 36.4% to 63.0% of imports, indicating roughly the importance of the capital inflow which took place during the German colonial period. Starting off as largely an official subsidy, this increasingly became commercial venture-capital on private account, the official budget being progressively strengthened by rising local revenues. By 1912 the private capital inflow appears to have reached the astonishing level of over 40% of imports (see Table 14 on page 44).

By modern standards the investors appear to have been venturesome and to have had high expectations. The profit outflow in 1912 was in fact about Mk.3.8 mn representing 12% of exports, some three times higher than the figure today. Moreover, head office expenses included a form of profit. The economic editor of the quarterly *Colonial Review* wrote:[2]

"The viability of many colonial enterprises is prejudiced right from the outset, in that the enterprise is burdened with excessive founders' profits. The

---

1 Sir Charles ELIOT: *The East Africa Protectorate*, 1905. But, see also Lord CRANWORTH: *A Colony in the Making*, 1912, on Kenya development.
2 *Koloniale Rundschau*, August, 1913. My translation, M.Y.

Table 14. *German East Africa, Balance of Payments, 1912*
Summary Estimates

	Thousands of Marks	
	Cr.	Dr.
Exports	31,418	
Imports		50,309
International Investment Income		3,712
Other Head Office Expenses		1,881
Military Grant from Germany	3,618	
Capital inflow, plus net errors and omissions (balancing item)	20,866	
Total	55,902	55,902

Source: Trade figures and Grant from official reports; investment income is my estimate based on company profits reported in contemporary journals. Head Office expenses are 50% of profits.

proof of this was given by the collapse of the 'Südküste' company, the 'Cotton Company', the 'German Rufiji Cotton Company' and in disappointments in the concern of Mertens and Co. A further source of problems is the fact that most of the enterprises are burdened with excessive costs in the home country; that the boards of directors over here receive much too high fees, while in the Protectorate itself, essential expenditure is subjected to economies."

This could have been written half a century later; it brings out the fact that balance of payments outflows of this nature are not merely the result of high local taxation, threat of nationalisation, exchange control, etc.

If we add for this a "guesstimate" of 50% of the (remaining) dividends we arrive at 18% of exports, or possibly 15% of monetary gross domestic product, which represents a severe burden on the economy, but for the fact of massive new capital coming in. It seems likely that, but for the War the economy would have developed characteristics, not of the "maturity" which was anticipated, but of those enormous debt burdens which are associated with South America.

The construction of lighthouses has already been mentioned. German shipping was further assisted by an annual subsidy of £67,000 to the Deutsche Ost-Afrika Linie (which never became profitable under the German Protectorate) and this line extended its service directly from Dar es Salaam to Aden and Bombay in order to by-pass Zanzibar. The deliberate shifting of the main trading port from Bagamoyo to Dar es Salaam was also intended to break the Arab trade routes. At the same time the introduction of a German rupee and the demonetization of the Mombasa and Zanzibar rupees in the German territory took place and these moves effectively shifted the trade routes so as to reduce substantially the reliance on Zanzibar as an entrepôt centre and to extend trade links directly with German ports and with German agents in Indian ports.

By 1911 Germany took 59% of the exports and Zanzibar 10% (compare with 22% in 1897, when 72% went to Zanzibar); and among the German share was most of the rubber, practically all of the sisal, cotton and gold, and all of the mica. Germany also supplied 53% of the imports including all the railway equipment, machinery, vehicles and instruments – though she never became the prime supplier of textiles[3].

Considerable changes took place in the commodity composition of trade. Ivory was the leading export up to 1898 followed by wild rubber. Ivory exports fell off rapidly through depletion (though the observed fall was partly due to smuggling through Kenya) and rubber became the leading export commodity reinforced by plantation rubber which came to market from 1908 onwards.

In the early 1890's there were many experiments in the planting of coffee, cotton, tobacco, tea and vanilla; also sisal, which was introduced from Florida in 1892 following a display in London. Sisal production rose after the gestation period from 1,368 Marks in 1906 to 7,359,000 in 1912. Sisal, hides and skins, coffee and groundnuts came into organised production together in the first few years of the century, closely followed by copra, timber and wattle bark. By the last decade of German rule the colony had a relatively well diversified pattern of exports; for instance, in 1910, when sisal was low in price, groundnuts were at a high price[4]. This has remained a permanent feature of the economy up to the present time.

The commodity structure of imports shows principally (a) a steady fall in the relative importance of *textiles,* from around 50% of imports towards the end of the nineteenth century to under a third after 1908; (b) heavy imports of iron rails and other railway equipment especially in 1900, and 1904 onwards; (c) imports of other engineering equipment fluctuating closely with the railway imports; (d) import of rice fluctuating decreasingly in accordance with the pattern of food-grain output and increasingly in accordance with the demands of railway-building labourers who received imported rice as a form of payment.

The railways were built inland from Dar es Salaam ("Central Line") and

---

3 The circumstances of commercial diplomacy are nicely revealed by a letter from the Hamburg Chamber of Commerce to the Dar es Salaam Council for Trade & Navigation dated 3rd July, 1894: "The disposal of German wares in the German colonies can best prosper, if German business as a whole develops in a natural, healthy and vigorous manner. For that purpose an understanding administration is necessary, which, without in any way impairing the equality of rights between German and foreign merchants, can nevertheless do a great deal to raise the German element in the colonies" (Letter in National Archives, Dar es Salaam).

4 Export price data are to be found in *Koloniale Rundschau* or (by calculation) in the official trade reports. Producer prices are not available.

Tanga ("Northern Line"). The Northern line served the sisal estates of the Tanga region, reaching Muheza in 1896, and was later extended north to the coffee areas, reaching Moshi in 1911. This was extended to Arusha much later, in 1929. The Central Line reached Morogoro (another sisal area) in 1907 but was aimed primarily at groundnut production in the central areas; Tabora was reached in 1912. It was also a strategic link to Lake Tanganyika: Kigoma was reached in 1914, offering links to Rwanda and Burundi to the north, which at that time were relatively rich provinces of German East Africa, and over to the Congo. The railways appear to have been commercial rather than military in nature, with no attempt made to drive up towards Lake Victoria or the headwaters of the Nile. It is significant for the economic development of subsequent years that Lake Victoria was first reached by the Kenya–Uganda railway (in 1902).

These were years, then, of a fairly vigorous development both of infrastructure and of agriculture, the latter including both plantation and (especially on the Central Line) peasant agriculture. It was stimulated by a massive capital inflow which (owing to the First World War which Germany lost) never paid off. By the end of the period, this ranked third in importance of Germany's seven colonies, after Kiautschou and South-West Africa; its exports remained considerably below its imports, and showed a lower growth trend[5].

The situation was transformed in August, 1914 by a British naval blockade and "ersatz" production was hastily undertaken both for military and for civil needs.

The list of commodities which were locally manufactured during the war includes quinine, blankets, dyestuffs, cigarettes, soap, bark sacks, palm wine, and even a kind of petrol ("trebol") made from copra.

Of particular importance was an excellent research station, the Amani Agricultural Research Institute, which went over to war production and in the first 18 months made "16 varieties of foodstuffs and liquors, 11 varieties of spices, 12 varieties of medicines and medicaments, 5 varieties of rubber products, 2 of soap, oils and candles" and so forth[6]. Some of these were produced in bulk, including 15,200 bottles of whisky and other spirits, 10,000 pieces of soap, and other items.

It was not to be expected, however, that this would generate an import-substituting impetus in the post-war period, since most of these commodities could not compete with imported commodities when the latter reappeared on the market, either because of poor quality or because of high production costs.

---

5 Between 1897 and 1911 the annual average compound growth rates were: exports $11^1/_2\%$; imports $12^1/_4\%$.
6 Report of the East Africa Commission, 1925.

2. The Separate Development of Zanzibar

Before pursuing the narrative of Tanganyika's external transactions under the British colonial rule, let us trace the separate course of Zanzibar which was effectively taken over in 1896. Briefly, this was rather a case of *non-development*.

The German efforts to bypass Zanzibar have been mentioned; because of these, the trade turnover actually declined absolutely during the period of German rule on the mainland. Furthermore, the export of slaves was gradually brought to an end. The slave trade, which in the decade 1895–1904 had permitted Zanzibar to run a merchandise trade deficit of half a million pounds sterling[7], left a gap which in the following decades had to be filled by a series of trade surpluses. This was assisted by the behaviour of the price of cloves, which over a thirty-year period (until 1931) showed a secular rise despite a concomitant secular rise in tonnage.

By the outbreak of the war, merchandise exports were slightly above merchandise imports, and a significant source of legitimate service earnings was beginning to emerge on the basis of items which nowadays would be classed in the travel account (port services, crews' expenditure, earnings from dhow

Table 15. *Zanzibar, Balance of Payments, 1914*
Summary Estimates

	Thousands of Pounds	
	Cr.	Dr.
Merchandise trade	749	747
Port earnings	8	
Investment income (official)	1	2
Transfers (official)		8
Long-term capital (official)	—	4
Basic balance	—	3
Monetary movements –		
bullion and specie	17	66
postal remittances	32	8
Balance of monetary movements	—	25
Services n.e.s.; private capital; and net errors and omissions	28	

n.e.s. means: not elsewhere specified.

Sources: Trade figures, from 1914 *Blue Book*. Port Earnings, estimated from Blue Book. Investment income receipts and outgoings, interest calculated at 3% on Sinking Fund and Public Debt respectively. Transfers (official) is £5,000 payment for King's African Rifles and £3,000 estimated pensions to retired European civil servants (this figure was to rise to £39,000 by 1947); source, *Blue Book*. Long-term capital is addition to Sinking Fund. Bullion and specie are trade figures; post office transactions in *Blue Book*.

---

7 £179,000 of this was financed by an outflow of silver currency.

traffic in third countries, etc.). On the other hand, outward payments for
colonial administration (pensions, support of King's African Rifles) which
ironically have to be classed as unrequited transfers were ominously mounting
up to become a noticeable feature of the colonial balance of payments, as was
to happen also on the mainland.

It is likely that most of the unrecorded £28,000 was service income. This,
added to the £8,000 port earnings gives a service sector income (ignoring
interest on the Sinking Fund) of £36,000 or:

		£'000
(1)	Export proceeds	749
(2)	Service proceeds	36
(3)	Total	785
	(2) as percentage of (3)	5%

This brings out the structural backwardness of the balance of payments of
this economy which lived almost entirely on the sale of primary products, as
indeed it still does, apart from recent heavy injections of foreign capital.

The domestic finances of the Sultanate had been weakened in 1892 when
Zanzibar was made a free port, which was helpful for the trading development of British East Africa; but the loss of import duty revenue, together
with the gradual disappearance of income from the slave trade, was too
heavy a blow to the public finances. In 1899 a 5% ad valorem duty was re-
imposed on most imports (to be raised to $7^{1}/_{2}\%$ in 1907, 10% in 1921 and
15% in 1927), and in 1901 a public loan of £100,000 was raised in the London market by floating 3% debentures at par; this loan was repayable by
1931, and was in fact gradually repaid over the period by regular additions
to a Sinking Fund. Apart from this early official capital there appears to
have been very little private capital input, judging from the state of industrial development. Thus, by 1919, there were in Zanzibar one ice factory,
7 soda factories, one electric generating plant, 6 bakeries, 3 oil mills and
2 flour mills, one railway workshop (railway building had covered eight
miles), 6 potteries, 4 rope-making machines, and 57 jewellers. Even after the
Second World War this sector had developed only slightly, there being in
1947, 7 soap factories, 5 more bakeries, 4 more flour mills, and a small clove-
oil distillery (sales ex-plant £88,216) in addition to the enterprises of 1919.
The 1919 list is virtually the same as the 1914 list, the only significant
increase being in the number of jewellers.

The £100,000 loan was used partly to pay compensation to old slave-owners
and partly for public works. Since the former would have a negative effect
on the balance of payments (by increasing imports of consumer goods) and
the latter would have a very doubtful effect, we can summarise by saying
that Zanzibar received little or no assistance on capital account. Even in the

post-war decade 1915–24 when exports were about doubled, the island was so ill-prepared to use its foreign exchange that it ran up a trade surplus of £1.6 mn and increased its stock of non-interest-bearing specie (silver) by £629,000.

This situation did not change fundamentally until the Revolution of 1964. At that time the economy was still dominated by cloves and the industrial sector was very much as it had been in 1914, 1919 and 1947.

The dependence upon cloves is a special characteristic of Zanzibar. In the West, these are used as occasional flavourings for apple pies, and while it is true that a rise in price will not deter the housewife from the insignificant expenditure involved, it is also true that demand is extremely limited and lacking in firm foundation. In the East cloves are used to flavour cigarettes, especially in Indonesia, which has become the main consumer: a particularly unfortunate trading partner to rely on because of her acute currency problems. London is the entrepôt even today. In Zanzibar itself, it is perhaps pertinent to remark, it is a crop suited to a stagnant social condition, requiring no labour except unskilled labour for harvesting.

Shortly after the Revolution, Zanzibar was united with Tanganyika, and its recent history is taken up as that of the country as a whole in our subsequent chapters.

3. International Transactions in the Inter-War Period

Historically, the mercantile development of East Africa was due in large measure to the importance of the area as a staging-post on the route between Western Europe and India; trade with India has been important, whether the Portuguese, the Omanis, the Germans or the British were in control of Tanganyika; and since independence too. Thus, when the British issued their first trade returns in 1920, imports from India were given as £322,026, as against imports from U.K. of only £189,781; exports to India were £108,983 (U.K. £686,326), but a large export trade to India is probably concealed in the Zanzibar figure (£442,143) since Zanzibar still acted as an entrepôt to some extent despite German efforts to by-pass it.

The currency in use here then was predominantly the silver rupee, the sterling value of which fluctuated with the London/India quotation and especially the London price of silver. After the War this rate was subject to marked fluctuations but the British authorities were not prepared to permit large fluctuations in the London/Tanganyika rate. Like the Germans before them, they considered this country's economy to be too small to justify the introduction of its own national currency; but unlike the Germans, they now had the opportunity to introduce a currency for the whole of East Africa, setting up the East African Currency Board, thereby beginning to integrate the mandated territory into the Empire. They naturally preferred to establish a fixed parity with the U.K., exposing the Indian trade to damaging fluctuations, rather than vice versa; and the local settlers, seeing their chief market opportunities in the U.K., tended to support this view.

"We now have in the balance against one another, the Imports from India principally Rice, Sugar, Chutney, etc., against the exports of a vast and inexhaustible sub-continent." (Editorial, "Tanga Post and Advertiser", 3. 1. 1920).

Ultimately the settler interests (aided by the newly-installed South African banks) succeeded in obtaining a complete demonetization of the silver rupee, with a fixed parity to sterling instead. On March 19th, 1921, the Secretary of State cabled the following orders to Nairobi:

- *"Demonetization of Rupee Coin* and replacement by Florin Notes.
- Period of redemption one month, with discretion . . . up to six months.
- East African shilling will be minted.
- Order in Council will be prepared making shillings standard coin and therefore legal tender for any amount. Do not consider it necessary or desirable to make sovereign standard coin, *as parity with sterling would be amply secured by operations of Currency Board.*
- Existing one cent, five cent and ten cent pieces will be marked down to cents of a shilling; existing 25 cent and 50 cent pieces remaining on Florin basis until redeemed by new 50 cents and shilling pieces respectively.
- Proclamation and redemption forthwith".

After considerable monetary disturbance, this process was completed and the shilling came into use. It should be emphasised that this did not amount to a *devaluation* of the rupee below its former "normal" level, but the rupee exchange was

- subjected to fluctuations[8] which had formerly been on the sterling exchange, and
- subject to wide buying and selling margins; the effect of which is similar to taxes on imports and exports. The effects can be seen from the following table.

More significant than the weakening of the link with India was the incorporation of Tanganyika into the sterling zone. Holding her reserves in London instead of Berlin, Tanganyika became an earner of foreign exchange for the U.K., and this policy was pursued irrespective of monetary and economic conditions in the territory.

---

8 After being steady through 1922 at 1s.4d., the rupee rose, with fluctuations, through 1923 and 1924, and thereafter held at 1s.6d. In 1927 it was fixed by the Government of India at 1s.6d. gold.

Table 16. *Tanganyika Trade with India and U.K., 1921–1923* [a]

	1921	1922	1923
India			
Exports as % of total exports	*8.85*	*4.90*	*2.83*
Imports as % of total imports	*20.48*	*21.90*	*16.55*
U.K.			
Exports as % of total exports	*16.42*	*18.99*	*20.96*
Imports as % of total imports	*23.24*	*21.08*	*29.69*

[a] Exports include re-exports. Trade via Zanzibar is unfortunately unrecorded but the Zanzibar trade as a whole was stable through this period. Bullion and specie excluded.

Source: Official trade reports.

Table 17. *Tanganyika Behaviour in Currency Bloc, 1920–1924* [a]
(£'000)

	1920	1921	1922	1923	1924
Balance of trade	+302	—172	+ 54	— 72	+602
Balance with rest of British Empire including U.K.	+ 78	—481	—301	—428	— 98
Balance with "foreign" countries	+224	+309	+355	—500	+700

[a] Exports include re-exports (estimated for 1920). Bullion and specie excluded. Imports are direct imports. Kenya, Zanzibar and Uganda trade is included in Empire.

Source: Official trade reports.

Despite the large fluctuations in the total trade balance, the progress in the non-sterling trade balance was steady, after the First World War.

After the Second World War, however, the non-sterling balance was negative and worsening; this was not checked until 1949, when sterling was devalued from $4.03 to $2.80, or over 30.5%. This had a powerful effect.

By 1960 the non-sterling trade balance had reached a positive figure of 10.8 million pounds.

The pattern of trade can thus be seen to have been decisively influenced by policy decisions, especially by the choice and parity of the currency. It should be remembered, however, that whereas the German currency decisions of the 1890's and anti-Zanzibar trading activities were conceived specifically for Tanganyika, those of the British Mandate were worked out for Kenya, Uganda and Tanganyika together, and do not imply the existence of an important settlers' pressure group in Tanganyika alone. Tanganyika alone was probably of marginal importance to Britain.

Table 18. *Tanganyika Behaviour in Currency Bloc, 1945–1951* [a]

	1945	1946	1947	1948	1949	1950	1951
Trade Balance with:							
World	+ 872	+ 956	—3,136	—6,574	—6,851	+1,056	+12,225
Empire	+1,229	+2,000	+1,149	+ 871	—6,715	— 889	+ 6,885
Non-Sterling Countries	— 357	—1,044	—4,285	—7,445	— 136	+1,945	+ 5,340

[a] Dotted lines indicate breaks in comparability, which, however, should have the effect of shifting all the figures in any one year in the same direction, approximately. Kenya and Uganda trade is excluded. As in the other tables Canada is included in Empire, although non-sterling; trade with Canada was sufficiently small to generate negligible error. Devaluation was on 18th September, 1949. Figures are in thousands of pounds.

Source: Official trade reports.

Tanganyika under the Currency Board became an integral part of the *British Empire* and so was open to a set of economic influences which had not operated in German East Africa. The characteristics of this new era may be summarised as: a greatly *reduced inflow of capital and grants-in-aid,* amounting at times to a very severe financial stringency and enforcing upon the territory for most of the time the necessity of a persistent *trade surplus; relatively high export prices* (not leading, however, to permanent improvements) *in the 1920's,* followed by a very heavy *collapse in the early 1930's;* and progressive *economic integration with Kenya on unfavourable terms,* especially because of the pattern of transportation routes.

One reason for the weak inflow of private capital was the unfamiliar constitutional status of the conquered territory, which was that of a Mandate under the League of Nations. In a report to the League of Nations on "The Practical Working of the Mandate System", Professor Rappard wrote:

"The obstacles which have undoubtedly in certain cases prevented capital from flowing into mandated areas appear to have been purely psychological and accidental, much more than real and permanent ... what is feared by would-be investors is that mandated territories may change hands and property titles therein be endangered. When it is fully realised, however, that ... no transfer can practically take place against the will of the Mandatory power, and ... if ... the Council of the League declares that it will authorise no ... voluntary transfer except on the condition that the transfer expressly recognises the validity of all existing property titles, then the security of investments in mandated territories will appear as great, if not indeed greater, than in colonial possessions which are under no such guarantee."

Quoting this with approval in reference to Tanganyika, Governor Cameron added: [9]

---

9 Legislative Council, 7. 12. 1926.

"All discussion as to the possibility of Tanganyika Territory or any part of it, passing from British control is superfluous and to be deprecated."

He went on to say that in discussions with plantation owners in Arusha who were particularly feeling this insecurity, he had warned them that by spreading these rumours they were depreciating their property titles, and "exhorted them to desist from it".

The fact remained that in the early British years — some might say, in all the years of British occupation — very little private capital came in, and the territory remained heavily dependent, for development and repair work, upon capital coming through official channels.

The dull state of the economy was described by the "Tanga Post and Advertiser":

"In direct contrast to our more fortunate neighbour Kenya, Tanganyika has not been boomed, and as far as is visible there is no intention that it shall be, so that we are not likely to suffer from reaction, but a similar affliction following on the dry rot and stagnation is slowly but surely eating up our Bank balances." (11. 9. 1920)

Official flows of capital and grants were quite favourable in the period of post-war reconstruction, and sizeable sums were received in 1925, 1928 and 1931, before the net flow turned outward in the bleak decade up to the Second World War.

Outright grants amounting to £408,000 were received in the years 1920/21 and 1921/22; subsequently £1.1 mn of debt was waived. The Territory also received "loan grants"; i.e., loans with neither fixed repayment dates nor regular interest payments. In addition the Treasury organised the issue in the London capital market of bonds to raise loans for Tanganyika; these bonds were guaranteed by the Treasury, and, but for the guarantee element, were in effect on hard terms. The loan grants would have been soft loans but for the financial stringency which supervened in the later 1920's and caused the British Government to require regular contributions to Sinking Funds plus regular interest payments at 5%; this was therefore more expensive than the Guaranted Loan. Arrears of interest were called up in 1926, and Sinking Fund contributions were regularised in 1927/28. More serious still was the virtual absence of new money; from 1932 onwards (and this coincided with low export prices) the annual *outflow* of repayments and Sinking Fund contributions regularly *exceeded the inflow* (if any). The official transfer account, in the absence of inward donations, became substantially negative because of colonial officers' pensions and gratuities.

While the lack of capital from London directly struck at the Development Budget, the depressed profits of the slump starting in 1931 accounted for reduced local revenue, with a further effect on the Budget. Development rather than recurrent expenditure was naturally the first to be hit. The Governor said to the Legislative Assembly:

53

"In these circumstances it is inevitable that there should be no money available for the further improvement of the necessary services ... We have been unable to find funds for extending the Medical and Sanitary work, the Educational and Agricultural Services, the campaign against the advance of the fly, for research, and for other public services which are of the utmost importance to the Territory. Owing to prolonged trade disturbances in Great Britain the financial situation there is more difficult even than our own..."

It should be borne in mind that the territorial government had no means of creating money. Its powers of borrowing were limited to what the authorities in London deemed advisable — and by its own estimation of its future debt-servicing capacity, which was a powerful consideration. Its cash reserves were held with the Crown Agents for the Colonies in London. A budget deficit was therefore a deficit with the Crown Agents (local bank balances and borrowing facilities being relatively negligible), and this was not permitted to any significant extent[10]. Nor was there any suggestion at the time that Tanganyika needed its own central bank, or that the private banks should be manipulated to assist the Treasury. In short, given the institutional set-up, no counter-cyclical policy was possible, and a sharp and painful curtailment of public expenditure was inevitable. A "Retrenchment Committee" was set up in March, 1931, and 18 months later was able to report that recurrent expenditure (alone) had fallen by over 16% (and by 40% on railway account).

Let us now look at the trade account. Sisal and cotton appear to have been the main commodities of interest to Britain; after some dislocation, they resumed their growth pattern in the 1920's in terms of volume, though at lower rates than in the German period. Rubber became progressively less important as Britain had already a source in South-East Asia; hides and skins became more important. Generally also the tonnages were increased by the extension of the railway lines to Mwanza (1928) and Arusha (1929); by 1930 the value of exports (£4 mn) was actually twice what it had been in 1920, and a steady stream of re-exports had emerged and built up to a level of £265,000. But then in 1930 Tanganyika was hit by an "economic hurricane", as Governor Symes called it. At this time there was an aggravating factor in the form of exceptionally heavy rains which caused serious and protracted washaways on the Central Railway line near Kidate, so that a recession had developed in Dar es Salaam even before the world recession made itself felt.

It can be seen that between 1929 and 1931 the export price index was approximately halved. Import prices also fell but not so sharply; the terms of trade worsened by about 40%, i.e. from an index figure of 177 to one of 108, over the same two-year period. It is to be noted, however, that only

---

10 To this day, the swing on the Crown Agent account is merely a working balance.

Table 19. *Import and Export Prices, 1924–1936* [a]

| Year | Exports | | | Imports | | | Implied Terms of Trade index 1924 = 100 |
	Tonnage 000 tons	Value £'000	Price £/ton	Tonnage 000 tons	Value £'000	Price £/ton	
1924	105	2,559	25.3	56	2,063	36.8	100
1925	108	3,008	27.8	90	2,864	31.8	127
1926	120	3,129	26.1	119	3,152	26.5	143
1927	141	3,441	24.4	158	3,672	23.2	153
1928	168	4,051	24.1	155	3,737	24.1	145
1929	180	3,988	22.2	236	4,286	18.2	177
1930	186	2,636	14.2	251	3,983	15.9	130
1931	155	1,645	10.6	174	2,496	14.3	108
1932	167	2,190	13.1	84	1,872	22.2	86
1933	191	2,543	13.3	105	1,947	18.5	105
1934	188	2,645	14.1	123	2,343	19.0	108
1935	228	3,445	15.1	153	2,990	19.5	113
1936	243	4,516	18.6	161	3,357	20.8	129

[a] Tonnages are bill-of-lading tons passing through Dar es Salaam, Tanga, Lindi, Mwanza and Bukoba ports. Values exclude bullion and specie; imports are direct imports, c.i.f. Terms of trade index is export price index divided by import price index. The long-run improvement in the terms of trade is presumably understated by reason of quality improvements in imports (export quality did not improve). The limitations of a crude £/ton index must be borne in mind.

Source: Customs.

in one year (1932) did the terms of trade indicator fall below its 1924 level, and there might be special reasons for the odd behaviour of the import price level in that year. To summarise, whilst the depression robbed Tanganyika of the benefits of the late 1920's conditions (in terms of import and export prices) the depression conditions were by no means unprecedentedly bad, and their main feature was the rapidity of the deterioration. By 1934 exports had fully recovered both in volume and in value to the 1930 level; the recovery of imports was much slower. In general, export prices were more flexible than import prices.

To return to the 1930 slump: sisal was not, of course, the only commodity affected — though it accounted for 40% of exports in that year. The price of coffee fell by one-third compared to 1929; export volume rose by 30% despite stockpiling. By 1936 the coffee price had fallen by about 65% or about 100£/ton on first-grade coffee, and the quantities going unsold at the London auctions were incurring extra costs for storage, insurance, and interest. The groundnut crop was a very large one but in view of the low prices part of it was retained for consumption by the growers. The fall in total export values led directly to a fall in commercial imports and so to a fall in government revenue. Revenue fell from £2.0 million in 1929/30 to £1.7 million the following year and to £1.5 million in 1931/32.

Throughout the inter-war period the inadequacy of government revenue gave rise to concern, first in the depression of the early twenties when the terms of London money were hardened, then in the thirties owing to the depression. It is understandable therefore that all official discussion of customs and excise policy was with a view to revenue; raising it, in the case of customs, or safeguarding it by countervailing duties, in the case of excise. Consequently the pressure which was exerted from time to time by Kenya for moves in the direction of a free trade area was to some extent resisted. The first of these took shape in December, 1926 when agreement was reached to remove internal tariffs between Kenya, Tanganyika and Uganda for certain goods on which the tariffs were identical. The second occasion arose in December, 1928 when a match factory in Tanganyika was under discussion. At that time it was estimated that each of the three territories was receiving £12,000 p.a. in customs duty from the import of matches. If the Tanganyika factory were to capture all three markets it was proposed to impose a countervailing excise duty and give rebates to Kenya and Uganda. The unofficial members of the Legislative Council protested that no such rebates came to Tanganyika from Kenyan or Ugandan manufacturing industry, but the Acting Governor, John Scott, emphasized that the proposal had the full approval of the Government of Kenya; and added: "We can assume confidently that if a similar case were to occur on this side, they will insert a clause in their legislation similar to the one which is already in our Bill." The Kenya Government had in fact promised to make similar arrangements respecting the manufacturing of beer in Kenya, and the Uganda Government had made a similar promise regarding cigarettes.

This resistance to a reasonable developmental proposal can be understood from the fact that duties on goods imported from overseas were regarded as vitally important for development; this revenue could not be given up without water-tight guarantees of a countervailing excise revenue.

The protection aspect definitely came second in importance. The official policy on protection was to ask the industry to prove its efficiency by establishing itself first before offering protection. This of course must have impeded development. In the case of the match industry referred to, and in the case of a meat processing industry, the machinery was installed, lay idle, and was finally dismantled and re-exported[11].

The same emphasis emerged in the discussions on railway policy matters. The revenue aspect came first, the developmental aspect second, and the balance of payments aspect, if at all, third. Nevertheless, railway policy has had (and still has) an important bearing on the balance of payments.

---

11 It must be added that the industries may have been of the hopelessly inefficient variety. The matches were produced at Shs. 418 per case; imported matches cost Shs. 135 per case plus Shs. 150 duty.

Two aspects of railway policy are important in this context: track layout, and tariffs.

The Germans had left Tanganyika with a Central Railway running westwards from Dar es Salaam to Kigoma on Lake Tanganyika. At Kigoma there were lake connections to the Congo, Ruanda and Urundi. Also there was the Tanga line running north-westwards from Tanga through Korogwe to Moshi (Arusha was linked up in 1924). Almost parallel with the Tanga line, a few score miles to the north in Kenya, was the "Uganda Railway" running north-westwards from Mombasa through Voi to Nairobi and on to Kisumu on Lake Victoria.

In 1916, the British forces invading Tanganyika from the north built a railway westwards from Voi, in Kenya, to Kahe, which lies south-east of Moshi, in Tanganyika. This was later joined to the Tanga line, despite considerable opposition. This meant that goods from Moshi (and, later, Arusha) could reach the sea either at Mombasa (Kenya) or at Tanga (Tanganyika). Mombasa is a superior port, with more efficient handling, deep-water berths, more frequent ships calling, etc., and as a policy has been adopted of charging equal freight rates to Mombasa and to Tanga the traffic naturally tends to go to Mombasa.

The tariff-equalisation policy was introduced gradually. So far as exports were concerned, it was the high tariffs in the early period which gave rise to complaints, and when later the tariffs were reduced to an equal level, the competitive advantage of Mombasa emerged. In September, 1920 the "Tanga Post and Advertiser" complained of high charges and published the following table:

Table 20. *Representative Freight Charges per Ton, in Rupees, 1920* [a]

| Commodity | Uganda Railways Nairobi to Coast | | East African Railways | | | |
| | | | Moshi to Coast | | Moshi to Voi | |
	Lots	Per ton	Per ton	Cheap Rate	Per ton	Cheap Rate
Sisal	1 ton	27/55	79/–	48/50	31/50	19/50
Coffee	1 ton	30/24	48/50	32/–	19/50	13/–
Wheat	10 tons	10/52	32/–	21/–	13/–	8/50
Flour	10 tons	18/59	48/50	32/–	19/50	13/–
Beans	10 tons	10/52	32/–	21/–	13/–	8/50
Flax	1 ton	16/57	79/–	48/50	31/50	19/50
Maize	10 tons	10/50	32/–	21/–	13/–	8/50
Hides	–	33/37	79/–	48/50	31/50	19/50

[a] Notes: Nairobi to Coast = 531 km.
Moshi to Coast (Tanga) = 352 km.
Moshi to Voi = 131 km.

There seems to be some bias in the way these rates have been selected. The cheap rate was for wagon-loads.

The present position is as follows:

Table 20a. *Representative Railway Freight Rates*
1960 and 1963
Charges, Shillings per 100 lbs.
(Rates are those in force since 1960
except where changes were made in 1963)

Freight Class:	Class 4	Class 7	Special Rate B.
Arusha to			
Mombasa	4/50	4/31	1/53
Tanga	4/50	4/31	1/53
Dar es Salaam	11/90	9/24	5/00
Dar es Salaam (1963)	6/96	5/87	2/04
Moshi to			
Mombasa	3/57	3/57	1/33
Tanga	3/57	3/57	1/33
Dar es Salaam	10/97	8/64	4/80
Dar es Salaam (1963)	5/94	5/26	1/82

This policy of equalisation to Mombasa and to Tanga has led to losses on the Tanga line[12], which have kept up the freight rates on the remaining (mostly sisal) traffic, has prevented the growth of Tanga port, assisted the growth of Mombasa harbour, and caused a continuous loss of foreign exchange to Kenya through the conveyance of Tanganyikan freight on the Kahe-Voi-Mombasa line.

A very similar arrangement was instituted on the Central Railway. It was an early ambition of the British authorities in Tanganyika to build an offshoot from the Central Line, northwards from Tabora, through the groundnut producing area around Shinyanga to Mwanza on Lake Victoria, giving access to the outlying areas of Tanganyika on the Lake, especially Bukoba and Musoma. The Kenyans already had a railhead on the Lake at Kisumu and regular steamer-services on the Lake; they protested to the Secretary of State for the Colonies against the building of the Mwanza line. It should be borne in mind that Tanganyika depended on the Secretary of State for permission to borrow the necessary funds. In the end permission was granted to build the line on the understanding that the tariff from Mwanza to Dar es Salaam was not to undercut the tariff from Kisumu to Mombasa. Accordingly most of the Bukoba and Musoma traffic continued to go via Kenya.

---

12 To what extent this tariff structure reflected the cost structure, and to what extent it is due to bias intentional (or otherwise) is not known. The present cost structure is subject of a study being undertaken by the Economist Intelligence Unit.

The question of Uganda traffic is also involved; Kenya's balance of payments is strongly supported by transit charges of various kinds on traffic between Uganda and Mombasa.

Table 20a continued

	Class 4	Class 7	Special Rate B.
Kampala to			
Mombasa (1960)	12/90	8/57	3/27
Tanga (1960)	13/63	10/15	4/06
Tanga (1963)	16/29	10/00	3/98
Dar es Salaam (1960)	17/31	10/43	4/19
Dar es Salaam (1963)	17/99	10/72	4/34

Freight rates are generally divided into classes from 4 (the dearest) to 10 (the cheapest) with certain special rates according to the nature of the cargo. This was an old-established British principle, that of charging what the traffic would bear, i.e. relating freight rates initially to the value of the cargo per ton, subsequently making minor adjustments according to pressures and protestations. This was the Uganda/Kenya principle. It meant, of course, that to some extent exports were subsidized while imports were taxed; this is still the case, an important point to bear in mind when discussing exchange rates and tariff protection. This had not been the case with the German Railway, and the captured German policy files were used by the British as a basis for determining post-war fares in Tanganyika. The gradual adjustment of the Tanganyika tariff structure to that of the Kenya system during the late 1920's and 1930's therefore meant for Tanganyika a considerable raising of import tariffs and only a slight lowering of export tariffs (no concessions were possible on the Tanga line, for the reason already mentioned; while revenue was the predominant consideration on the Central Line). There was therefore a negative effect on up-country development through a deterioration of the effective income terms of trade at the point of production[13].

The charges for goods travelling from the Congo were (and still are) about equal whether they go via Dar es Salaam or via Mombasa. This also seemingly gives Mombasa a slight advantage but much depends on the exact point of origin in the Congo.

This was evidently the best arrangement Tanganyika could make, and the British authorities in London evidently preferred to consider the development of East Africa as a whole (and to take the static viewpoint of comparative cost advantage)[14] rather than equity as between territories.

---

13 Apparently the Uganda Government was also opposed to what they considered to be in effect a subsidy for Kenya exports.

14 This is to place an economic interpretation upon their actions, ignoring the effect of political pressures.

In one respect perhaps Tanganyika could have done better. There was until 1961 no link between the Northern and Central lines. Communication was by sea between Tanga and Dar es Salaam; services were irregular, and the shipping agents' charges were unpredictable; no through bookings were possible. The Government did not establish its own steamer service because it did not wish to interfere in a domain given to private enterprise. Had it done so, or had it made a rail link as was done in 1961, the viability of the whole railway system and especially the Tanga line would have certainly been improved, and the prosperity of Dar es Salaam and Tanga relative to Mombasa would have been enhanced. Instead the prospects for development were conceived as further offshoots of the Central Line, both branch line possibilities in the groundnut area and southward extensions into Northern Rhodesia. In 1929 Tanganyika asked the Secretary of State to approach Northern Rhodesia to look into the possibility of exporting copper by rail through Tanganyika via Singida (or Dodoma); this was the so-called "Imperial Link". There was, however, no response; the period of retrenchment supervened, and a delay of 40 years followed before this project went ahead (with Chinese finance).

By 1938 the traffic passing through Mombasa, and the charges levied on it (road freights, railway freights, storage, insurance, breaking-bulk and repackaging, port charges and profits) were considerable, whereas the transit trade through Tanganyika (Dar es Salaam/Kigoma chiefly) was small.

Table 21. *Development of Mombasa by 1938*

	Cargo tonnage inward	Cargo tonnage outward
Mombasa	559,660	610,779
All Tanganyikan ports together	139,820	228,786

Source: Customs reports.

The balance of payments effects must have been cumulative as the development of Mombasa proceeded.

The trade recorded as "transit trade", with no breaking-bulk, to Tanganyika through Kenya and Uganda in 1938 was £2,527 only; but the broken-bulk trade, classed as re-exports, was £955,395. The "transit trade" out of Tanganyika was £35,268 and the "re-exports" of Tanganyikan origin were £687,985.

By 1938 Tanganyika's balance of payments must have been roughly as follows.

Apart from the margins on merchandise trade transactions, the main item of interest here is the behaviour of net private capital. The object of constructing this balance of payments account has been to attempt to measure private

Table 22. *Tanganyika's Balance of Payments in 1938* [a]
(thousands of pounds)

	Credits	Debits
Merchandise trade		
Exports	3,118	
less Value added on indirect exports		34
Re-exports	343	
Imports		3,448
plus Value added on indirect imports		133
Transit trade: value added		
in Kenya/Uganda		2
in Tanganyika	3	
Services		
Travel and tourism	319	306
(of which: crews' expenditure)	(29)	
Port earnings	35	
International Investment Income		
i) Government	46	140
ii) Post Office Savings Bank	6	
iii) Other		?
Other services		?
Transfers		
Pensions and gratuities		104
Private remittances	24	49
Private capital (net) (residual)		364
Government long-term capital		
i) Public Debt	44	
ii) Sinking Funds		113
iii) Joint Colonial Fund	181	
iv) Post Office Savings Bank		4
Government short-term capital		
Crown Agents (i) London		1
(ii) Bombay	1	
Monetary Movements		
Remittances through E. A. Currency Bd.	225	166
Movements of bullion and specie	607	88
Change in banks' external position	?	?
	4,952	4,952

[a] The following margins have been applied: on transit trade, 5%. On other imports via Kenya/Uganda, 14%. On other exports via Kenya/Uganda, 5%. Port income is estimated from revenue data. Crews' expenditure is Shs. 5/– per man, assuming a longer turnaround than is customary nowadays. Tourist revenue (offship) is 10 times crews' expenditure. Travel outgoings are £100 per European every 3 years. Private remittances are remittances by money-order only (therefore probably understated).

Sources: Currency Board remittances are from EACB reports (1937/38 and 1938/39 divided by 2). Bullion and specie from trade return. Remaining items from public accounts.

capital as a residual. It is interesting to note that it appears here as a net *outflow*. This is, however, to be taken in conjunction with the various sources of error — at least the obvious ones – in the accounts. These are as follows. (1) Imports are direct imports as measured at ports plus inter-territorial movements as noted by Mombasa and inadequate posts on or near the border with Kenya. Known "re-exports" from Kenya to Tanganyika are given (in the Kenya trade return) as £952,868. If we assume a possible 30% understatement then true imports will be £286,000 larger and the capital (residual item) will be only minus £78,000 instead of £364,000. "Other services" may be another missing debit item; if we assume a possible 25% of the relevant services of 1961–1964 (average) this gives a further £82,000 to offset. Then there is profit outflow: in 1961–64 this was exactly 7% of adjusted exports; in 1938, following the depression, it was probably smaller, but if we allow a possible 7% of £3,427,000 we can adjust the residual item by a further £240,000. These adjustments have the effect of converting an outflow of £364,000 to an inflow of possibly as much as £244,000. There could be a further error in the same direction arising from the omission of changes in the external position of the commercial banks; but it seems very unlikely that this item would be (net) on the debit side seeing that the other monetary movements are preponderantly on the credit side — heavily so. It is probable that this error is therefore in the opposite direction, indicating a capital outflow or smaller capital inflow. We may therefore conclude with a fair degree of confidence that if there was a net capital inflow at all it was not more than £244,000 which represents nearly 7% of the value of imports. This may be contrasted with the figure already calculated for 1912, another pre-war year, of 40%. The comparison in absolute terms is between £244,000 (at best) in 1938 and a little over one million pounds in 1912. Granted the existence of further statistical errors and omissions in these calculations the difference between the two is very striking. It shows the contrast between a boom year and a semi-depression year; it shows the more cautious attitude of investors in the 1930's as compared with the extravagant enthusiasm of the colonizing heyday; politically, perhaps, it shows the demotion of Tanganyika from being the only foothold in the region of one imperial power to being only one (and a marginal one) of several footholds of another; or some combination of these factors. Perhaps the most important feature was that Tanganyika was no longer on an equal footing with Kenya. In effect Tanganyika was a conquered territory, and Kenya (politically) a part of the conqueror, the British Empire. This has permeated Tanzania's balance of payments ever since both on capital account (capital is attracted against Kenyan competition) and on current account (especially in respect of the merchandise transiting and handling as described above).

4. The Second World War and Post-War Controls

The Second World War in its economic effects on Tanganyika differed from the First World War in the following respects: it did not encourage import substitution[15]; the scarcity of shipping space was met by a system of planned "commodity priorities"; many commodities were price-controlled and their prices did not reflect their scarcity value until a year or two after the end of hostilities. It was like the First World War in that it was followed by a spirit of optimism and a new emphasis was placed on economic development; and for a few years this brought with it some official capital funds. From about 1948 onwards, the physical supply of railway equipment and other capital goods had recovered sufficiently to begin to make some use of available funds, but both 1948 and 1949 were bad weather years; 1950 marked the real upturn.

In 1950 the impact of the events of September 1949 (when the shilling followed sterling in a devaluation of over 30%) was one of rising export prices and to a lesser extent rising import prices. Also in 1950, the meat factory "Tanganyika Packers" was opened by Liebig's Extract of Meat Ltd. The Tanganyika Government put in £1/4 million which in turn it had borrowed from Barclays Overseas Development Corporation. Previously virtually all meat exports went through Liebig's factory in Kenya. Also in 1950 came first disbursements of a £23 mill. loan raised on the U.K. capital market for East African Railways and Harbours. It was also around this time that considerable incomes were generated by the well-known Groundnut Scheme of the United Kingdom Overseas Food Corporation, which, though it failed in its purposes, left behind (at U.K. expense) physical capital in the form of Mtwara port, the Southern Railway, a number of roads in the hinterland of Mtwara and land clearances at Kongwa, Urambo and Nachingwea. The World Bank Report of 1961 says: "The injection of purchasing power by way of the expenditures of those engaged in the scheme appear to have given a certain stimulus to the economy of Tanganyika[16].

Back in 1949, Governor Twining had stated his economic priorities as:

- self-sufficiency in food;
- water development;
- improvement of communications;
- solution of labour problems.

---

15 Though it did stimulate new crops for export, namely pyrethrum and castorseed. However, 1942 and 1943 were years of bad weather and in 1943 famine conditions necessitated the import of foodgrains. 1946 was again bad.

16 IBRD: *The Economic Development of Tanganyika,* Baltimore, 1961. See also: J. F. R. HILL and J. J. MOFFETT: *Tanganyika, A Review of its Resources and their Development,* Tang. Government, 1955; and Legislative Council debates.

He stressed the difficulties of achieving these objectives with the Government's cash balances exhausted and the drought situation of that year. It is noteworthy that the development of industry did not figure among these modest objectives. Two years later, however [17], he referred for the first time to industrial promotion policy, speaking specifically of import substitution and of processing industries, based on local raw materials as far as possible, exporting primarily to the markets surrounding the Indian Ocean. He hoped for a self-sufficiency in gunny-bags and other containers, for industrial growth zones in Dar es Salaam, Tanga, Mtwara, Moshi, Morogoro, Mwanza and Iringa (not Mbeya, Lindi or Arusha however) and for laid out industrial estates with road and rail access, water supplies, and power. His Development Budget rose from £1.7 mill. in 1949 to £3.4 mill. in 1950 and £3.8 mill. in 1951; in 1952 it reached a peak at £5.0 mill. before declining as the Colonial Development and Welfare Grants ran down and the proceeds from the Korean War boom dwindled.

The year 1950 is something of a dividing line between the post-war period of shortages, stagnation and controls, and the period of steady growth and development. It is perhaps significant that the most serious labour troubles of Tanganyika occured in February 1950 — 5 months after the devaluation — when rioting, especially by Dar es Salaam dockworkers, led to shootings and pangaslashings [18]. This would be at the period when rising prices affected living standards but the beneficial effect of high export earnings had not yet been felt. It will be contended in the following pages that the stimuli of the early 1950's lifted the economy to a new stage of development — in terms of infrastructure, linkages and income — in which, despite adverse external conditions later, some self-sustaining growth could proceed.

5. External Transactions from 1950 to Independence

Driven chiefly by the sisal price following post-war decontrol, the export price index rose sharply after the war and was further spurred by the devaluation of sterling in September 1949 and subsequently by the Korean War.

The export price index rose by about 50% between 1950 and 1951 alone. This was not altogether due to the Korean War boom; it was also due to the general rise in prices as expressed in sterling, and to diversion of exports

---

17 Address to the Legislative Council, 31st October, 1951.
18 A dock strike was defended by pickets who, though not violent, were found to be numerically "in force sufficient to intimidate". This legal ruling escalated the dispute.

to non-sterling area countries following devaluation, a shift which also raises export prices as expressed in sterling; conversely a diversion of imports towards sterling-area origins would tend to cause the import price index to rise by *less* than the export price index. The devaluation was on 18 September 1949; between 1950 and 1951 the export price index rose by 52%, the import price index rose by only 23%. The terms of trade improved by 22%. To some extent, of course, the abnormal export proceeds were taxed away from the public, but owing to delays in the collection of taxes, especially income tax, the peak in government revenue did not occur until 1954/55, i.e. 2–3 years after the peak in export proceeds. There was therefore an abnormally high import potential in the years 1951–53, which presumably was the major factor (besides the change in direction of trade already referred to) in raising the import price index during those years:

Table 23. *External Trade Price Indices, 1950–1956*

Indices (1956—1958 = 100)	1950	1951	1952	1953	1954	1955	1956
Export price	110	167	148	114	113	102	108
Import price	91	112	121	110	98	99	103
Terms of trade	121	149	123	104	115	103	105

Source: *The Economic Development of Tanganyika*, op. cit. These indices exclude Kenya and Uganda trade (as do all other existing foreign trade price indices).

The Dar es Salaam Cost of Living Index (1958 = 100) jumped from 70 in 1950 to 80 in 1951 and 86 in 1952 (subsequently rising by at most 3 points per year).

This hypothesis concerning the behaviour of imports implies a remarkable inelasticity of supply; not in the sense of rigid production conditions, nor of rising production costs (since the price index fell after 1952) but in the sense of a particular behaviour by manufacturers. Most imports, it will be remembered, are handled by agents or manufacturers' representatives; the manufacturers were able, and chose, to raise prices to the extent described when purchasing power was unusually high, and lower them again later.

The import prices reached their peak in 1952, whereas export prices had peaked in 1951, (around the middle of the year)[19] and fell until 1954 as the abnormal purchasing power was siphoned off.

---

19 Legislative Council Debates.

At about the same time some stringency developed on capital and official transfers account; external loans and grants stagnated between 1952 and 1956 with grants falling as a percentage of the total.

The combination of falling recurrent domestic Government revenue and a hardening of the terms of British finance gave rise to a policy of austerity in Government expenditure comparable in kind, though not in degree, to the situation of three decades earlier. In this case a further factor was the rising recurrent expenditures unavoidably necessitated by the large capital expenditures of the previous boom. According to the World Bank Mission[20]:

"This gave rise to a feeling of acute budgetary difficulty, resulting in deliberate measures, sometimes even of an emergency nature, to hold current expenditures down to the approximate level of revenue: for example, in October, 1958 the Government imposed a freeze on recruitment of staff."

Public sector investment after reaching a peak in 1955 declined steadily right up to the end of the decade; private sector investment succombed a little later to the unfavourable climate, after peaking in 1957[21]. The extent of the disaster can be seen in the fact that total investment fell from 30% of monetary GDP in 1955 to 20% in 1960–62.

It was in 1955 that the East African Currency Board regulations were changed to permit domestic money creation through a Fiduciary Issue, an innovation which could only be useful in the context of, and may be regarded as a recognition of, a viable local non-export monetary sector. This Fiduciary Issue (the local lending of shillings, with which sterling could be purchased, to territorial Governments against the security of territorial Treasury Bills or other security) was extended to Tanganyika in 1957 (Shs. 20 mn), but did not reach a significant level until 1960 when it rose from 22 to 72 million shillings.

The Fiduciary Issue may be regarded as an artifical creation of money permitting the territorial Government if it so desired to utilise foreign exchange reserves for the importation of Government stores or services — reserves which were built up by earlier balance of payments surpluses. Though this was not a form of external aid, it did release reserves which would not otherwise have been spendable. It is unfortunate that this one available counter-cyclical institution was not utilised on any significant scale until 1960, when the export price index, the terms of trade index, and the availability of outside finance were clearly recovering.

The last years before independence, 1959 onwards, were characterised by an improvement in the terms of trade; as mentioned earlier, this was due to a recovery in the industrialised nations, and brought a sharp response:

---

20 IBRD: *The Economic Development of Tanganyika*, Baltimore, 1961 and J. F. R. HILL & J. J. MOFFETT, *op. cit.*
21 Paul G. CLARK: *Development Planning in East Africa*, Nairobi, 1965.

Table 24. *External Trade Indices, 1957–1963*

Indices (1954 = 100)	1957	1958	1959	1960	1961	1962	1963
Export price Index	87	81	85	89	86	87	100
Export volume Index	124	142	147	169	157	162	174
Import price Index	95	95	94	99	95	90	99
Terms of trade Index	92	85	90	90	91	97	101

Source: Statistical Abstract, 1964.

The Government was able, in the last pre-independence Budget, to push up its capital expenditure programme to £7.3 mn., an increase of 29.4% over that of 1960/61:

Table 25. *Development Budget 1958/59 to 1963/64*
(£'000)

Year	Capital Expenditure	Financed Domestically	Externally
1958/59	5,159	1,529	3,630
1959/60	3,939	852	3,087
1960/61	5,672	866	4,806
1961/62	7,341	189	7,152
1962/63	5,674	626	5,018
1963/64	7,263	2,233	5,030

Source: Statistical Abstract, 1964.

The £7,341,000 was financed almost entirely from external sources (£7,152,000); of this, £3,182,000 was the Colonial Development and Welfare grant and £3,970,000 was external borrowing. The latter was chiefly short term; between mid-1961 and mid-1962 the Tanganyika Government took £2,901,000 of external short-term finance [22] mostly from Crown Agents in London and sold a further £0.4 mn. of Treasury Bills to the East African Currency Board [23].

The change also brought new attitudes towards development. In a late pre-independence Budget (1960) the Finance Minister advocated investment in agriculture rather than in manufacturing:

22 This is a swing on current account, plus discounting of bills if need be, or lending on the security of British Government Stock.
23 E.A.C.B. Report, 1966.

"The first aim of the Government ... must be to expand our market by increasing the incomes of our people, and this means expanding first and foremost our agricultural production for sale. To give an example, a ten per cent expansion of agricultural marketed production — which is certainly feasible — means an increase of almost £4,000,000 in the Territory's national income and could be achieved with comparatively and certainly relatively little additional capital investment. But a ten per cent increase in manufacturing output would add only £700,000 to our national income and would probably require a capital outlay of the order of £4,000,000. A study of figures of the initial amounts of working and fixed capital required per worker in certain West African industries will underline this point. For the cement industry the figure is £13,150 per worker. For textile mills £1,375 and for a vehicle assembly plant £3,000 per worker. Similar ratios are likely to apply in East African circumstances. But the numbers employed are also interesting. Based on West African experience it is believed that a singlet factory employing about 200 people could supply all Tanganyika's requirements. Now let me be not misunderstood. I am not saying that industrialization is not necessary nor welcome in Tanganyika. On the contrary, there are a number of industries which could operate with profit even within the present Tanganyikan market and the Government will actively encourage their establishment by assisting them in every possible way. But industry will seek us naturally when it sees, through the growth of the purchasing power of our people, an expanding market which will assure them a reasonable prospect of profitable operation, and we may have to await that time before we see a really big increase in industrial manufacturing. "Import substitution" is useful when fighting a battle in a balance of payments difficulty, but it is doubtful whether it would be wise to indulge in this on a very large scale if that meant the use of limited resources from Government funds. In those circumstances Government money would be more wisely and profitably used in developing our natural resources, in expanding our agricultural production and providing the communications which will open up the country and ensure a freer, more certain and cheaper method of getting that production to the point of sale or export."

This raises the question of whether, by independence, the economy was ready (in terms of purchasing power and distribution facilities) for an upswing in investment in manufacturing, or whether, as the Minister believed, a further period of preparation was necessary, in which the market would be extended (by increasing rural incomes) and distribution would be facilitated by additional infrastructural amenities. In other words, whether or not conditions had matured for "take-off".

There is in fact considerable evidence that conditions had matured for some kind of take-off. The low export prices which had characterised the recession had encouraged larger export tonnages, and a number of physical (transportation) bottlenecks had been widened; thus, in 1961, 39,000 road vehicles were licensed, as compared with under 19,000 outstanding road licences ten years before. In addition to vehicles, over £3 mn. per year of road transport equipment was imported throughout the recession years. Mileage of classified roads rose by 20% between 1950 and 1960 to reach 20,464 miles. Electricity consumption over the same period rose by almost 60% (though cement consumption stagnated). In short, the real *recurrent economic activity* continued to expand, though *profit and investment* did not; commercial bank deposits at end-1960 were £1 mn. below the end-1954 level. This resilience of the real recurrent activity, together with the rapidity of development after Independence, constitute the evidence that the 1945–54 boom had brought a new set of conditions into being within the economy. However, to describe these new conditions as being the conditions for self-sustaining growth *given favourable external conditions* is to introduce a difficult concept which need not be pressed here. It is sufficient to note that the post-Independence changes are not to be explained solely on the basis of a new constitutional environment.

The revival, when it came in 1959–60, was not due to the emergence of any economic forces in Tanganyika which had been in gestation, but simply to increasing overseas demand. The Minister for Finance stated[24] in June 1961:

"Last year's recovery in the Western world has exceeded all expectations. Britain's industrial production rose by about 2% each quarter ... Tanganyika's economy responded well to the recovery in the industrial countries, perhaps better than many other primary producers ... our gross domestic product increased by £10 mn. in 1959 to £177.6 mn." He attributed the response first and foremost to the diversity of the economy in agricultural, livestock and mineral products; and secondly to the behaviour of the sisal price. Grade I sisal rose during 1959 by 24% because of excellent harvests in Europe which created a strong demand for twine at a time when Brazilian sisal production had declined.

6. Independence and After

Independence came, therefore to an economy already capable of accelerated growth. As we shall see, however, the growth in the first two years was no better than could be accounted for by an improvement in the terms of trade; later, the Five-Year Development Plan gave the economy a new impetus.

In 1961 weather conditions were extremely adverse[25] and the value of exports fell by 11% of which only 3% was attributable to a fall in prices. 1962 was a better year though the weather did not favour tobacco, and oilseeds and nuts were also adversely affected. Exports from Tanganyika rose from £52,834,000 to £55,966,000 (an increase of 6% with an increase of about 1% in the price index). It is believed, however, that the proceeds on a payments basis did not increase, owing to changes in the timing of payments. Meanwhile there was a modest 5% increase in tourist receipts[26] and

---

24 Budget Speech.
25 "A severe drought in the spring was followed by unseasonal rain and floods." Budget Speech, 1962.
26 Excluding harbour and airline earnings.

a useful boost in local expenditure by foreign diplomats (which jumped after independence from £450,000 in 1961 to £800,000 in 1962 and £1,303,000 in 1963). The capital account moved adversely however since the Railways and Harbours had borrowed £2,500,000 in 1961 which was not repeated, and there was a reduction of about £1¹/₄ million on central government long-term borrowing from the U.K. The result was that total foreign exchange receipts actually declined from £77.5 million to £77.3 million. The result of these unfortunate factors was a period of "restraint and sacrifice" [27]. Government imports fell from £5,854,000 in 1961 to £4,727,000 in 1962 and in 1963 were to fall further to £2,670,000. If food imports for famine relief (which were free of charge) be deducted, the figures are £4,530,000 in 1961, £3,283,000 in 1962 and £2,469,000 in 1963. The cuts were in:

Table 26. *Retained Imports – Government, 1961–1963*
(£'000)

	1961	1962	1963
Producers' materials	1,124	708	569
Producers' capital goods	2,302	1,558	978
Consumers' goods	843	539	511

Source: Statistical Abstract, 1964.

No such austerity was suffered by the private sector, however.

Table 27. *Retained Imports – Commercial, 1961–1963*
(£'000)

	1961	1962	1963
Producers' materials	8,509	8,819	9,729
Producers' capital goods	7,137	6,287	7,721
Consumers' goods	10,997	12,059	13,042

Source: Statistical Abstract, 1964.

Consumer imports increased sharply while there was a fall in capital goods imports. The estimates of actual capital formation show a decline in investment which was not made good until 1964.

The total imports, commercial and government, plus imports from Kenya and Uganda (which are treated separately in the statistics) rose from £50,292,000 in 1961 to £51,502,000 in 1962.

It seems likely that the explanation of this rise in imports and stagnant total foreign exchange receipts was simply one of changes in inventories. Consumption of such items as khangas, for example, depends largely on weather

27 Budget Speech, 1963.

70

Table 28. *Gross Fixed Capital Formation, 1961–1964*
(£ million)

	1961	1962	1963	1964
Government	12.0	12.4	10.4	12.9
Private	14.5	12.0	13.9	17.2
Total	26.5	24.4	24.3	30.1

Source: Background to the Budget, 1966–1967.

conditions (since agriculturists who can see that their crops will be poor reduce their spending on non-food items) and importers judge the market from year to year. Imports of cotton fabrics rose from £3,828,000 in 1961 to £4,021,000 in 1962 but fell back to £3,940,000 in 1963; this indicates some "over-stocking" in 1962.

Other significant increases in usage of foreign exchange were in interest on external public debt (up from £354,000 to £835,000) and emigrants' remittances (up from £571,000 to £788,000), a move into foreign securities by resident companies and local government amounting to some £988,000. At the same time the central government paid subscriptions to the IBRD, the IFC and the IDA totalling £223,000 [28]. Total foreign exchange outgoings rose from £74,563,000 in 1961 to £78,869,000 in 1962. The monetary reserves after rising by £2,809,000 (net) in 1961 rose by only £1,261,000 (net) in 1962. (The "residual item" was positive.)

In 1963 conditions for primary producers improved further, with a further boom in the U.S.A. and the U.K. The export price index rose by 13 points and the import price index rose by 9 points. The sisal price in particular reached the high level of £148 per ton (for No. 1 grade c.i.f. London) in April and remained at that level throughout 1963; the average price of all Tanzanian sisal through the year was £106, 47% higher than the comparable figure of 1962. Cotton and coffee fetched fairly high prices despite record harvests, and there was some recovery in cashew and groundnut prices. Tea and tobacco remained depressed.

The weather was favourable over most of the country and every major crop increased in volume, reaching record levels. The net output of monetary agriculture, both from estates and from smallholdings, rose by over 11% in real terms [29]. The total gross output of crops rose from £105,590,000 to £118,570,000 in money terms, an increase of 12.3% [30]. Total exports rose from £55,966,000 to £68,562,000, an increase of 22.5%.

---

28 E.A.C.S.O. balance of payments data. Budgetary data (Budget Speech, 1963) show a payment of £1,055,000 to these bodies together with the I.M.F. in the financial year 1962/63.
29 *Background to the Budget, 1964–1965.*
30 Ibid.

Tourist receipts rose by 16% and transportation earnings (harbour and airways) rose by 28%. This was undoubtedly the year in which tourism emerged from the status of accident and became a field of public policy. The Tanganyika National Tourist Board was set up in 1962 and the 1962/63 Budget provided for a levy of Shs. 2/- per adult traveller per night, to be paid to the Board for the development of the tourist trade.

Diplomatic expenditure in Dar es Salaam rose further, and was consistently more than Tanzania spent on similar objects abroad.

Table 29. *Diplomats' Expenditure, 1961–1965*

	Foreign, in Tanzania (Credits) £'000	Tanzanian, abroad (Debits) £'000
1961	450	nil
1962	800	71
1963	1,303	187
1964	1,433	333
1965	1,485	400

Source: E.A.C.S.O. data (estimates of credits, reports of debits).

There appears to have been a considerable gross inflow of private long-term capital in 1963: £873,000 of equity sales, and £2,554,000 of loans, in particular. The total gross inflow was £5½ million as compared with £2½ million in 1962 and slightly less in 1961. This was paralleled by an inflow of short-term private funds[31]. The central government succeeded in borrowing £2,675,000 long-term from foreign governments, at the same time repaying £749,000 on short-term account. The Currency Board distributed £2 mn. of its reserves as compared with £1¼ mn. in previous years. Total foreign exchange receipts[32] were £91.0 mn., fully £14 mn above those of 1962.

All categories of national income increased. The average cash earnings of African employees rose by 35%[33] and although this, together with the introduction of more capital-intensive techniques, led to a fall in numbers employed, total remuneration of employees rose from £56.4 mn. to £64.2 mn., an increase of 11.4%. Enterprise profits, after payment of increased direct taxes, rose from £26.3 to £33.2 mn., an increase of 12.6%; this mainly reflects sisal profits. Peasant monetary income rose from £28.9 mn. to £32.8 mn., an increase of 13.5%.

On the expenditure side, public capital formation fell (largely because of the completion of the Ruvu-Mnyusi railway link), but private capital

---

31 Mainly swings on inter-company accounts.
32 Excluding retained profits. These are normally shown both as a current outflow and as a capital inflow. Here however they have been netted out.
33 *Background to the Budget, 1966–1967.*

formation rose from £12.0 mn. to £13.9 mn. (still short of the level reached in 1961) and private consumption expenditure increased from £174.1 mn. to £182.0 mn.; a rise of $4^{1/2}$%. Imports however rose by only 2.5 or possibly 2.6 [34] per cent; it will be remembered that there was some "overstocking" in 1962, (also there was some import-substitution under way); and there was a considerable rise in other forms of consumption of foreign exchange. Tanzania's share of overseas expenditure of the airways rose by £$^{1/2}$ mn. Private investment income (profits, dividents and interest) debits rose from £5,623,000 to £8,139,000 (including the undistributed profits). There was a further rise of £$^{1/2}$ mn. in pensions, gratuities and allied payments; and a significant purchase of foreign securities by individuals resident in Tanzania, amounting to £5,157,000 in 1963 as against £4,300,000 in 1962. This was to jump to £8,763,000 in 1964. Also there was a substantial unidentified outflow of £6,587,000 [35]. The monetary reserves [36] rose by £3,004,000.

Thus, of the £14 mn. increase in foreign exchange receipts, £3 mn. went into official reserves, a little over £1 mn. went into increased merchandise imports, and most of the remainder went into capital outflow [37] — £5 mn. of it identified, and a large unidentified outflow which may be presumed to consist mainly of private capital outflow.

Such a result indicates the absence of modern balance of payments *management,* which indeed was not commenced until 1965 when a major step was taken to control certain capital movements.

The additional spending on imports, moreover, probably did not produce any increase in imports in real terms. The import price index rose from 91 to 100 (1960 = 100) and, although there was a slight shift towards Kenya-Uganda sources to which the index does not apply, the overall volume almost certainly fell. Assuming no change in the price level of Kenya-Uganda imports, the total imports in real terms fell by 4.6% in this exceptionally good year. Assuming an identical change, the fall was 6.6%.

Private capital formation, it will be recalled, rose in 1963 from £12.0 mn. to £13.9 mn. (an increase of over 15%) and this was reflected in the commodity composition of imports.

The contribution to manufacturing investment was clearly a small one.

The chief gain from the favourable circumstances of 1963 was, therefore, a strengthening of the official foreign exchange reserves.

Between 1963 and 1964 there is a distinct dividing line, (and incidentally the statistics shift here from pounds to shillings). In and after 1964, the

---

34 2.5% on customs clearance basis, 2.6% on payments basis (E.A.C.S.O. data).

35 E.A.C.S.O. (East African Statistical Department), Balance of payments calculations.

36 In this case this refers to external net assets of monetary institutions.

37 There could be a further capital outflow concealed in higher import prices and in higher profit remittances. This is, indeed, very likely.

Table 30. *Retained Imports by End Use, 1962 and 1963*

Category	1962 £'000	1963 £'000	Percentage increase
Capital goods and spares for:			
industry and commerce	2,461	2,648	*7.6*
agriculture	2,151	2,963	*37.7*
Producers' materials:			
mineral oils	1,772	2,066	*16.6*
other	4,134	4,756	*15.0*
Chemicals and fertilizers	1,380	1,494	*8.3*

Source: Statistical Abstract, 1964.

Government was working to a new plan — the Five Year Development Plan. In 1962 and 1963, it was attempting to work to a Three Year Plan, which, however, came to grief, partly because of lack of hoped-for external finance[38], and in 1963 a number of projects were deliberately stopped for this reason. In fact, the foreign exchange reserves showed a rise in 1963, as has been pointed out, and had the Government had adequate means of

---

38 Budget Speech, 1963:
"At the outset of the Plan we were assured of the support promised by the British Government in the Financial Settlement which so far as capital finance for development was concerned amounted to a firm promise of grants totalling £9¼ million spread over the period of the Plan together with a promise of a loan of last resort of up to £4 million. Soon after the Plan commenced encouraging promises of aid from other sources were received and we proceeded with the Plan, optimistic that the majority of finance required would soon be negotiated. By March, 1962, however it became apparent that it would take considerably longer than expected to negotiate assistance from the main sources to which we were looking. In the event virtually no external aid other than that from the British Government became available in the first year of the Plan and out of a total expenditure that year of £7,341,000 no less than £3.9 million had to be financed internally, largely by short-term borrowing. Even so, the figure achieved although smaller than had been hoped for, represented a substantially greater programme of work than had been previously attempted or achieved in a single year in Tanganyika under colonial rule.
"In the 1962/63 Estimates — the second year of the Plan, we budgeted for a capital expenditure of £8.34 million. By July, 1962, however, negotiations with various aid sources was still in progress and the Government had no option but to impose a standstill on much of the second year's programme. It was only possible to allow works for which finance was assured or for which there was a reasonable expectation of receiving support, to proceed. Although by November many of the projects which had been halted were allowed to proceed, valuable time was lost and inevitably expenditure this year has shown a disappointing drop and I now estimate a programme of only £6 million is likely to be achieved."

domestic borrowing at its disposal, these reserves could have been utilised. However, the fact that the economy was not geared to take advantage of unexpected foreign exchange windfalls was merely a feature of its general underdevelopment; a Central Bank was to be instituted only in 1966.

While the Treasury was wrestling with its problems of financial uncertainty, and erring (as it turned out) on the side of prudence so far as the public sector was concerned, it greatly assisted the private sector by extending protective customs duties in order to promote import substitution. The main protective duties (ignoring purely revenue duties) were extended, in and after 1961, as follows:

Principal Protective Duties	*Budget*
1. Shoes, leather or plastic, Shs. 5/– per pair or 22%	1961
2. Yarn, cotton or synthetic, 22%	1961
3. Screws, wood, $12^{1}/_{2}$%	1962
4. Galvanised gutterings and ridgings, 25%	1962
5. Cigarettes, pipe tobacco, Shs. 44/– per lb.	1962
6. Sugar, Shs. 16/– per 100 lbs	1962
7. Cloth, cotton, finished, Shs. –/90 per sq. yard or $36^{2}/_{3}$%	1963
8. Blankets, Shs. –/70 per sq. yard	1963
9. Shirts, pullovers and other garments Shs. 1/85 each	1963
10. Stockings, hose, Shs. –/35 per pair	1963
11. Builders' requisites, metal or plastic, windows, doors, baths, sinks, locks, etc. 25%	1963
12. Tanks, aluminium or stainless steel, $12^{1}/_{2}$%	1963
13. Paints, ready-mixed, 33%	1963
14. Cement, portland, 25/– per ton with suspended duty of Shs. –/65 per 100 lbs (antidumping device)	1963
15. Cloth, cotton, grey and unbleached, Shs. –/75 per sq. yard or $36^{2}/_{3}$%	1964
16. Other cotton piece goods, 1/0 per sq. yard or $36^{2}/_{3}$%	1964
17. Blankets, Shs. –/80 per sq. yard or 40%	1964
18. Shirts, pullovers, and other garments, 2/– or 40%	1964
19. Stockings, hose, –/40 per pair or 40%	1964
20. Soap, 50/– per 100 lbs. or $33^{1}/_{3}$%	1964
21. Razor blades, 3 cents per blade	1964
22. Sugar, 19/– per 100 lbs.	1964
23. Beer, cider, Shs. 18/– per gallon	1965
24. Aluminium products, $33^{1}/_{3}$%	1965
25. Steel products substitutes, 25%	1965
26. Screws, wood, and nails, 30%	1965
27. Polythene (certain types), 30%	1965
28. Stockings, hose, 1/– per pair or 40%	1965
29. Plywood, $37^{1}/_{2}$%	1965
30. Leather –/90 per sq. ft or 25% (whichever greater)	1965
31. Radio receivers, suspended duty 50/– each or $37^{1}/_{2}$%	1965
32. Mills, plate and hammer, 15%	1965
33. Sugar, 21 cents per lb	1966
34. Clothing, 3/– or 40% (whichever greater)	1966[a]

35. Piece-goods: cotton, grey, 1/– per sq. yard or 40%; other cotton or synthetic, 1/25 or 40%; silk, 2/75 or 40%; knitted, 3/30 per lb, or 40% (whichever greater in each case)   1966[a]
36. Radio receivers, 50%   1966
37. Soap, 80/– per 100 lbs.   1966
38. Biscuits, 1/25 per lb.   1966
39. Coffee extracts, 30% + 7½% suspended duty   1966
40. Steel bars and rods, round, Shs. 175/– per ton   1966
41. Nuts and washers, black steel, 30%   1966
42. Paint brushes, 30%   1966
43. Electrical cables, 15% suspended duty   1966
44. Electric lamps, 30% + 7½% or –/40 suspended duty   1966
45. Pipes and fittings, 15%   1966
46. Liner board, 15% suspended duty   1966
47. Beer, 19/– per gallon   1967
48. Breakfast foods, ghee, jams, pickles, preserved fruits, spices, confectionery, nuts, macaroni, tomato puree and foodstuffs not specified elsewhere in the tariff list, 50%   1967
49. Wines, still, 20/– per gallon (in bottle) or 16/– (in cask)   1967
50. Cloth, cotton, grey, Shs. 1/25 per sq. yard or 40%   1967
51. Other woven fabrics, 1/50 per sq. yard or 40%   1967

[a] Special April Budget.

Source: Extracted from successive Budgets. Some of these duties are partly offset by excise duties. Protection given by freeing industrial inputs from duty is excluded.

A perusal of this list will indicate (a) the increasing coverage and degree of protection (no protective duties were *reduced* during this period), and (b) the increasing sophistication of the protected industries. This was particularly marked in 1966 which was in some respects a year of a "Great Leap".

In addition to protective tariffs, further protection was given by import licensing and, from 1968 onwards, by the "transfer taxes" (tariffs on Kenya and Uganda goods). These are described elsewhere.

The growth of manufacturing, partly no doubt because of this protection[39], has been impressive:

Table 31. *Gross Domestic Product from Manufacturing, 1960/62–1966*

	1960—1962 average	1963	1964	1965	1966
At current factor cost					
Shs. mn.	134	156	194	222	271
Index (1960 = 100)	123	143	178	204	249
At constant prices					
Index (1960 = 100)	119	145	155	171	197

Source: Statistical Abstract, 1964.

39 The extent of protection has been shown to be great in D. KESSEL "The Effective Protection of Tanzania's Industry", E.R.B. Paper 67/8.

These figures refer, of course, to value added.

The annual average growth rate between 1960–62 and 1966 in money terms has been 15.1% and in constant prices has been 10.6%.

This industrialisation effort is reflected in the pattern of imports, from which the turning point after 1963, already remarked on, can again be seen from the commodity classification of imports (see Table 5).

From these figures it can be seen that the percentage of imports of consumer goods (which were boosted in 1961–62 by famine) continued in 1963 at a higher level than in 1961, and showed a significant decline only in the later years (1964 onwards). The percentage share of capital goods was slightly better in 1963 than in 1962 but did not regain its 1961 level until 1965. In 1966 it apparently fell back but in that year there were very heavy imports of transport equipment much of which was of a "capital" nature. Moreover the jump in 1965 may partly be due to the inclusion under "capital goods" of items of an intermediate nature; the "intermediate goods" category shows uninterrupted growth except for that one year.

With this digression to show how imports were affected by the post-1963 development effort, we may return to the historical narrative.

In 1964, GDP rose to Shs. 4,194 million at 1960 prices, an increase of 6.6% over 1963 in real terms. A very small part of this increase was due to higher world commodity prices: the export price index rose by a mere 1 point. Prices did rise significantly, however, for cashew nuts and coffee, and in these crops there was at the same time a big jump in production. In cotton and sisal there were similar jumps in production but not in actual exports; quantities were withheld at a time of falling prices.

The output of tea declined as a result of adverse weather, but a larger quantity was actually sold (4.4 as against 3.9 thousand tons); export proceeds remained static at Shs. 31 million.

Diamond exports increased in volume from 588.9 to 664.0 thousand carats, 1963 having been the nadir from which volume was to expand to reach 905.7 thousand in 1966. The value rose from 99 to 136 million shillings, an increase of 37%. Gold, by contrast, declined from its 1963 peak value of Shs. 26 mn. to Shs. 23 mn. and has continued to decline since, as known reserves are progressively exhausted.

The total export proceeds rose from Shs. 1,371 million to Shs. 1,531 million, an increase of over 11%.

Other sources of additional foreign exchange were tourism and port earnings (up from Shs. 90 mn. to Shs. 99 mn.), interest on sinking funds and other official investments in the U.K. (up from 23 to 29 million Shs.), a further growth in diplomatic expenditure in the country (from 26 to 29 million), additional borrowing by East African Railways & Harbours attributable to Tanganyika (from 1 to 24 mn. Shs., including both long- and short-term borrowing).

Total foreign exchange receipts rose from 1,819 mn. Shs. in 1963 to 2,043 mn. in 1964 (undistributed profits excluded), an increase of 12.3% — achieved with the export price index almost stable.

Unfortunately there was a heavy outflow of private capital in 1964. This is attributable to (1) the army mutiny, (2) the revolution in Zanzibar which shortly afterwards was united with Tanganyika, (3) independence of Kenya and Uganda which caused some withdrawal of expatriate capital operated on an East African basis.

It is, as usual in such cases, impossible to determine accurately the extent of the outflow. In addition to the data given by the company survey (included in Appendix I), there was a very large "net errors and omissions" entry in the 1964 accounts, showing an unidentified outflow of Shs. 251 mn. net. We may adopt the IMF (unofficial) convention of assuming that this is private capital flight except for some which is unidentified current account debits, equal to [40] 10% of imports.

The private capital account allowing for all this shows a net outflow of Shs. 279 mn. as compared with approximate equilibrium for 1963. Since gross fixed capital formation in 1964 was valued at Shs. 602 mn.[41], this capital flight was clearly of a serious magnitude; we may suppose that Tanganyika lost about one-third of potential capital formation in the private sector.

On the other hand, Government achieved a net inflow of Shs. 92 mn. whereas in 1963 there had been a net outflow of Government capital of Shs. 126 mn. (to strengthen the short-term position).

Besides the capital flight, other significant increases in the consumption of foreign exchange were in personal remittances (emigrants' and family remittances) as non-citizens left, and pensions, gratuities and compensation (for loss of office) as their monetary entitlements followed them. Some other (minor) items, however, fell.

Total consumption of foreign exchange other than for imports rose from Shs. 703 mn. to Shs. 1,006 mn., an increase of 303 mn. for which the capital flight was almost entirely responsible in all probability.

The commercial banks drew on their correspondents abroad to produce Shs. 81 mn. in 1964, and the other monetary institutions (particularly the Currency Board) released a further 8 mn. from reserves.

Imports, in this situation, were allowed to rise by 13% (the total annual wage bill rose by 10.6%, and capital formation was up by 24% at current prices) from 1,056 to 1,194 mn. Shs. Unfortunately 9% of this 13% increase was a rise in prices only. Real imports therefore rose by only 4% in a year when real exports rose by 11%.

All this is summarised in the following table.

---

40 At most.
41 *Background to the Budget, 1966–1967.*

Table 32. *Major Foreign Exchange Movements, 1963 and 1964*

	1963 Shs. mn.	1964 Shs. mn.	Comments
Credits			
Exports	1,371	1,531	Rise of 11% with 1% price rise
Travel and transport	90	99	
Interest on sinking funds, etc.	23	29	
Diplomatic	26	29	
Other current	157	182	
Capital: Rise in external liabilities, net:			
Public	35	102	Of which, inter-governmental drawings on loans were 53 (1963) and 79 (1964)
Private	117	71	
TOTAL CREDITS	1,819	2,043	Rise of 12.3%
Debits			
Imports	−1,056	−1,194	Rise of 13% with 9% price rise
Emigrants and family	− 32	− 38	
Pensions, etc.	− 90	− 93	
Other current	−339	−328	Of which, investment income 116 (1963) and 118 (1964)
Capital: Rise in external assets, net:			
Public	− 26	− 10	Minus sign shows rise in assets, i.e. outflow of capital
Private (non bank)	− 84	−218	
Errors and omissions:			
Presumed current	−106	−119	
Presumed capital	− 26	−132	
TOTAL DEBITS	−1,759	−2,132	
Monetary Movements			
Commercial bank funds net recorded inflow	− 29	+81	Minus sign indicates rise in reserves; plus sign indicates borrowing
Other monetary institutions, net inflow	− 31	+ 8	ditto
TOTAL MONETARY MOVEMENTS	− 60	+89	

Source: E.A.C.S.O. (East African Statistical Department), Balance of payments calculations.

In still briefer summary, we may say that there was both a very heavy demand for imports and a serious capital flight; the foreign exchange requirements for this were met by a strong lift in exports and import substitutions, a more vigorous public-sector external borrowing programme, and a large commercial bank overdraft in London. The reserves (largely external assets of the Currency Board attributable to Tanzania) fell slightly.

A higher degree of control is noticeable here as compared with 1963. True, the capital flight remained uncontrolled: appropriate measures were introduced in 1965 and reinforced subsequently. But the public sector borrowing was much more effective. The public capital accounts showed a swing between 1963 and 1964 of Shs. 83 mn.; and it should be borne in mind that only the latter 6 months of 1964 fell officially within the period of the Development Plan.

Still beyond control was the import price index, which robbed the 13% rise in expenditure of 9% of its real value. Real imports thus rose only 4%[42]. Obviously having no national monetary institutions and virtually no parastatal importing agencies, the Government could not put pressure on import prices. This could be said to be a manpower problem. What it could do, and did, with only a small team of experts, was to extend the number of countries from which government-to-government finance was sought, and to develop the system of residual financing so to make better use of such funds as were available. More domestic tax was also collected.

1964 clearly emerges as the year in which the Treasury became an effective developmental force.

Basically the development effort as it was at that stage may be appraised (as seen through balance of payments analysis) as being built around two forces: the mobilisation of manpower in agriculture and the mobilisation of foreign finance through the Treasury[43]. These two ingredients were injected into a system of largely uncontrolled market forces. The more detailed control of the economy had to await the solution of various high-level manpower problems[44]. Consequently a large part of the potential benefits was unavoidably lost. Real imports, as has been said, rose by only 4%, while the external liquid assets/liabilities position deteriorated.

The circumstances of 1965 were very different, both because of changes in the structure of the economy and because of changes in the forces which impinged upon it.

The export price index fell by 9%. This was largely because of sisal, the price of which collapsed from 2,167 Shs./ton (1964 average) to 1,394 Shs./ton

---

42 Assuming that the price of imports from Kenya and Uganda, not covered by the index, behaved similarly.
43 Reference is made to later progress by the Treasury in the Budget Speech of June, 1966.
44 It is not suggested that these are now solved.

(1965 average), a fall of over 35%. The price had indeed been unusually high; but at 1,394 Shs./ton it was lower than at any time in the sixties. (In 1966 it was to fall further, to 1,232 Shs./ton). The reasons for this will not be discussed at this point. The tonnage exported rose slightly (though production tonnage began its decline) but total value of sisal exports was only 286 as against 437 million shillings the year before. Cotton and coffee, the other major crops, also went down in price; cashewnuts (a much smaller crop), on the other hand, continued its price rise which went on from 1962 until 1966.

Table 33. *Unit Export Price* [a] *of Principal Commodities, 1961–1966*
(Shs./ton)

Commodity	1961	1962	1963	1964	1965	1966	Change 1965/66 %
Cotton, raw	4,580	4,538	4,481	4,445	4,420	4,127	— 6.6
Coffee, unroasted	5,522	5,129	5,255	6,726	6,155	6,045	— 1.8
Sisal fibre	1,431	1,472	2,179	2,167	1,394	1,232	—11.6
Cashewnuts	902	790	940	1,174	1,290	1,406	+ 9.0
Tea	8,900	8,266	7,760	7,091	7,159	7,236	+ 1.1
Cloves	5,752	5,448	5,448	5,454	5,441	6,051	+11.2
Meat and meat preparations	6,716	6,794	7,994	7,973	6,830	7,284	+ 6.6
Castor Seed	1,026	890	870	898	821	911	+11.0
Sesame Seed	1,316	1,366	1,264	1,238	1,364	1,676	+22.9

[a] F.o.b. including export levy.
Source: Background to the Budget, 1966–1967.

As a result of these price changes the export price index (1960 base) fell from 113 to 103. The volume index also declined (from 113 to 111) owing to the much poorer weather of 1965, and total Tanganyika exports fell in value from 1,531 to 1,400 mn. Shs. This drop was only 8.5% (the two indexes are not fully accurate).

For Tanzania as a whole — Zanzibar was linked with Tanganyika by this time — exports fell from 1,563 to 1,434 mn., a drop of 8.3%. However, as Zanzibar balance of payments data are not yet fully integrated with those of the mainland, and are relatively very small, the statistics used here will be confined to mainland Tanzania unless otherwise stated.

The capital flight was greatly reduced. This was partly because of changes in Exchange Control regulations introduced in June, 1965, whereby capital outflows to destinations outside East Africa were no longer permitted. Formerly such flows were permitted within the Sterling Area, and undoubtedly the U.K., India and South Africa were the main havens of the capital flight. Partly responsible, also, was the non-recurrence of the special political disturbances which had caused capital to leave East Africa in 1964.

The private long-term capital, as recorded (rather badly) by the banks, showed the following movement after the new Exchange Control measures:

Table 34. *Capital Movements, 1965–1966* [a]
(£'000)

Month	Inflow	Outflow	Net Inflow
July, 1965	190	188	+ 2
August	858	582	+276
September	319	310	+ 9
October	357	51	+306
November	391	116	+275
December	422	218	+204
January, 1966	718	118	+600
February	586	93	+493
March	1,053	161	+892

[a] These figures refer to capital movements between Tanzania and countries outside East Africa channelled through the major banks.
Source: Background to the Budget, 1966–1967.

These figures show a net inflow of Shs. 21 mn. in the latter half of the year. Comparable [45] figures in the balance of payments accounts show a net inflow over the whole year of Shs. 3 mn., which indicates a net outflow of Shs. 18 mn. in the first half and a remarkable turnaround thereafter. If this is roughly correct, the Exchange Control measures must have been exceptionally effective, and the changed political circumstances may have been relatively unimportant.

Private short-term capital showed a net outflow of Shs. 14 mn. as the overseas cash position was strengthened, and this strengthening of the short-term position together with the net inflow of long-term money might be regarded as a healthy sign but for the fact that the *overall* private capital position registered a net *outflow* (Shs. 11 mn.).

The public capital account showed a substantial inflow both long-term and short-term. On long-term account external liabilities rose by Shs. 68 mn. and a further 26 mn. was obtained by the sale of external assets, making Shs. 94 mn. in all. The opportunity was taken to strengthen the short-term position by building up external net assets by Shs. 20 mn.; the overall public capital flow was therefore inwards, to the value of Shs. 74 mn.

Public and private capital movements together showed a net inflow of Shs. 63 mn., which went half-way towards offsetting the fall in exports. These capital flows are tabulated in the following table:

45 I.e. long-term private capital. Though in principle comparable, the two series show major differences for a variety of reasons.

82

Table 35. *Capital Flows, 1965*
(Shs. mn.)

	Long-Term	Short-Term	Total
Public:			
liabilities	+68	—17	+51
assets	+26	— 4	+22
net inflow	+94	—20	+74
Private:			
liabilities	+ 2	+ 2	+ 4
assets	+ 1	—15	—14
net inflow	+ 3	—14	—11
Total:			
liabilities	+70	—15	+55
assets	+27	—19	+ 8
net inflow	+97	—34	+63

Source: E.A.C.S.O. (East African Statistical Department), Balance of payments calculations.

The net errors and omissions item for 1965 was Shs. 68 mn. (debit), which is well within the limits of what could be explained by errors and omissions on current account. It may be mentioned in passing that for certain reasons there is a permanent negative bias in the residual item which has nothing to do with capital flow. However, even if part of the Shs. 68 mn. was capital outflow, it would probably not be sufficient to offset the Shs. 63 mn. recorded capital inflow. We can therefore state with reasonable confidence that the capital flight of 1964 was arrested in 1965.

There was also an increase in grants received by the Government from external sources. Commitments for such grants had reached the level of Shs. 97 mn. in the last year before independence, so that receipts peaked in 1962, but subsequently declined.

Of the 1965 sum (Shs. 113 mn.), Shs. 22 mn. was an exceptional grant for famine relief (it will be remembered that 1965 was a year of bad weather).

A further Shs. 44 mn. was earmarked to pay British civil servants' salaries under an arrangement with Britain which was part of the independence "package". E.A.C.S.O. received a further Shs. 7 mn. Besides these the "hard core" of the grants was technical assistance worth Shs. 15 mn. and other grants mostly towards the development budget of Shs. 24 mn.[46]. Grants were made available from the Governments of Canada, China, Ireland, Israel, Netherlands and the U.K.[47].

46 E.A.C.S.O. (East African Statistical Department), Balance of payments calculations.
47 *Background to the Budget, 1965–1966.*

Other developments, of lesser significance, were as follows:

Tourist receipts fell off, due to political changes (especially in Zanzibar), from Shs. 47 mn. to Shs. 40 mn. but airways' receipts rose, and taking transportation earnings together with foreign travel, total earnings in 1965 were at Shs. 102 mn. almost unchanged since 1964 (99 mn.). The outflow of investment income, net of retained profits, rose from Shs. 118 mn. to Shs. 155 mn. This change was entirely on the private account, up from Shs. 70 mn. to Shs. 117 mn. (a rise of two-thirds). This was presumably due to the exceptional profits earned in 1964 (especially on sisal) and to a preference for retaining very little profit in Tanzania (indeed, retained profit was negative) in the mood of capital flight which existed in 1964 and into early 1965.

We may sum up these main changes so far as follows:

Exports fell by Shs. 131 mn. and investment income inflow also deteriorated by Shs. 37 mn. This deterioration of Shs. 168 mn. was more than offset by a swing in the capital accounts of Shs. 240 mn. and an improvement of Shs. 17 mn. in government donations. Ignoring minor changes, this left the foreign exchange availability position some Shs. 100 mn. better off than in 1964, despite the worse weather.

This was taken up by a rise in imports of Shs. 141 mn. and a slower deterioration of commercial bank reserves abroad.

The rise in imports was as follows:

Table 36. *Imports by Category, 1964 and 1965*

	1964 Shs. mn.	1965 Shs. mn.	% change
Consumer goods	528	543	+ 2.8
Intermediate goods	185	205	+10.8
Transport equipment	112	129	+15.2
Capital goods	340	427	+25.6
Miscellaneous	29	31	—
Total	1,194	1,335	+11.8

Source: Background to the Budget, 1966–1967.

This massive shift towards capital goods imports, within one year of a substantial capital flight and at a time of such bad weather that P.L. 480 assistance was received for famine relief, is quite remarkable.

The small rise of 2.8% in consumer goods imports (while the import price index rose by $4^1/_2$%) reflects both reduced export earnings and import substitution. The category can be further broken down as follows:

84

Table 37. *Consumer Goods Imports, 1964 and 1965*

Description	1964 Shs. mn.	1965 Shs. mn.
Food, including live animals	109.6	127.3
Beer	17.5	15.9
Other beverages	4.8	5.8
Tobacco	27.0	14.9
Oils and fats (non-mineral)	4.7	11.2
Leather goods	1.5	1.8
Textiles (non-industrial)	197.7	195.0
Radio receivers	12.3	9.9
Miscellaneous manufactures	122.0	127.1
Medicines and cosmetics	31.1	34.3
Total	528.2	543.2

Source: Background to the Budget, 1966–1967.

The most significant falls were marked in tobacco, beer, and textiles. In all three cases vigorous growth is apparent, under conditions of considerable protection by tariffs and other means. However, another feature noticeable in all three cases is a slackening of the pace of expansion in 1965 when the reduction of export proceeds evidently caused an easing of the domestic consumer goods market.

These three industries comprised the first major import substitution programme. Many smaller enterprises were started up during this period, the *output* of which is generally however not recorded.

The percentage increase in consumer goods other than those three was 11.1% (from Shs. 286.0 mn. to Shs. 317.4 mn.). This may be compared to the increase in national income (monetary sector) or to the rise in monetary GDP, both of which worked out at 3.0%. Considering that 1965 was a bad year for exports, and that the new sources of foreign exchange were mostly tied to capital goods imports, this high figure of 11.1% requires explanation. Owing to local shortages, foodgrain imports were increased; imports of wheat, rice and maize rose from 15.9 to 27.2 mn. Shs.[48]. Without these, the increase of the other consumer goods was 7 1/2 %.

The 25.6% increase in capital goods imports, though reflecting the Government's efforts to secure external finance for public sector capital formation, also reflected an increase in private capital formation:

48 Customs and Excise, Annual Trade Reports.

Table 38. *Gross Fixed Capital Formation by Sector, 1964 and 1965*

	1964 Shs. mn.	1965 Shs. mn. (Provisional Estimates)	1965 Shs. mn. (Final Figures)
Public sector	208	224	313
Parastatal sector	50	41	
Private sector	345	473	525
Total	603	738	838

Source: Budget Surveys, 1966/67 and 1967/68.

The percentage increase in the private sector appears to have been about 38–40%, while the overall increase was 39%. This is considerably more than the recorded increase in capital goods imports (25.6%) and more than the increase in transport equipment (15.2%). The categories of imports do not, of course, correspond with the categories of capital formation, but it is significant that capital formation apparently increased much more rapidly than *any* category of imports. This may be simply because the import category is not sufficiently pure and includes consumer or intermediate items with a lower growth rate; another computation [49] of imports of "capital goods and spares for industry and commerce" shows an increase of 78.0%, which seems to err in the other direction. By any calculation, however, the increase in capital goods imports was remarkably large.

The increase in imports of intermediate goods was 10.8%. It is very doubtful if this reflects any significant degree of import substitution under way at that time. Between 1961 and 1966 intermediate goods imports rose at an annual rate of 13.3% while GDP in manufacturing rose at 14.4%; the difference is very small, and other sectors in which some of the intermediate imports were presumably used grew at lower rates [50]. The most promising field for import substitution is clearly consumer goods.

With these underlying factors, imports rose in 1965 by Shs. 141 mn.

The reserves of sterling held by the Currency Board rose by Shs. 32 mn., largely bought from the commercial banks. The latter found it necessary, however, to run down their (already overdrawn) positions in Europe by a further Shs. 71 mn., the reasons for which will be discussed elsewhere. A subscription of £331,000 (Shs. 7 mn.) was paid to the African Development Bank.

The current account (including transfer payments) as a whole was in deficit in 1965 after two years of surplus. Undoubtedly, this can be ascribed to the

49 E.A.C.S.O. (East African Statistical Department), calculation of "Retained Net Imports". Import from Kenya and Uganda excluded.

50 For example, Agriculture 5.1%, Commerce 12.8%, Transport 7.0% (*Background to the Budget, 1966–1967*).

agricultural situation — bad weather and falling prices; if exports had merely been as high as in 1964 the current account would have shown a substantial surplus (over Shs. 100 mn.). This implies that, but for unexpected factors, a situation would have existed which is not appropriate to rapid economic development, since there was no necessity for such a surplus. Although there was a large increase in the inflow of grants and loans from abroad, which had an approximately equal negative influence on the current account [51], the inflow of capital and intermediate goods was still over Shs. 100 mn. short of what could have been accommodated by the balance of payments constraint, had exports remained at their 1964 level. Since exports *actually* fell, it was fortunate that imports were not Shs. 100 mn. larger, but this exposes a weakness in the sense that capital goods imports were much smaller than *ex ante* could have been provided for without depletion of reserves. The explanation is, of course, that one cannot create Shs. Δx of capital formation simply by offering Shs. Δx of foreign exchange to the banks. The manpower constraint has to be reckoned with (and others such as borrowers' risk) and certain time-lags are unavoidable. In the conditions of Tanzania in 1965 an increase of 25.6% (or more) [52] was a remarkable achievement.

In 1966 the weather was much more favourable for export crops than in 1965 and exports rose by no less than 27.5%, from Shs. 1,400 mn. to Shs. 1,785 mn.

The behaviour of the main crops was as follows.

Table 39. *Four Main Crops, 1965 and 1966*

	Cotton		Coffee		Sisal		Cashew	
	1965	1966	1965	1966	1965	1966	1965	1966
Tonnage								
Production ('000 tons)	66.0	77.6	33.6	48.6	214.2	221.5	73.1	81.2
Exports ('000 tons)	55.3	84.8	27.9	50.3	210.2	195.8	63.6	71.1
Value								
Production (Shs. mn.)	212.4	252.8	204.9	305.4	279.9	254.2	62.6	79.6
Exports (Shs. mn.)	244.2	349.9	171.8	302.7	285.6	234.7	82.5	100.0
Price								
Export (Shs./ton)	4,420	4,127	6,156	6,018	1,570	1,199	1,297	1,406
Change per cent	−6.6%		−2.2%		−23.6%		+8.4%	

Source: Production figures are estimates based on marketed quantitites (*Background to the Budget 1967/68*); export figures are from Customs returns. "Sisal" here includes flume, tow and waste as well as fibre. "Coffee" includes cherry-buni. "Cashewnuts" are unprocessed nuts only.

51 Ignoring second-round effects, e.g. the impact of external finance on domestic savings.
52 Depending on the calculation used, as explained above: see Table 5, note, and footnote 49. Lowest figure is 25.6%, highest is 78%.

All four crops increased in output, though three of them were subject to falling price. The output increase reflected the development effort[53], combined with the great improvement in weather conditions. Cotton rose by 17.6%, coffee by 44.6%, sisal by 3.4%, and cashewnuts by 11.1%. Exported tonnage of cotton and coffee actually rose by 53.3% and 80.3% respectively: a logical response to a falling market price situation. The sisal industry, however, increased its stocks, refusing to accept the inevitability of a further fall in price, and trying to hold out for better prices. Sisal fell from first place to third place as a source of foreign exchange, at this period (1965–1966). Cashew exports rose in line with marketed production (the local offtake remaining approximately constant at 10,000 tons).

The export of diamonds shot up in 1966 to a degree which offset more than half of the decline in sisal.

Table 40. *Diamond Exports, 1963–1966*

	1963	1964	1965	1966
Quantity ('000 carats)	589	664	828	906
Price (Shs./carat)	171	204	172	199
Value (Shs. mn.)	100.5	135.6	142.3	180.0

Source: *Background to the Budget, 1967/68.*

It can be seen that an even larger percentage increase (25%) had occurred the year before, in output, but this had been partly negated by a fall in unit price. In 1966 both output and price rose (by 9.4% and 15.7% respectively). Price per carat depends largely on quality (size, shape, purity of stones).

Large increases were also recorded in exports of tea, meat products, hides and skins and various minor commodities.

A considerable effort was made during 1965 and 1966 to find non-traditional markets for the extra output. The important cases with the main crops were: (see Table 41 on page 89).

There was no significant diversification in cashewnuts.

The improvement in exports to Japan was achieved "following measures which restricted Tanzanian imports from Japan to a level not exceeding exports to that country"[54].

---

53 The increase in the cotton crop "can be attributed in part to favourable weather and the virtual absence of any serious outbreaks of disease but is largely due to increased acreage and improved crop husbandry. The continued provision of subsidies has encouraged further progress in the greater application of fertiliser and insecticide" *(Background to the Budget, 1967–1968).* The increase in coffee was "largely due to extensive use of copper spraying by smallholders but also to the favourable weather conditions" (ibid).

54 *Background to the Budget, 1967–1968.*

Table 41. *New Outlets for Major Crops, 1965–1966*

	1965 Tons	1966 Tons
Cotton		
Japan	2,414	15,392
(For reference:)		
Hong Kong	23,065	33,365
China	16,182	12,388
Coffee		
Japan	506	1,243
GDR	–	1,177
Poland	71	2,077
China	299	716
Sisal		
China	3,453	6,984
USSR	2,528	7,414
(For reference:)		
Japan	7,261	6,555

Source: Data from customs returns.

As a result of all these factors, exports in 1966 reached Shs. 1,785 mn., an increase of Shs. 385 mn. above the 1965 level.

At the time of writing only tentative estimates are available for most of the other sources of foreign exchange in 1966[55]. Travel and transportation are believed to have shown a substantial improvement, from Shs. 102 mn. in 1965 to around Shs. 132 mn.; and borrowing on public account is believed to have reached Shs. 141 mn. (as against Shs. 52 mn. in 1965), despite the last-minute failure of a Shs. 150 mn. British loan arrangement (withdrawn when diplomatic relations were severed over the Rhodesian issue). These factors would put the balance of payments some Shs. 500 mn. better off.

Imports rose by Shs. 278 mn. to Shs. 1,613 mn., and the monetary movements were Shs. 162 mn. better (in the sense of adding to reserves) than in 1965. This suggests a worsening amounting to some Shs. 440 mn. in all the other items.

The 20.9% rise in imports involved a rise of only 3% in the import price index (provisional)[56] so that the increase in real terms was a large one. It could, of course, have been larger still had it not been advisable to replenish the liquid foreign exchange reserves. Consumer goods imports are estimated to have risen by about 22%[57]; this compares with a rise in cash wages (of

55 East African Statistical Department estimates dated May, 1967, and Bank of Tanzania reports.
56 *Background to the Budget,* 1967–1968.
57 Ibid.

adult male citizens) of 13%[58]; however, the picture is distorted by fluctuations in the stock of imported textiles[59]. If textiles be excluded, consumer goods imports rose from Shs. 348 mn. to Shs. 372 mn., a rise of just 7%. The actual rise in consumer offtake would be somewhere in between 22% and 7%.

Imports of transport equipment rose from Shs. 129 mn. to Shs. 197 mn., an increase of no less than 53%. One of the main factors underlying this development was the "Zambian emergency oil and copper lift"[60]. This involved the importation of a large number of exceptionally expensive lorries and trailers.

This increase of 53% is paralleled by an increase of 54% shown in the national income accounts as capital formation (broken down by type of asset), "transport equipment". The increase of investment in machinery (other than transport) is shown as 18%; the two together show an increase of 30%.

Table 42. *Gross Fixed Capital Formation by Type of Asset, 1965 and 1966*
(At current market prices)

	1965	1966	% change
Building	254	253	− 0.4
Construction	255	262	+ 2.7
Equipment	329	428	+30.1
of which:			
Transport	110	169	+53.6
Machinery	219	259	+18.3
Total:	838	943	+12.5

Source: Background to the Budget, 1967–1968.

It is clear that the building trade underwent a slackening of activity in 1966. This impression is reinforced by a study of the import statistics in detail[61]

---

58 Ibid. The number employed was stagnant.
59 In 1965 the importation of textiles was confined to the Co-operative Supply Association of Tanganyika Ltd. (COSATA) which at that time was unable to cope fully with its responsibilities. The 1965 textile imports were insufficient to meet demand (prices rose). By 1966 new arrangements had been made and imports were correspondingly heavy in that year (a position which led to difficulties in the recession of early 1967). See Chapter 3.
60 See *Background to the Budget 1967–1968* for details.

61 For example:

	1965	1966	%
Imports of Iron and Steel:	Shs. mn.	Shs. mn.	Change
Bars, roads, angles, sections	7.4	5.0	−48
Universals, plates, sheets	23.4	19.4	−21
Tubes, pipes & fittings	18.2	14.8	−23

Source: Bank of Tanzania: *Economic Report*, July-December 1966, p. 28.

for 1965 and 1966. Consequently the figure for imports of capital goods as a whole shows considerably less expansion than that of equipment: Shs. 427 mn. in 1965, Shs. 455 mn. in 1966, a 6% increase [62].

The imports of intermediate goods rose by 24% to Shs. 254 mn. This is sufficiently large to require some explanation. Mineral oil formed a large part of this:

Table 43. *Imports of Intermediate Goods, 1965 and 1966*

	1965 Shs. mn.	1966 Shs. mn.	% change
Intermediate goods, imports	205	254	+24
of which			
S.I.T.C. 3	82	108	+32
Other	123	146	+19

Source: *Background to the Budget, 1967–1968.*

Imports of S.I.T.C. 3 (mineral oil and gas) rose substantially both because of the expanded transport programme and because of the opening of the TIPER oil refinery with its associated re-export of refined oil to Zambia. Re-exports of S.I.T.C. 3 rose from 16 to 96 million shillings.

The other intermediate goods imports recorded an increase of 19% which probably reflects much more accurately the rise in industrial activity. GDP originating in manufacturing rose by 22%, and in mining by 17% [63].

The rise of 22% in manufacturing output represents a vigorous programme of *import substitution* and explains why the imports of consumer goods (other than textiles) rose by a mere 7% when the cash wage bill rose by 13%.

In beer brewing, for example, Tanzanian production rose from 2,673 to 4,137 thousand gallons between 1965 and 1966. Total domestic consumption rose by 1,076 thousand gallons (or 24%) and if this extra gallonage had been imported at the 1964/1965 average import price of Shs. 7/75 per gallon it would have added a further Shs. 8 mn. to the import bill [64]. This alone would have put the 7% figure up to 11%.

There was also a considerable increase (42%) in local textile production, but

---

62 See *Background to the Budget, 1967–1968*, for details.

63 *Background to the Budget, 1967–1968*. The other sectors are also shown in the source.

64 Faced with an increase in consumption of as much as 24%, we may wonder whether this is appropriately described as import-substitution. A large part of the increase may be a shift away from a near-substitute (pombe) which is not imported; that would be substitution of one domestic product for another. The net rise in recorded manufacturing output would nevertheless take place since pombe is partly left unrecorded and is cheaper per gallon than beer produced under factory conditions.

that did not immediately have the effect of substituting against imports for the reasons already stated. Over-stocking resulted instead [65].

In order to assess the importance of import substitution in 1966 it is necessary to resort to various estimates.

First it is necessary to estimate the actual demand for imported consumer manufactures by correcting the actual imports to allow for fluctuations in textile stocks. On the basis of imports over the period 1961–64, linearly projected, the 1965 imports were some 15–20 million shillings below requirements and we may assume that this shortfall was belatedly made good in 1966. We thus have:

Table 44. *Demand for Imports (Consumer Goods), 1965 and 1966*

	1965 Shs. mn.	1966 Shs. mn.
Actual consumer imports	543	660
Textile adjustment	+15 or 20	−15 or 20
Adjusted imports	558–563	640–645

Secondly it is necessary to estimate the value of domestic production of consumer manufactures for the domestic market.

For 1965 the Survey of Industries shows the gross output value of each branch of industry. It is possible to pick out those branches which produce consumer goods [66]. Taking the combined gross output of these industries in 1965 (Shs. 874 mn.) we can deduct exports of consumer manufactures which by inspection of the Customs returns appear to have been some Shs. 80 mn. in 1965 [67]. That leaves Shs. 794 mn. Had this demand been directed to imports, customs duty would have been payable, which we can conventionally assume at 30% [68]. The import substitution in 1965 (for manufactured consumer goods) was therefore worth Shs. 556 million (or thereabouts) in foreign exchange.

There is no Survey of Industries available for 1966 and the only recourse is to gross up the figure of Shs. 556 mn. by an appropriate percentage. The increase in monetary national income (an indicator of the demand side) was

---

65 These facts are known in the trade, but no statistics of stocks of imported goods are available.
66 I.e. using the code references of the "Survey of Industries, 1965", all items except 2310, 233, 2390, 2391, 2510, 2511, 259, 300, 311, 313, 3190, 3192, 3195, 331, 334, 339, 342, 350, 360, 370.
67 £1,578,951 to Kenya and Uganda, £2,394,826 to the rest of the world — according to the writer's method of summary classification!
68 In fact, import duty amounted to 21% of the c.i.f. value of all imports in 1966 but clearly the duty on consumer goods is well above the average. Some further details are available in *Background to the Budget, 1967–1968*.

10.8%; the increase in GDP originating in manufacturing [69] (an indicator of the supply side) was 22.1%. This gives us a range, as follows:

Table 45. *Effect of Import Substitution in Consumer Manufactures, 1965 and 1966*

	1965 Shs. mn.	1966 Shs. mn.	% change
Adjusted imports	558– 563	640– 645	+14–16%
Import substitution	556	616– 679	+10.8 or +22.1%
Total demand	1,114–1,119	1,256–1,324	12.2 to 18.9%

This range, especially its upper register, of increase in total demand is quite consistent with a 13% increase in the cash wage bill, and is of the order one would expect in comparing a boom year (1966) with a bad-weather year (1965). It is unfortunate that one cannot be more precise, however [70].

From the above estimates we can draw the tentative conclusions that (a) about half of the demand for consumer manufactures was met by imports, and (b) about half of the 1965/66 *increase* in the demand was met by imports.

If the average propensity to import (for this major category of goods) did in fact diminish over this period, as one would hope given a 22% increase in manufacturing value added, it did not fall sufficiently to be visible in these statistical estimates. If it did fall, the increase in import-substituting output must have been in the upper half of its suggested range, i.e. between about 15% and 22%. In absolute terms this would imply an increase of at least Shs. 80 mn.

1966 was a remarkably good year for the balance of payments as compared with previous post-independence years. The withdrawal of the British loan was met with prompt action, in obtaining aid from elsewhere (chiefly China). Not only did foreign exchange earnings rise considerably, but the disposal of these earnings was fairly well-balanced: a moderate rise in consumer imports, without giving away more than 3% in rising import prices, a steep rise in imports of intermediate goods, a large jump in imports of transport equipment which was mostly [71] of an essential character, a reasonable increase in capital goods imports [72], and a rebuilding of foreign exchange reserves

---

69 Value added. Data from *Background to the Budget, 1961–1968*.

70 If private consumption estimates (in the Social Accounts) for 1966 were available, an alternative method of estimation might conceivably be attempted.

71 The reference here is to lorries for the Tanzania/Zambia road. There was also, however, an increase of 37% in the imports of motor-cars, some of which could be considered an unnecessary luxury. This was mentioned in the Bank of Tanzania's Economic Report and dealt with by the Minister of Finance in the following Budget (June, 1967).

72 Only 6%, but the Wazo Hill cement factory opened during this period. The completion of the TIPER oil refinery and of parts of the University College also had an effect on reducing imports of capital goods components in 1966.

including those of the commercial banks. Nevertheless some weaknesses can be discerned:

1. The rise in the import price index from 114 (1960 = 100) to 117 (provisonal) might not seem large, but it brought the index to 29% above its 1962 (post-independence) level. Even without any further rise one might suspect that a disguised outflow of capital was continously taking place in the form of unnecessarily high import costs.

2. The rise in capital goods imports, at 6%, was too small. The completion of the more obvious import-substituting projects — textiles, beer, tobacco, petroleum, cement — may, one fears, have preceded a gap during which new viable projects would be sought with difficulty in 1967. This in turn would lead to a reduction in the pace of the import-substituting programme. At the same time consumer demand, especially that of organised wage-earners involved in annual negotiations, might have acquired a certain momentum, thus producing a rise in the average propensity to import in 1967. Measures were in fact instituted, in 1967 and 1968, to restrain the growth of urban incomes but these did not "bite" in time to affect the 1967 figures.

3. The deterioration of some Shs. 440 mn. between 1965 and 1966, in balance of payments items not yet identified by the sketchy 1966 data, is disturbing. In view of the Bank of Tanzania's favourable opinion on the long-term private capital account, this may well be a matter of invisible imports. Another speculative possibility is that there may have been an adverse swing in private short-term capital owing to the rise in interest rates in London and elsewhere. This is a particularly difficult field to cover statistically and administratively, even in developed countries, requiring as it does either a very elaborate and expensive statistical service (as in Federal Germany) or rigid controls over methods of payment (as in Japan).

4. The export proceeds, though they rose by 27.5% were not as large as could have been obtained by better marketing particularly of sisal.

These weaknesses are, however, less serious than those which have been pointed out (above) in respect of earlier years.

At the present time, no balance of payments data are available for 1967, with the exception of the official foreign exchange reserves[73].

---

73 These rose by Shs. 8 mn. during the year; the change due to regular transactions was a drop of several millions of shillings. This, however, has no special significance since the end-year figures are subject to considerable fluctuations because of the pattern of timing of exports. Furthermore the foreign exchange (net assets) position of the National Bank of Commerce (not published) ought properly to be taken together with that of the Central Bank, under present operating arrangements.

An increase of Shs. 8 mn. does not mean that Shs. 8 mn. worth of foreign currency was purchased from the commercial banking sector and the Government. There was also an accrual of foreign assets through the conversion operation whereby the old East African currency notes were progressively

1967 was, however, a year of great changes which may be qualitatively described, briefly, at this stage.

Following the Arusha Declaration of socialism and self-reliance, the Government nationalised a number of private activities important in the balance of payments: the commercial banks (which formed the National Bank of Commerce), certain import and export firms (which formed the State Trading Corporation), and insurance (whereby private companies now operate as agents of the National Insurance Corporation). In Zanzibar, imports were progressively placed under the control of official bodies there (Bizanje and the Zanzibar State Trading Corporation). Furthermore the Government took majority or complete shareholdings in a number of manufacturing enterprises, which, together with the ensemble of the above-mentioned measures, had — for a time at least — a negative effect on potential foreign capital investment in Tanzania; i.e. the investment climate was changed. Industries open to private investment were listed. The actual effect on the capital account will not be measurable for some time to come.

In balance of payments terms these measures could be described as a drive against invisible debits. The nationalisation of the banks will stop a profit outflow of Shs. 16–20 mn. per year[74]; the reorganisation of insurance could (when satisfactorily completed) have almost as great an effect; the State Trading Corporation may have a smaller effect in terms of stopped profit remittances but could well have an even bigger effect upon hidden remittances, by reducing the import prices, upon which adverse comment has already been made.

Another drive on invisibles occurred as a result of the Rhodesia problem whereby Zambia was obliged to look to Tanzania for merchandise transiting on a significant scale for the first time, especially for the outward movement of copper and the inward movement of oil[75]. This began in 1966 but developed in 1967 with the expansion of harbours in Dar es Salaam and Mtwara, and the increased use of road and airport services. This should greatly strengthen the services account in the balance of payments — at the expense, of course, of the merchandise account to the extent that Tanzania

---

withdrawn and handed over to the vestigial Currency Board in exchange for an equal claim upon the Board's sterling reserves in London. Between the end of 1966 and the middle of 1967, Shs. 13.6 mn. had been converted in this way, with a possibility of several millions more during the latter half of the year, for which statistics are not released. This means that the change in official reserves *due to regular transactions* fell over the year by at least 5.6, and probably several more, millions of shillings.

74 Data from National Bank of Commerce (Chairman's speech to Economic Society of Tanzania, February, 1968).

75 Oil is not merely a transit item since the TIPER refinery is now supplying some oil to Zambia.

finances the imported component of capital investment in roads, harbours, etc.

It was also in 1967 that the East Africa National Shipping Line was established. The final agreement was signed in mid-1966 by Government representatives from Tanzania, Uganda, Kenya and Zambia, and in early 1967 the Line took delivery of its first ship (other than its 8 hired vessels). The difficulties of slotting in the new sailings so as to obtain the most profitable cargo have been a major preoccupation up to the present.

It was also in 1967 that the first sailing occurred of a new Chinese-Tanzanian joint shipping line, the first ship being under Tanzanian ownership (purchased with an interest-free loan from China). Whilst the E.A.N.S.L. serves the North-West Europe ports, which were relatively well served already, this other line will augment the Far Eastern service. The infrequent landings from all ports other than Mombasa and North-West Europe make it extremely difficult for importers to go freely to the world's cheapest sources, especially for semi-perishable consumer articles.

East African Airways in 1966/67 introduced Super VC–10's on its intercontinental routes with a fleet of 3 at Shs. 30 mn. each; these replace Comet IV's which were unattractive to passengers in competition with BOAC's VC–10's on the same routes. Cost per capacity ton-mile is officially expected to decline from Shs. 2/47 to Shs. 2/18 with an increase in capacity of over 40%[76].

Another significant development in 1967 was the decision by the Governments of Tanzania, Kenya and Uganda to maintain the value of their currencies, when the pound sterling was devalued from $2,80 to $2,40 in November. Most of Tanzania's foreign trade — virtually all except trade with the Americas — is invoiced in sterling, and such was the faith in the 44-year old sterling/shilling parity that almost none of the contracts included any provision for exchange rate fluctuations, such as gold clauses. There was not even the practice, among East African banks, of offering their customers forward exchange cover: this was introduced after the change of rate. Importers therefore made windfall gains, and exporters made windfall losses, though some of the latter — in the case of cotton contracts — were voided by successful renegotiation of the contracts, on an East African basis. Apart from this windfall effect upon business "in the pipeline", *new* business entered into a period of "tâtonnement" as new price levels were worked out. Export orders came almost to a standstill for a few weeks, as U.K. buyers sought to reduce the shilling price, and other buyers held off in the hope that they would succeed. On the import side, efforts were made (by the State Trading Corporation, which brings in about 20% of the imports, and by public opinion acting through private importers on the other 80%) to pre-

---

76 *Background to the Budget, 1967–1968.*

vent sterling prices from being raised by the full 16²/₃ per cent. It is too early as yet to assess the outcome, but it appears that Tanzania may have come out about square on the whole. This has focussed attention on import prices, an attention which is linked to the Government's policy of regulating the retail prices of essential mass-consumption articles, several of which are imported (tinned milk, textiles, bicycles for example). The very process of "tâtonnement" brings into the sphere of public interest what might otherwise be regarded as technically determined, and stimulates the development of instruments whereby the Government's intentions are made effective.

7. Summary and Overview

The latter years of the 'fifties were years of near-stagnation, with contradictory movements in the main economic indicators[77]. An up-turn in export prices in the early 'sixties, however, produced a sharp response in export volume and it is interesting to note that as the economy revived the Government was able to obtain increasing amounts of foreign finance for its Development Budget.

In an overview of the whole period from 1945 to the period after independence when non-British sources of aid were tapped, it is noteworthy that *more aid was received in periods of export-led expansion* (1949–52, 1960–62), and less in periods of stagnation. A similar pattern, though less marked, can be discerned in the inter-war period.

Private capital inflow, which — until independence at least — was mainly interested in production for export[78], perhaps behaved with similar perversity, but no statistics are available before 1961 for Tanganyika. Such as are available reveal the following pattern.

Bearing in mind the quality of the data, it seems that the vigorous injection of capital in the German period was not sustained, and by 1938 had become a mere trickle if indeed the net direction of flow was inward at all. By the early 1960's it was definitely outward, and the Treasury was successfully offsetting the flow by *increasing doses of official capital.*

---

77 This was common through East Africa. See Peter von MARLIN, *The Impact of External Economic Relations on the Economic Development of East Africa,* IFO-Institut, 1966, p. 70.

78 By 1964, paid up equity capital in Tanzania was £23,225,000. 52% of this, £12,229,000, was held by residents outside East Africa (how much was owned by Kenya/Uganda residents is not known). Of this latter sum, 60% was invested in mining, agriculture and services incidental to agriculture. Comparable figures for loan capital were £20,485,000 total, £18,730,000 (91%) foreign; £9,685,000 (52%) in the sectors mentioned. Source: East African Statistical Department, quoted by MARLIN, op. cit., Tables 14 and 15. Tanzania is, of course, not exceptional in this regard.

Table 46. *Private Capital Inflows: Evidence of Trend*

Date	Net Inflow	% of Imports
1912	+20,866,000 M.	+40%
1938	Between —364,000 and +244,000 stg.	Between —10% and +7%
1961	— 1,327,000 stg.	
1962	— 819,000 stg.	
1963	— 2,686,000 stg.	— 6%
1964	—12,844,000 stg.	
1965	— 933,000 stg.	

Sources: Calculations for 1912 and 1938 are mine; see Tables 14 and 22 for details. Data 1961–1965 are taken from E.A.S.D. using their "net private long-term" and "net private short-term" capital account figures plus net errors and omissions to the extent that they exceed 10% of imports, and are negative. The private long-term flows include undistributed profit. Imports for 1961–1965 are adjusted (E.A.S.D. adjustments) to payments basis, for better comparability with 1912 and 1938.

The propensity of the early colonial companies, such as operated in 1912, to invest exuberantly, rashly and often "erroneously" is widely agreed upon; though in the Tanganyika case the atmosphere of exuberance might arguably have proved sufficiently stimulating to justify itself, had it not been rendered "erroneous" by the event and outcome of the First World War. The greater powers of calculation and circumspection of experienced international corporations of the modern age, pointed out by ARRIGHI[79], may have erred on the side of pessimism, creating a negative climate of business opinion (even though their investments, perhaps for this very reason, did not constitute a preponderance of the expatriate "presence") which prevented the development of a great drive and break-through of the Rosenstein-Rodan variety, such as may be held to have occurred *after independence* (1964–66) under the moral leadership of a dynamic Government determined to economically mobilise the rural population, armed also with an energetic National Development Corporation in the processing sector and other new institutions determined to make their mark, and under the technical leadership of the Five-Year Development Plan.

Private capital, having trickled in (partly in the form of settlers' savings) the past, and having established a considerable annual outflow of investment income, registered a net outflow in the early-independence years, thereby shifting the emphasis to public capital, so that the present predominance of the public sector — quite aside from any domestic reasons — became an

79 G. ARRIGHI, in: *The Corporations and the Cold War* (ed. HOROWITZ), London, 1968.

economic necessity [80]. The private outflow was reversed in 1965 by Exchange Control measures, but still showed signs of weakness (late 1966) and by no reckoning could it be expected to show a substantial annual growth at the rate necessary to offset the negative balance of payments effects of its own amortization [81]. A path of development of the early Latin-American type is therefore out of the question [82].

With the growth of foreign official capital inflow and donations, the Government has achieved an increasing measure of control over the economy. This is seen in its control over the balance of payments.

1962 was a period of "restraint and sacrifice" especially in Government imports though consumer goods imports rose sharply.

In *1963* exports rose $22^{1}/_{2}$%, tourist receipts rose 16% and transportation earnings rose 28%. But of £14 mn. increase in foreign exchange receipts, perhaps £10 mn. was lost in capital outflow; £3 mn. went (usefully) into reserves, and the remainder was lost in higher import prices. However, from 1963 onwards the share of capital goods in imports increased.

In *1964,* exports rose 11% and total foreign exchange receipts by over 12%, but there was a heavy outflow of capital and emigrants' funds of various kinds. Reserves fell substantially, but imports were allowed to rise by 13% — of which 9% was a rise in prices only. Thus, while real exports rose 11%, real imports rose by only 4%. However, the situation would have been much worse if public capital inflow had not come to the rescue; the public capital accounts between 1963 and 1964 improved by Shs. 83 mn.

In *1965* coffee and sisal prices fell sharply and weather was bad. Export receipts fell by $8^{1}/_{2}$%. Tourism declined and profit outflow rose. But the private capital account was immensely strengthened by new Exchange Con-

---

80 It is possible for capital from foreign official sources to be attracted through local private enterprises, but the absence of Tanzanian large-scale enterprises makes this untenable. Capital from foreign official sources used by foreign private enterprise in Tanzania is recorded in the private capital account — which, as has been shown, was negative and had to be supplemented by public capital and transfers.

81 Estimated by ARRIGHI (op. cit.) as 11–14% well over the probable rate of growth of exports (with which the investment tends to be associated). ARRIGHI's calculations assume a net yield of 15–20% per annum which is perhaps on the low side for Tanzania. With a yield of 25% and a maturation period of up to 3 years the growth rate would need to be at least 16% per annum. In fact it is by no means certain that the 1965/66 performance will be improved upon at all in the remainder of the 'sixties.

82 These facts are reflected in the official Party policy of "Socialism and Self-Reliance". This programme *followed* the exodus of expatriate capital around 1964, and did not cause it. It may conceivably prove a deterrent to capital from fresh sources, which might conceivably be attracted, despite its circumspection, by the high rates of growth recently achieved, but, as remarked above, the inflow of such capital is unlikely to rise at a rate much in excess of the growth rate of exports.

trol regulations, and the official capital and transfer accounts continued to be fruitful — the transfer account alone produced Shs. 113 mn. in foreign exchange, half of it from non-sterling sources. Despite the fall in exports, foreign exchange receipts rose by some Shs. 100 mn. over 1964. Imports were allowed to rise by 12% and it is significant that in this difficult year capital goods imports rose by 25%. There was, by this time, a definite programme of import substitution, behind a rising wall of protective tariffs.

In *1966* the weather was favourable; exports actually rose by $27^{1}/_{2}$% (not entirely due to the weather, of course). Imports were allowed to rise by only 21%, and of this, 18% was a "real" benefit. A large U.K. loan was lost at the last moment because of the Rhodesian crisis, and the Government was prepared to lose it; fortunately it was largely made up from other sources. Import substitution was in full swing, and able to hold down the average propensity to import consumer manufactures even with a substantial rise in incomes — though it is arguable that the latter should not have been allowed to occur to the extent it did. A start was also made on dealing with various invisible items in the payments balance, and this was reinforced in 1967, the year of the Arusha Declaration, when the major nationalisations took place and a drive on prices including import prices began.

The growing degree of control, since independence, is quite obvious. This has been achieved partly through the development of new institutions — the Bank of Tanzania, the National Bank of Commerce, the National Development Corporation, the shipping lines, the State Trading Corporation — and partly through the greater experience of the Ministries, improved statistics, etc. Those who analyse economics in terms of models may regard this period as one of transition from one type model to another; 1962 could be approximated by a laissez-faire model with exports as the main autonomous explanatory variable, and automatic responses in capital movements, import prices, tax receipts, etc.; the model towards which the economy is tending is one in which a large number of variables are policy variables, including the trend[83] of export volume of certain commodities, official inflow of capital and donations (though not the terms thereof), tax receipts, the level and commodity-pattern of imports (in conjunction with Kenya and Uganda), and to some extent prices, certain invisible items in the balance of payments, and the size and rôle of the parastatal sector.

---

83 Only the trend, because of weather conditions.

III. MERCHANDISE EXPORTS

1. Agricultural Produce

Agricultural produce, raw or subjected to a simple preliminary form of processing or treatment, makes up about 70% of total merchandise exports. The three leading crops — cotton, coffee and sisal — accounted for about 50% of the total in 1966, a figure which stood at about the same level in 1961 though it was temporarily raised in the intervening years, touching 58% in 1963, by the high sisal prices of that period; in 1967 it fell to 40% due to greater diversification within agriculture, some industrialisation, and diamond sales ex-stock.

Table 47. *Value of Exports, 1962–1967, and Major Commodities*
(Shs. mn.)

Principal Commodities	1962	1963	1964	1965	1966	1967	Change 1966/67 %
Coffee	132	137	221	172	301	237	—21.3
Cotton	148	214	198	244	350	251	—28.3
Sisal	315	453	437	286	235	201	—14.5
Diamonds	109	99	136	142	186	223	+19.9
Cashewnuts	47	40	66	83	100	92	— 8.0
Meat and meat preparations	46	39	43	38	57	48	—15.8
Cloves	42	61	43	46	74	90	+21.6
Oil seeds, nuts and kernels	46	80	61	57	53	45	—15.1
Tea	32	31	31	29	45	43	— 4.5
Hides & skins	30	33	26	30	43	29	—32.6
Petroleum products	—	—	—	—	5	133	+2,560.0
Tobacco	2	2	1	10	16	34	+112.5
Other domestic	127	156	193	176	203	219	+ 7.9
Sub-total (outside E.Af)	1,076	1,345	1,456	1,313	1,668	1,645	— 1.4
Exports to Kenya & Uganda	65	72	107	121	98	83	—15
Total exports	1,141	1,417	1,563	1,434	1,766	1,728	— 2.2
Re-exports	52	42	34	31	112	32	—71
Grand total	1,193	1,459	1,597	1,465	1,878	1,760	— 6.3

Source: Background to the Budget 1967–1968 and 1968–1969.

Table 48. *Marketed Output of Principal Export Crops, 1957–1967*
(Thousands of Tons)

	1957	1958	1959	1960	1961	1962	1963	1964	1965	1966	1967	Average compound growth rate (%) 1962–1967
Cotton	31.6	30.2	36.2	33.6	29.9	38.2	46.9	52.4	66.0	77.6	71.0	13.2
Coffee	20.7	22.5	22.7	26.2	19.3	26.5	28.2	33.3	33.6	48.6	50.0	13.5
Sisal	186.0	194.0	209.0	205.0	195.0	214.0	214.0	230.0	214.0	222.0	215.0	—
Cashewnuts	23.4	20.6	28.4	56.3	26.6	55.4	56.5	72.9	73.1	81.2	80.0	7.6
Tea	6.3	6.3	8.1	8.3	9.8	9.5	11.1	10.6	12.5	15.0	15.3	10.0
Tobacco	16.1	17.0	21.0	17.9	26.3	24.6	23.2	21.0	50.9	52.2	71.9	23.9
Groundnuts	15.3	9.7	15.9	22.8	8.3	16.5	20.1	16.8	9.3	8.3	6.0	−18.3
Castor	13.9	6.9	6.2	10.9	12.0	10.0	26.8	14.6	13.1	12.8	13.0	5.4
Sesame and Sunflower	19.1	15.8	14.9	10.8	13.4	10.5	17.5	13.9	16.2	12.8	12.5	3.5
Pyrethrum	3.1	2.7	3.6	8.5	5.8	8.5	10.3	10.3	16.1	19.6	22.3	21.3

Source: Background to the Budget 1967–1968 and 1968–1969.

It is not within the scope of a balance of payments study to look far into the great complexity of factors which go to determine agricultural output; but mention may be made of the effect of prices upon output, i.e. producer response to price changes. This is unfortunately also something of a maze, since in addition to the official export taxes, and charges by marketing boards, cotton ginneries, etc., there are local levies which vary in each district, and it is in many cases impossible to determine the price actually received by the grower. The whole system is under review and is expected to be simplified and rationalised. Under these circumstances the setting of export taxes (by the Treasury), which is with minor exceptions a post-independence institution, has been very much a process of trial and error, and these taxes have been drastically altered from one year to the next.

Before considering the general results of export taxes, and other budgetary provisions, we shall take a description of each of the leading export commodities.

a) Sisal

Sisal was until 1966 the leading export crop. Its main market is in Western Europe where it is principally used for making into string for binding and baling, i.e. reaperbinders and combine harvesters use it for tying corn into bales. It is also used, to a much lesser extent, for tying newspapers into bundles, and for making ropes, mostly for marine purposes.

The total potential demand in Western Europe is therefore, broadly speaking, limited to the growth rate of agricultural production, which may be 3–5% per annum, depending on weather. The other major markets have independent sources of supply; the USA relies on Brazilian and Haitian fibre, while the U.S.S.R. and China are almost self-sufficient. China uses mostly "true" hemp.

This limited total market is gradually being invaded by the synthetic substitute, polypropylene, which has a number of advantages. Given the necessary know-how, it is produced from what is virtually a waste product of oil refining, namely propylene gas. Polypropylene crystals are easy to handle and store, in bags, being unaffected by humidity. A simple extruder costing a few thousands of pounds converts the crystals into either a string, for baling, or a strip, for heavier industrial packaging. The polypropylene string, used in agriculture, may be accidentally eaten by cattle without ill-effects. For marine ropes, nylon and terylene are coming into use, which last 2 and 3 times as long as sisal, respectively, and so work out cheaper except for special once-only uses. The introduction of synthetics in the marine trades is delayed only by the process of modifying the customs and practices of labour and supervision, associated with the care, preservation and testing of ropes. For light marine purposes, polypropylene ropes are available which float on water.

Table 49. *Destination of Tanzania Sisal, 1964–1966*
(Sisal including flume and tow)

Country to which consigned	1964 Tons	1965 Tons	1966 Tons	1967 Tons
United Kingdom	61,709	56,648	48,577	44,445
Australia	14,810	14,243	13,348	12,936
Canada	13,252	11,068	10,446	8,340
New Zealand	4,711	6,229	5,373	4,503
Belgium	23,577	25,092	21,608	22,774
China	5,229	3,453	6,984	3,000
Denmark	7,074	8,553	5,535	7,146
Eire	4,741	5,615	5,436	6,081
France	6,083	6,626	4,748	5,055
Germany (Fed. Rep.)	14,409	16,655	15,874	14,269
Japan	4,303	7,281	6,560	10,862
Netherlands	10,719	14,759	18,643	25,342
U.S.S.R.	614	2,528	7,414	2,369
Other countries	37,699	31,485	25,266	34,780
Total:	208,930	210,235	195,812	201,902
Of which: Western Europe:	140,906	147,849	124,260	137,611
equals (%)	67	70	63	68

Source: East African Customs and Excise, *Annual Trade Returns.*

The future price of polypropylene depends largely on the scale of its output, i.e. on investment decisions, which in turn depend on the sisal marketing policy. This means that, so long as sisal commands less than a certain price, the invasion of polypropylene can probably be virtually halted. This critical price level was a subject of discussion at a sisal conference held in 1967, at Rome, under the aegis of the F.A.O. It was decided that a sisal price of £73/10/- per ton was a suitable target price (maximum "safe" price), though the buyers' representatives originally proposed £68. This price relates to a low grade of sisal known as East African Rejects, selected as a key or indicative grade.

Shortly after this conference, sterling was devalued, and since polypropylene is produced in the U.K., the maximum "safe" price is somewhat lower than before in Tanzanian shilling terms, probably around Shs. 1,260/-.

Recent research by French technologists has shown that sisal can be made into a high-quality writing paper; and important investment in a factory to make use of this process is under study by the N.D.C. The economics of this process, as against the use of flax or ramie (soft fibres) or for that matter abaca and the other hard fibres, is still unclear. In any case it can scarcely account for a high proportion of the Sisal output of Tanzania.

While sisal is subject to all these difficulties, Tanzanian sisal is under pressure from Brazilian and other sisal. Brazilian sisal is produced mostly by

Table 50. *Sisal Production, 1960–1967*

Calendar Year	World Production [a] '000 tons	Mature Acreage [a] '000 acres	Tanzania Production tons	Total Export tons	Estimated Local Sales [b] tons	Change in Stocks tons	Value of Gross Output Shs. mn.	Price of Sisal No. 3L [c] (£ sterling/ton)
1960–62	567	530	205,623	209,658	—	− 4,035	285.3	103
1963	599	544	214,274	214,388	—	− 114	441.9	146
1964	655	560	229,852	209,554	770	+20,472	468.7	98
1965	610	549	214,152	210,510	4,900	+ 1,248	279.9	83
1966	612	565	221,529	196,736	11,700	+13,093	254.2	74
1967	590	587	216,618	201,936	17,400	− 2,718	216.3	70
Percentage change 1966/67	−3.6	+3.9	−2.2	+2.6	+48.7	..	−14.9	−5.4
Annual growth rate 1960–62/67	+0.7	+1.7	+0.9	−0.6	..	..	− 4.5	..

[a] Estimate
[b] In Tanzania
[c] December c.i.f. U.K. price

Source: Background to the Budget 1967–1968 and 1968–1969.

independent small-holders, who have been encouraged to diversify out of coffee; Tanzanian sisal is produced mainly on organised estates, with relatively heavy and incompressible overhead costs. At the present depressed prices, the Brazilian small-holders are prepared to increase their plantings, while the Tanzanian estates are in difficulties, mostly unable to operate profitably, cutting back on maintenance expenditures, and totally unable to invest new money in such new, cost-reducing techniques as are available.

In 1963/64, owing to exceptional world demand, Tanzanian sisal fetched over £100 per ton, and this situation undoubtedly provoked the swing towards synthetics which has subsequently depressed the world market. Cordage companies not only invested heavily in extrusion equipment but instructed their salesmen to urge farmers to experiment with polypropylene twine. Major polypropylene producers sought to establish themselves in the new market by offering attractive prices. In the falling sisal market, the U.S. strategic stockpile authorities (G.S.O.) decided to sell substantial quantities of sisal, and the stocks accumulating within Tanzania and Mexico have had a further depressing effect.

The 1967 conference decided to impose country quotas, applying a reduction of 4.8% to the agreed producing capacity of each country[1]. Both the agreed capacities and the agreed reduction were somewhat arbitrary, and indeed, if this scheme were perfectly implemented, the effect would probably be barely to sustain the price level rather than to reach the agreed target. In fact, since the quota applies to actual shipments while the price level is negotiated on the forward market, the tendency will be for each country to sell out competitively on the forward market first while waiting to see how far other countries have adhered to their quotas as regards deliveries. This condemns the scheme to a bad start; present forward prices reflect no confidence in it. Basically the problem is one of a conflict of interests between Brazil and other producers.

On 1st January, 1963 when prices were clearly rising, an export tax was imposed of 5% ad valorem, with a floor level of £60 per ton. In the 1963 Budget, following complaints by producers based on rising costs, the floor level was raised to £75, but the rate was made into a sliding scale rising after £100 per ton to 10% at £110 and 20% at £125 or above. In 1963 the average export price of sisal fibre was in fact £109 per ton, and in 1964 £108; the price collapsed towards the end of 1964, so that the 1963/64 Budget year was the year of largest tax base so far as sisal was concerned. The duty collected was £846,856 (Shs. 17 million). In the following budget the rate of duty was increased but revenue fell. The incidence of duty became:

---

1 The implied reduction for Tanzania is greater because of the existence of large stocks. The peasant producers of "hedge-sisal" are not expected to participate in the reduction.

Price	Duty
£75 to £95	5%
£95 to £100	£4/15/0 plus 10/- for every £1 over £95
£100 to £105	£7/15/0 plus 15/- for every £1 over £100
£105 and above	£11/0/0 plus £1 for every £1 over £105

This higher, and in the words of the Minister of Finance "more progressive" scale of taxation was expected to increase the revenue, on the assumption that current prices would persist, by a further Shs. 12 mn. In fact the revenue from sisal fell from 17 to 14 million shillings.

In the following Budget of June, 1965 the scale was made "progressive" below the level of £95 per ton as well as above, but the average price of sisal during both 1965 and 1966 was below the "floor" level, and the revenue was only Shs. 186,673/-. At the same time, however, sisal came into the scope of a new tax, the Development Levy, at a flat rate of Shs. 20/- per ton. This presumably produced some Shs. 4 mn. in 1965/66. In the 1966 Budget the Development Levy was slightly reduced by exempting locally processed sisal. In the 1968 Budget a complicated sliding scale was introduced designed to discourage the production of inferior grades of sisal.

The policy of taxing sisal exports at a time of higher prices was justifiable on the grounds that *either* the profits of the estates would otherwise be remitted to Europe (they were mostly European-owned) and so lost to Tanzania, *or* they would be inflationary. It does not seem likely that the taxes significantly aggravated the price fluctuations since other exporting countries and other fibres with which Tanzania was in competition did not impose such a tax. Under the circumstances, failure to tax would have been surprising. The only criticism one might make of this tax policy is that it suffered from the rigidity of the annual budgeting system.

The marketing policy has also been a rational one. This has been shown by PATEL and RIORDAN[2] who, after pointing out that Tanzanian sisal tends to fetch less foreign exchange than Kenya sisal of equivalent quality, demonstrate that this is a logical result of Tanzania's greater dependence on sisal: "It is concluded that Tanganyika foregoes some export earnings in order to reduce uncertainty of earnings, and to minimise substitution against sisal in the sisal industries ..." at a time of high prices, but takes more than Kenya from a weak market.

Tanzania, until recently the world's largest producer of sisal, has attempted to form a cartel (in effect) by declaring a minimum price. This experiment was made in 1966. The other producers, it was hoped, would follow the price

---

2 H. D. PATEL and E. B. RIORDAN: "Making the Most of Sisal Exports: An Analysis of Prices Paid to Tanganyika and Kenya", Rural Development Research Project Paper No. 22, Makerere, 1962 (mimeographed); and their article in *East African Rural Development*, Vol. 1, No. 1., 1968, with the same title.

lead. But they undersold Tanzania leaving her with heavy stocks; in 1967 the experiment was discontinued. Despite its failure, this experiment was clearly a rational, and indeed a text-book type, expedient. Further attempts were then made to regulate prices in 1967, through the Rome conferences, and a measure of agreement was reached as described above. The application of the quota (i.e. reduction) to Tanzania is now proceeding[3].

The spinners, who buy the sisal, have also behaved with rationality. GUILLEBAUD writes[4]:

"It is noteworthy, and entirely characteristic of the behaviour of commodity markets, that sales of sisal continued to be very small throughout the period of falling prices. It was not until some degree of stability had been reached that buyers began to place orders again in any substantial quantities."

In others words, the buyers forced the market down by holding off. Their ability to do so, i.e. to minimise their stock requirements, to act in unison, and to command the psychological tone of the market, is remarkable. A similar strength was demonstrated at the end of 1967 after the devaluation of sterling, when the buyers' desire to reduce the shilling price (as nearly as possible, by 14.3%) was pitted against the sellers' desire to "talk the market up" on the basis of the recent Rome agreement. The sales which have taken place in these last few months were at prices which do not reflect any Roman influence. This is probably because of the devalution of the Brazilian cruzeiro.

The first weakening of the sisal market early in 1964 was seen in Brazilian prices. A rally towards the end of that year was broken by the devaluation of the cruzeiro on December 2nd, 1964. The new rally which seemed possible three years later was again broken by the cruzeiro. Under these circumstances the chances of a firm producers' agreement seem slight. It seems more likely that Tanzanian sisal output will fall substantially. The urgent task is therefore one of diversification, and this is (at last) being actively pursued in Tanzania wherever possible: oilseeds and cattle seem to be the main new outlets, according to location. It is to be hoped that these will offset some of the loss of foreign exchange earnings but the capital outlay is substantial. The nationalisation of the majority of the estates (60% of the capacity) has provided the administrative machinery for this relief operation.

---

3 Though Brazil has now overtaken Tanzania as the world's largest sisal producer, Tanzania is still playing the rôle of would-be price leader.
4 C. W. GUILLEBAUD: *Economic Survey of the Sisal Industry of Tanganyika,* 3rd edn. 1966.

b) Cotton

Since the decline of sisal, cotton has come to the fore as Tanzania's leading export crop, and its value is approaching that of Uganda's crop. The quantity exported in 1966 exceeded that of Uganda.

Table 51. *Cotton Exports: Tanzania and Uganda, 1965–1967*

	1965	1966	1967
Tanzania: mn. lbs.	123.8	189.9	133.9
Uganda: mn. lbs.	152.8	153.9	158.6
Tanzania: mn. Shs.	244.2	349.9	251.4
Uganda: mn. Shs.	335.6	306.8	303.2

Source: East African Customs and Excise, *Annual Trade Returns.*

The quantity retained for local processing is however rising rapidly. The textile mills now in production have a full-capacity off-take of about 58 thousand bales of cotton per annum, which is only 13% of Tanzania's 1966/67 crop. Thus the local off-take is unlikely to remove cotton from its leading position in the export list.

As Table 52 shows, the output of cotton, which in the few years to independence fluctuated with no discernible upward or downward trend, has since independence grown from 168 to 436 thousand bales, with no deterioration of quality. This represents a growth rate of 21% per annum. Ruthenberg[5] traces the post-war expansion of cotton production in the main region back to 1947 when a development grant of £520,000 was given to Sukumaland. The desire of the Wasukuma to enter the cash economy, the work of agricultural officers, and the enterprise of Asians (investing in ginneries) and of local co-operatives brought production in Sukumaland up from 40,000 bales in 1950 to the levels given in our table. It seems likely, however, that producer price has also been a significant factor. According to Ruthenberg the producer price rose from 34 cents/lb in 1950 to 62 in 1954 and 1955. This accompanied an increase in output from 40 to 109 thousand bales over the same period. The price then declined gradually from 62 to 54 in 1961, while output rose unsteadily to 160 thousand bales in 1961, representing a trend growth rate of only 6.6% per annum as compared with 22% in the earlier period. In 1962 the price rose slightly to 55 cents but since then has declined sharply and for the 1966/67 crop stood at 46 cents. It is remarkable that in this later period the post-war growth rate has been regained, the more so as the decline in price is to be taken in conjunction with a fall in the purchasing power of the money.

---

5 H. Ruthenberg: *Agricultural Development in Tanganyika*, Afrika-Studien No. 2, IFO-Institut, Springer-Verlag, Berlin–Heidelberg–New York, 1964.

Table 52. *Cotton Crop Statistics*
(Thousands of 400 lb. bales)

Region	1958	1959	1960	1961	Crop year 1962	1963	1964	1965/66	1966/67
Lake and West Lake	150	182	161	158	192	230	257	323	377
Western	1	1	2	3	5	9	13	15	28
Eastern	14	13	17	7	15	18	18	27	23
Northern	3	4	5	2	3	5	3	2	3
Tanga	2	2	4	1	1	2	3	3	4
Total	170	202	189	171	216	264	294	370	435
Of which: AR grade	154	185	169	154	188	226	262	341	394
BR grade	16	18	20	14	26	37	31	29	42
AR grade as % of total	*91*	*91*	*89*	*92*	*88*	*86*	*89*	*92*	*91*

Source: Lint and Seed Marketing Board, *Annual Report, 1967*. More recent crop estimates indicate a fall in 1967/68 due to adverse weather conditions.

The decline in producer price since 1962 has been caused chiefly by a decline in the export price:

Table 53. *Cotton Prices, 1962–1966*

	1962	1963	1964	1965	1966
Average export price Shs./ton	4,538	4,481	4,445	4,420	4,127
Producer price, "A" grade, Lake area, cents/lb.	55	50	50	48	46

Source: Export prices, *Background to the Budget 1967–1968 and 1968–1969.* Producer prices from Lint and Seed Marketing Board.

The export price declined over this period by 9% while the producer price fell by 16%; the Lint & Seed Marketing Board incurred deficits (except in 1966) but costs and margins between producer and Board (co-operatives, ginneries, railways) rose. In 1966, faced with a severe decline in export price (more severe in anticipation than in the outturn) the Government decided on drastic measures; not only did it reduce the Grade "A" grower price by 2 cents, but the Development Levy was reduced from 2 cents to 1 cent, the Co-operative Societies' remuneration was reduced from 5 cents to 3 cents (with other cuts in the Co-operative Union levies and Victoria Federation of Co-operative Unions levies), and ginning fees were reduced. The Board made a profit for the year of Shs. 4.3 mn. On a crop of some 520 mn. lbs an extra cent to the grower would not have been possible without incurring a deficit.

In view of the poor prospects for sisal and the limited prospects for coffee, it is important not to discourage cotton production. Tanzanian cotton output is not so significant a part of total world output of long-staple cotton that a problem of disposal arises. Indeed, it is the Government's policy to increase cotton production, and the present target (500,000 bales by 1970) could well be largely surpassed providing the incentive is not destroyed. It is therefore to be hoped that further economies in handling and ginning will prove possible; if not, the grower price is likely to decline further, since the long-term export price prognosis is downward.

At present the main alternatives to cotton in Sukumaland are maize — not attractive as a cash crop; rice, which requires irrigation, and cattle, which is a long-term prospect involving both heavy investment and changes in economic organisation. It therefore seems likely that, for several years, the cotton producer's response to falling prices will be one of increasing output.

This situation has undoubtedly influenced official policy in the field of export taxation. In 1965, when prices were firm, i.e. virtually unchanged since 1964, cotton was caught in the net of the Development Levy, with a duty of 5% ad valorem. In the following (1966) Budget, however, this was withdrawn, and an export tax of 3 cents per lb (12/- per bale) substituted, equivalent to under 2% ad valorem, or about one third as severe as the levy. In 1967 this duty was raised to Shs. 18/- per bale, an increase which was however to be covered by reductions in ginning and handling charges, not by a further reduction in the grower price. The latter remained at 46 cents per lb.

The main aim of the Treasury, understandably, is to raise revenue; estimated revenue from the cotton duty for 1967/68 is Shs. 25 mn.; for 1966/67 Shs. 15 mn.; for previous years, nil. It is necessary to offset the loss of revenue from sisal. At the same time the Treasury clearly wishes not to depress the grower price, but rather to press upon handling charges and ginnery profits.

c) Coffee

Coffee, Tanzania's most important foreign exchange earner after cotton, is both protected and limited in its earning potential by Tanzania's membership of the International Coffee Agreement, which operates a form of price stabilisation by restricting sales from those exporting countries, and into those importing countries, which are members of the Agreement. Tanzania's basic quota when the Agreement began was 435,458 bags of 60 kg., or 25,715 tons. This includes both arabica, which is the main form of coffee produced in Tanzania, and the robusta type. This basic quota has been subject to quarterly adjustments and in 1966 it was extended to 461,000 bags[6] or 27,223 tons by a one-year "waiver". In September, 1967 the

6 *Background to the Budget, 1967–1968* and *1968–1969.*

Agreement was renegotiated and Tanzania obtained a new quota of 700,000 bags, 41,337 tons, beginning on October 1st, 1968.

Tanzania's position in the market can be judged from the new basic quotas.

Table 54. *Basic Coffee Quotas*
(60 kg. bags)

Brazil	20,926,000	Uganda	2,379,000
Columbia	7,000,000	Kenya	860,000
Ivory Coast	3,073,000	Tanzania	700,000
Portugal	2,776,000	Others	17,327,000
		Total:	55,041,000

Tanzania percentage: *1.27%*

Source: Press reports.

In the absence of any Agreement, Tanzania would probably follow the price-leadership of Columbia, the major producer of the chief type of coffee produced in Tanzania. Under the working of the Agreement, however, the price is kept relatively stable, and the volume is expected to grow slowly.

In addition to quota sales as described above, no restriction is placed on sales to "Annex B markets", otherwise known as "new markets" or "non-quota markets" which are listed in the Agreement. The exports to quota and non-quota countries from 1964–67 are analysed in Table 55.

Table 55. *Total Coffee Exports, 1964–1967*

	1964	1965	1966	1967
Tonnage				
Annex B	3,550	5,256	9,823	7,789
Quota	29,200	22,500	39,985	35,942
Total	32,750	27,756	49,808	43,731
Value (Shs. '000)				
Annex B	21,467	28,580	57,161	36,954
Quota	198,799	142,471	243,915	199,582
Total	220,266	171,051	301,076	236,536
Price (Shs./ton)				
Annex B	6,047	5,438	5,819	4,744
Quota	6,808	6,332	6,100	5,553
Total	6,726	6,163	6,045	5,409
Differential	761	894	281	809
Annex B tonnage as				
percentage of total tonnage				
Arabica	*10%*	*19%*	*22%*	*10%*
Robusta	*19%*	*20%*	*12%*	*53%*
Total	*11%*	*19%*	*20%*	*18%*

The quantity of coffee *produced* was (in thousands of clean tons):

31.3 in 1964
37.6 in 1965
48.7 in 1966
47.7 in 1967

It is fairly clear that the original quota of 25.7 thousand tons was an immediate constraint in 1964 and 1965. The tonnage exported on quota markets in those two years fully absorbed the quota, with annual production running at some 7.6 thousand tons in excess of this. Some of the excess was accounted for by home sales, some by rising stocks, but the overspill to the non-quota market rose from 3,550 to 5,256 tons.

Although Tanzania is in general desirous of exploring new markets, this type of sale is well described as an overspill, since it fetches a lower price, being in effect a forced sale. As stocks were increasing, the discount widened, and in 1965 on the average it amounted to Shs. 894 per ton. The official discount is in 1968 Shs. 800/ton.

In connexion with the 45% rise in production in 1966, it is necessary to bear in mind not only the wide difference in weather conditions between the two years, but also the efforts of extension workers and other officials to encourage insecticide spraying and other husbandry improvements. There is little new planting taking place, as the main area (Kilimanjaro) is already fully planted. The emphasis is on yield per tree. In view of the previous poor yields the quota may be said to have been too low for Tanzania, and this fact led to its being raised at the 1967 negotiations.

The tonnage exported to quota countries in 1964, 1965 and 1966 appears from the foregoing table as 91,685 tons, or 30,562 as an annual average. This is substantially more than the original basic quota of 25,715 tons and even more than the extended figure of 27,223 tons; it may therefore be regarded as the maximum sale tolerable under the Coffee Agreement, if not more.

Under these circumstances the production levels of 48.7 and 47.7 thousand tons reached in 1966 and 1967 give rise to *serious problems*.

A small factory, "Tanica", has been established to process Robusta into instant coffee, but such is the world market for instant coffee that this scarcely alleviates the problem. The factory is working under-capacity. Domestic consumption, though stimulated by low selling prices (with a subsidy of Shs. 2,800 per ton to local roasters) is still virtually negligible. Attention must therefore be given to the Annex B market; as the above figures show, this market took 20% of the exports in 1966, despite a record sale of 40,000 tons to the quota market.

The rise in the price of coffee sold to the non-quota market under these circumstances is odd, the more so as the quota-coffee price was falling. The willingness of Annex B importers to go up to Shs. 5,819 per ton (admittedly still lower than the 1964 price) leaving an average differential of only Shs. 281 per ton over the year suggests that they may have had intentions of re-selling the coffee on the quota market ("tourist coffee"). In this connexion a closer examination of the trade statistics shows up the following.

Table 56. *East African Coffee Exports to Bahrein, Jordan and Saudia Arabia, 1964–1967*

| | | Kenya | | Uganda | | Tanzania | | East Africa | |
		Tons	Shs. '000	Tons	Shs. '000	Tons	Shs. '000	Tons	Shs. '000
1964									
Arabica	B	391	2,373	18	120	180	1,136	589	3,629
	J	432	2,691	78	375	168	1,098	678	4,164
	SA	524	2,938	7	41	272	1,674	803	4,653
Robusta	B	–	–	366	1,446	117	470	483	1,916
	J	–	–	2,764	8,039	124	490	2,888	8,529
	SA	–	–	1,608	4,469	226	980	1,834	5,449
Total								7,275	28,340
1965									
Arabica	B	242	1,596	–	–	316	2,072	558	3,668
	J	1,039	7,057	18	105	1,911	11,084	2,968	18,246
	SA	238	1,399	–	–	523	3,239	761	4,638
Robusta	B	–	–	950	3,190	181	671	1,131	3,861
	J	–	–	7,848	22,766	944	3,787	8,792	26,553
	SA	–	–	270	884	–	–	270	884
Total								14,480	57,850
1966									
Arabica	B	155	900	–	–	1,004	6,104	1,159	7,004
	J	11	54	15	81	1,304	7,996	1,330	8,131
	SA	359	1,985	–	–	1,721	10,383	2,020	12,368
Robusta	B	–	–	4,877	10,026	25	116	4,902	10,142
	J	–	–	4,170	12,286	214	934	4,384	13,221
	SA	–	–	7,114	19,319	–	–	7,114	19,319
Total								20,908	70,185
1967									
Arabica	B	440	1,864	–	–	392	2,067	832	3,931
	J	1,179	5,193	84	476	1,979	9,562	3,242	15,231
	SA	2,339	10,986	–	–	4,757	21,375	7,096	32,361
Robusta	B	–	–	8,452	20,445	127	521	8,579	20,966
	J	–	–	3,883	10,188	783	3,004	4,666	13,192
	SA	–	–	3,832	9,544	80	263	3,912	9,807
Total								28,327	95,488

Source: East African Customs and Excise, *Annual Trade Returns.*

Trade statistics cannot be conclusive in such a matter. It is clear that consignments of both Uganda Robusta and Tanzania Arabica to Bahrein, especially, have shot up to heights which cannot possibly represent anything but re-sale or redirection, but whether the coffee found its way to the quota market or to the non-quota market is not clear. In any case, the 1967 figures (Table 55) indicate a return to normal so far as Tanzania is concerned.

Since 1967 the ICA authorities have introduced stiffer regulations intended to ensure that quotas are adhered to. Insofar as these are effective, they will reduce the off-taking capacity of the Annex B countries and so reduce the price at which coffee — including Tanzania's coffee — is sold to them. A discount in the region of Shs. 800 per ton, effective, is therefore to be anticipated; i.e. the present official discount is reasonable.

With a productive capacity in the region of 50 thousand tons, and a quota in the region of 41 thousand tons, Tanzania therefore faces a marginal revenue of under Shs. 5,000 per ton for her coffee.

To compare marginal revenue with marginal costs one requires more data than research has yet produced, for each type of coffee[7]. Nevertheless, the Government arrived at the view that, if not reduction, at least containment of coffee production was desirable[8]. For that reason the export tax on coffee was extended in the 1967 Budget to cover coffee sales to non-quota markets also; the rates at present (1967/69) are Shs. 560 per ton on mild arabicas, Shs. 520 on hard arabicas, Shs. 440 on robustas, and Shs. 280 on cheri-buni and tex. This extension has the effect of raising the estimated tax yield from Shs. 15 mn. (1966/67) to Shs. 25 mn. This is intended to encourage diversification, which, in the Kilimanjaro area, takes the form mainly of dairy cattle husbandry, a traditional activity in that part of Tanzania and one which has bright marketing prospects. At present the Kilimanjaro milk production is locally consumed, but as supply grows fresh milk is expected to become available first for Tanga and later for Dar es Salaam in place of the KCC milk which at present arrives daily from Kenya. In 1966 Kenya supplied 314,000 gallons of fresh milk to Tanzania, valued at Shs. 1.3 mn. There will also be import substitution against tinned milk.

In 1966/67 the effective rate of taxation on coffee was the heaviest of all major export crops, according to Dr. HELLEINER's calculations[9].

As a means of discouraging additional planting, and replanting, these taxes should be effective; but the rise in output has been mainly due to increased

---

7 Ralph CLARK: "Economic Considerations in determining Coffee Policies in East Africa", mimeographed, Nairobi 1967.

8 "Common prudence and concern for the future of the industry calls for the exertion of self-discipline, not to cut back output but to halt the explosive rise in production." Minister of Finance, Budget Speech, June, 1967.

9 G. K. HELLEINER: "Agricultural Export Pricing Strategy in Tanzania", paper presented to the Social Science Conference, University of East Africa, Nairobi, December, 1966.

Table 57. *Aggregate Tax Rates (Central, Local and Marketing Boards)*
on Major Export Crops, 1966/67

	Tax on gross potential income	Tax on net value added
Coffee, arabica	*14.6%*	*17.4%*
Coffee, robusta	*20.2%*	*26.1%*
Sisal[a]	*3.4%*	*10.4%*
Cotton	*2.5%*	*4.3%*

[a] Excludes taxes on sisal estate profits (negligible).

yields per tree, as described above. In the cases of sisal and cotton, falling incomes are expected to lead to rising yields. In this case, however, a distinction must be drawn between increasing yields per plant by more intense labour, likely for sisal and cotton, and increasing yield per plant due to higher inputs of fertilisers, insecticides and other monetary inputs — as is required for coffee. The latter response is unlikely to occur, especially since dairying provides an attractive alternative for many producers.

d) Some Minor Agricultural Exports

Cotton, coffee and sisal exports in 1961–1966 fetched about 50% of Tanzania's total exports; this fell to about 40% in 1967. None of the other export commodities approach these three in importance, but the next in importance (after diamonds; minerals are discussed below) is cashew nuts.

The cashew tree, Anacardium occidentale, is a native of Brazil. It is believed to have been introduced in India by the Portuguese in the sixteenth century and may have reached the Portuguese territories in East Africa at the same time. It now grows mainly in Mozambique, Tanzania, India, Kenya and Brazil.

While the shell of the cashew nut contains a valuable oil[10], most of the value of the commodity lies in the kernel, which is a highly nutritious delicacy, exported mainly to the U.S.A. The extraction of the kernel, or decortication, was until recently confined to factories in India. Performed entirely by hand to avoid damaging the kernel, this monotonous task is carried out by women at wages which are well below the legal minimum wages in Tanzania.

The cashew trade in Tanzania developed since 1938, therefore, in the following pattern:

---

10 Cardol, used as a friction modifier in brake linings, etc. See, *Indian Cashew Nut Journal,* passim.

African producers, Southern Region

↓

Indian exporters, Mtwara and Dar es Salaam

↓

Indian importers, brokers, Bombay

↓

Decortication in India

↓

Export to U.S.A. and elsewhere.

The authorities here have naturally been concerned at the low proportion of value-added which this structure brings to Tanzania; best grade kernels ("dessert wholes") may fetch up to 8 shillings per kilo, f.o.b., and second grade ("white splits") may fetch up to six shillings, while the grower receives about Shs. 0/70 per kilo for undecorticated nuts.

In 1950, before minimum wage laws existed in Tanganyika, an attempt was made to start a processing factory in Mtwara. It was hoped that the workers would acquire the necessary skill to decorticate 10 lbs of kernels per day per head, a fair average for India; a modest start was made with a seasonal throughput of 20 tons. This failed due to the instability of the labour force; in the Southern Region the employment opportunities on the land can provide a more comfortable livelihood than is available to the unfortunate women in the Indian factories.

To process Tanzania's present crop of around 80,000 tons of raw nuts, by hand, would require a labour force of over 15,000 persons. Quite apart from the minimum wage law which makes hand decortication uncompetitive (against Indian female labour), it would not be possible to find such numbers in one place, or in a few places; since the Tanzanian Southern Region economy, unlike the Indian economy, is not burdened with heavy overpopulation and female underemployment caused by the depression of cottage industry.

In 1966 another attempt was made to establish a decorticating factory at Mtwara, this time using a new technique of mechanical handling developed in Italy. This scheme, capitalised at Shs. 30 mn. is taking about one-tenth of the crop. Using a new technique, it has run into difficulties, being apparently unable to handle the smaller nuts satisfactorily. The price of kernels being outside Tanzania's control, this has meant a reduction in the price at which the National Agricultural Marketing Board is contracted to deliver raw nuts to the factory. The factory cannot be allowed to close, since most of the capital — reportedly over Shs. 26 mn. — was provided by the Tanzania partners (NDC). It is expected that the second plant will be of Japanese manufacture, with a different technique, and appropriate guarantees of per-

117

formance. Negotiations with the Cashew Company of Tokyo are at an advanced stage.

Export taxes have been imposed on cashew nuts, as on other crops, as a matter of trial and error. In 1965 a Development Levy of 5% was imposed; in 1966 this was removed and replaced by a less severe export duty, with a sliding scale, whereby any excess over a floor price was taxed at a percentage rate of 5 multiplied by the number of 20/- units in the excess. The floor price was set at Shs. 1,000 per ton. Above a ceiling price of Shs. 1,280 a fixed marginal rate of Shs. 15/- of every Shs. 20 excess was applied. Even this was found to deplete the reserves of the paying agent (National Agricultural Products Board) and in 1967 the tax was further modified. Three grades of nuts were established, with floor prices of Shs. 1,150, Shs. 1,050 and Shs. 950 per ton, and the top tax rate was set at Shs. 10/- in Shs. 20/- above Shs. 1,330, Shs. 1,230 and Shs. 1,130. The revenue estimated for 1967/68 stands at Shs. 5.9 mn. as compared with Shs. 9.6 mn. for the previous year.

Table 58. *Cashew Nut Prices, 1962–1967*
(cents/kg.)

	1962	1963	1964	1965	1966	1967
Export price	79	94	116	128	138	120
Producer price, Mtwara	52	67	75	81	68	71
Marketed output, index	100	102	132	132	147	156

Source: Export prices from *Background to the Budget 1967–1968* and *1968–1969.* Producer prices from Ministry of Agriculture and Co-operatives.

As the above table shows, the export price has risen every year since independence up to 1967; the producer price has risen each year except 1966, when the effects of export taxation were worrying the N.A.P.B. Output has risen in a spectacular manner and, with producer prices at their present levels approximately there is little prospect of the Southern Region farmers diversifying to other crops. A survey of 45 farms, conducted by P. WESTERGAARD[11] in 1967 showed that 70% of their acreage was under cashew which provided 85% of their income and required relatively little cash input; 28 of the 45 farmers had cleared new land during the year, and of the 17 who did not, none gave as the reason the inadequate remuneration of cashew.

Should the export price of cashew decline as is anticipated it might be possible to protect the producer price by narrowing the gap between the two. As the above table shows, this gap (which includes the export duty) rose from 27 cents/kg. in 1962 to 70 cents/kg. in 1966. This implies both compressible margins and accumulated reserves.

11 P. WESTERGAARD: "Cashew Nuts: The Quality Problem." E.R.B. Paper, 68.8, Dar es Salaam, 1968.

118

Cashew has been a star performer for Tanzania with substantial increases in both price and quantity and it is unfortunate that the world market is entering into a depressed phase. In 1966/67 world production rose by 15% (to 277,000 tons) an increase which could not be matched on the demand side, and the U.S. kernel price fell by 25% from $73.00 per 100 lbs to $55.00. The latter is equivalent to Shs. 8/66 per kg., c.i.f. U.S. port; this is still over five times the price of Tanzania's *raw cashew* exports, which in turn is more than double the price received by the grower.

It is to be concluded therefore, that although the demand is highly elastic (a feature which may stem from the U.S. practice of marketing cashew kernels in tins of mixed nuts), Tanzania still has a powerful incentive to proceed with a further expansion of output and with domestic decortication.

Some improvement in marketing could probably be achieved by organisational changes. The marketing is done neither by the NAPB nor (to a large extent) by the State Trading Corporation; it is conducted through brokers who are unco-ordinated. The fact of the Tanzania crop coming to market 1–2 months before that of Mozambique is not exploited and Mozambique remains the price leader. To some extent Tanzania has benefitted from weak marketing on the part of Mozambique, the latter following a minimum price policy which allowed underselling; Tanzania's relationship to Mozambique in the cashew market may be compared to Brazil's relationship to Tanzania in sisal. The demand situation is not comparable to that of sisal, however, since cashew has prospects of mass selling in the non-luxury market with some further reduction in price.

A final point about cashew is that there should be a possibility of reducing the freight charges out from Mtwara as the port becomes more important. At present, exporters have to pay premia in order to ensure the off-take. In 1966 only 176 ships called at Mtwara as compared with 311 in 1961; however, the Zambia transit trade has rejuvenated Mtwara and necessitated additional handling and storage capacity.

Another crop handled by the NAPB, one which has seriously declined in recent years, is groundnuts. The quantity marketed has fallen from 20.1 thousand tons in 1963 to 8.3 thousand in 1966; this appears to have been due to unattractive prices.

Table 59. *Groundnut Prices, 1962–1966*
(cents per kg.)

	1962	1963	1964	1965	1966
Average export price, f.o.b.	120	128	138	185	144
Average producer price	100	91	87	99	87
Index of marketed output	100	122	102	56	50

Source: Export prices from *Background to the Budget 1967–1968* and *1968–1969*. Producer prices from Ministry of Agriculture and Co-operatives.

In this crop the difference between producer price and export price has widened considerably, from a 20% margin in 1962 to a 65% margin in 1966. To some extent this is due to export taxation, which began in 1965/66 with the 5% Development Levy. This was modified in the 1966 Budget to an export tax of the type used for cashew nuts. With export prices up to Shs. 1,200 per ton (edible grade) or Shs. 1,000 per ton (crushing grade), no tax was imposed; at prices in excess of these, the rate of tax rises by 5% for every 20/- excess, up to a maximum of 10/- in every 20/- above the levels of Shs. 1,380 and Shs. 1,180 for the two grades. The exact effect of these taxes cannot be calculated from available data but it is evident that, apart from these taxes, the distribution mark-up between the producer price and the export price must have averaged at least 50% as compared with 20% in 1962 before the NAPB began operations. How far this is positively reflected in an accumulation of NAPB financial reserves is also not known, since no report is available as yet, but certainly the effect on production has been negative.

In 1967 there was a further fall in output due largely to drought in Tabora and Dodoma areas.

It is interesting to recall that groundnut production potential has been responsible for the building of two railways in Tanzania: the main line from Dar es Salaam, under the German Governor's policy which at one time was characterised as "the peanut economy", and the short-lived line from Mtwara which was the main infrastructure of the British "Groundnut Scheme" fiasco. Cotton and cashew respectively are the main products of these areas today, one with an enormous potential for forward linkages towards domestic industry, which groundnuts never had, the other with a limited linkage potential, beset with difficulties, but with probably better price prospects as an export crop than groundnuts. Also both cotton and cashew are said to be easier to grow than groundnuts.

It is likely that in the course of the Second Five Year Development Plan a highway will be built linking the Southern Region directly with Dar es Salaam and the northern half of the country. This should open up possibilities of, and incentives for, new crops or livestock in the Southern Region geared to industrial or consumer demand in Tanzania itself. Neither groundnuts nor cashewnuts can be regarded as a satisfactory basis for the long-term development of the Southern Region.

The products discussed above, together with diamonds, account for 65% (1966) of Tanzania's total exports, or 60% if re-exports be included. Among the many other minor agricultural exports with seemingly good prospects on a small scale are tea, pyrethrum, flue-cured tobacco, cloves, hides and skins and anato. Among those with seemingly poor or dubious prospects are fire-cured and aromatic tobacco, kapok, allenblackia nuts, macadamia nuts, cassava, cocoa, wheat-bran and pollards, crocodile skins, cardamoms, beeswax, mangrove bark, wattle extract, limes and chillies. Little factual infor-

Table 60. *Nuts and Oilseeds Production in 1960's*
(Shs. mn.)

	1960—1962 Average	1963	1964	1965	1966	1965/66 Change %	Growth Rate 1960/62— 1966 %	1970 Target
Cashew Nuts	26.5	28.2	46.6	62.6	79.6	+27.2	+24.6	62
Groundnuts	16.0	17.9	15.6	10.1	7.7	—23.8	—15.7	50
Castor Seed	10.6	16.1	9.3	6.8	6.1	—10.3	—11.7	..
Sesame and Sunflower	13.5	12.0	9.9	9.9	9.3	— 6.1	— 7.7	..

Source: Background to the Budget 1967–1968 and 1968–1969.

mation is available about these, though some appear to present fascinating economic problems in miniature.

Meat and meat products are discussed separately below.

2. Export Duties in General

The foregoing summary of major crops, together with Table 61, give a good picture of the attempts made in recent years to experiment with export taxation. Export duties were in fact originally established in 1946, on beeswax, hides and skins, and Lake Province coffee; after the 1949 devaluation and in the 'fifties, duties were temporarily imposed on some other commodities (copra, coconut oil, copra cake, sisal and cotton) in times of exceptionally high export prices. The World Bank mission of 1959 proposed a more systematic adoption of export duties suggesting "... the adoption of export taxation. With the exception of minor levies on exports of hides and skins and beeswax, no such tax is at present imposed in Tanganyika. This is in sharp contrast with the many other underdeveloped countries which rely rather heavily on export taxes as a source of revenue. The experience of these countries has on the whole been satisfactory, at least so long as the rates of export tax have been kept rather low. While comprehensive export taxation in Tanganyika would raise certain problems, none of these seem serious. It seems that a tax equivalent to not more than, say, 5% ad valorem would have no perceptible tendency to discourage exports or to divert productive effort and sales from export to the home market. In assessing these effects, it must be remembered that the export tax would be compensated in varying degrees for different commodities and in different areas by the abolition of produce cesses" [12].

12 I.B.R.D.: *The Economic Development of Tanganyika*, 1961.

Table 61. *Summary of Export Duty Revenues*

	1959/60 £	1960/61 £	1961/62 £	1962/63 £	1963/64 £	1964/65 Shs.	1965/66 Shs.	1966/67 Estimate Shs. mn.	1967/68 Estimate Shs. mn.
1. Beeswax	45,940	62,410	55,000	649,372	5,929	1,548,180	336,932	1.6	2.0
2. Hides and skins					26,857		1,631,914		
3. Tea	—	—	—	—	19,438	881,340	1,241,853	0.9	1.2
4. Sisal	—	—	—	—	846,856	13,970,460	186,673	—	—
5. Coffee	—	—	—	—	8,169	12,712,041	8,918,952	15.0	25.0
6. Cotton	—	—	—	—	—	—	—	6.0	7.0
7. Oilseeds and nuts	—	—	—	—	—	—	—	1.4	2.6
8. Cashew nuts	—	—	—	—	—	—	—	9.6	5.9
9. Pyrethrum	—	—	—	—	—	—	—	0.8	0.6
10. Meat products	—	—	—	—	—	—	—	1.2	2.0
11. Timber	—	—	—	—	—	—	—	0.4	0.3
	45,940	62,410	55,000	649,372	907,249	29,112,020	12,316,324	36.9	46.6

Source: Appropriation Accounts, annual; Financial Estimates, 1966/67 and 1967/68. Ministry of Finance.

In the 1965 Budget the Development Levy was announced (Act No. 42 of 1965, amended by Act No. 41 of 1966) imposing a 5% tax on a wide range of exports. Between the publication of the Mission's report and 1965, parastatal institutions had been formed which, but for deficiencies in their operations, would have made ideal collectors of these taxes (NAPB, COSATA, etc.). Far from abolishing the produce cesses, however, these bodies had added to the "bewildering variety" of taxation, and in general it was found necessary in the following Budget to reduce the overall incidence. The abolition or substantial reduction of these cesses and levies requires drastic institutional change, which cannot be performed in a year or two. Some further rationalisation can, however, be expected in due course. In the meantime, the export duties do not constitute a major source of central Government revenue (under 5% in 1967/68 estimates) nor a large impost on total export earnings (currently around 2 3/4 %).

Their main function at present is rather one of guiding agricultural effort towards the most promising crops. Further changes from year to year are therefore to be expected.

3. Mineral Exports

Official figures for the value of mineral production in Tanzania (mainland) show a long-term growth which is substantially larger than that of agricultural production, though the absolute level is still small (17% of GDP in 1966).

Table 62. *Value of Mineral Output, 1884–1967*

Period	Millions of Shillings
German administration 1884–1918	10 (est)
1923–1927	10.2
1928–1932	16.8
1933–1937	46.4
1938–1942	113./
1943–1947	122.2
1948–1952	292.0
1953–1957	486.0
1958–1962	725.7
1963–1967	973.2

Source: a) J. F. HARRIS: "Summary of the Geology of Tanganyika", 1923–1959, Part IV., Memoir No. 1., 1961.

b) *Background to the Budget 1960–1967*, various issues.

The increase in recent years has, however, been due to one mineral and to one company, Williamson Diamonds.

Table 63. *Diamond Exports, 1961–1967*

	1961	1962	1963	1964	1965	1966	1967
Weight, '000 carats	685	648	589	664	828	906	988
Value, Shs. mn.	116	109	99	136	142	186	223
Price per carat, Shs.	169	168	168	205	171	205	226

Source: Background to the Budget 1960–1967, various issues.

This places diamonds in the fourth rank of Tanzania's exports (third, in 1967).

Over 100 kimberlite pipes, associated with igneous rock formations[13], have been located in Tanzania, lying in well-defined clusters mostly in the Shinyanga, Nzega and Iramba-Singida areas. Some of these may contain workable concentrations of diamonds but in general they are too poor to be economic; the mining takes place in the gravels and other superficial deposits which overlie and surround the kimberlite pipes. Thus, in the main mine at Mwadui, while the true pipe is 1,200 feet down, the diamond production is effected mainly from the 30 feet of material immediately below the surface soil. Further investigation of the pipes continues, however, in an effort to find a type of primary kimberlite of workable grade.

Small diamond discoveries began shortly before the First World War but the large Mwadui deposit was discovered by J. T. Williamson in 1940. During the Second World War diamond exports rose from under 5 to over 100 thousand carats; the 1945 export value was £638,000.

Williamson's mine, situated in 347 acres of flat country which in 1940 bore no surface indication of kimberlite, excavates the subsoil, gravel, etc. by digging, and by explosives. Ore is transported by trucks and by conveyor belting to the treatment plant which is capable of reducing 7,000 tons a day to a concentrate of a few hundred tons, and eventually after further crushing and screening to a final concentrate of a few pounds' weight from which the diamonds are directly extracted. A 99% extraction rate is claimed.

The present output of Mwadui is around one million carats. The value of a carat depends not only upon market conditions but also upon the rarity of each stone, involving such factors as purity, colour and shape. The average price realised, as shown in Table 63, has been around Shs. 200 per carat, but one stone of exceptional size (241 carats, found in 1956) was valued at Shs. 2,297 per carat.

The marketing is done through the world diamond cartel of De Beers. It is

---

13 For the source of the mineralogical and petrological information in this section see J. F. HARRIS, op. cit.

of course unpalatable for Tanzania to work with this South African organisation, but as GREEN and SEIDMAN[14] remark: "A unilateral break with De
Beers could cost Tanzania up to £5 million annually without breaking the
cartel's power or significantly weakening the South African economy." The
figure of £5 million may be exaggerated, but it is certainly true that Tanzania needs to proceed further with a diamond-cutting and jewellery manufacturing industry before she could confidently expect to reduce the risk of
loss to reasonable proportions. In this connexion the special importance of
Mwadui profits should be mentioned: they are the main source of income of
the National Development Corporation, a 50% shareholder in Williamson
Diamonds, Ltd. In 1965 Mwadui contributed Shs. 10 mn. or 71% of NDC's
income; in 1966 Shs. 9.5 mn. or 75%[15]. Thus diamond revenues not only
represent foreign exchange but also a particularly leading area of capital
formation.

The company is reported[16] to be undertaking prospecting surveys outside
Mwadui itself, and in addition the Soviet geological survey team provided
for in the Tanzanian-Soviet treaty of May 26th, 1966 can be expected to
give diamond reconnaissance a high priority. The Siberian diamond discoveries make the USSR a highly suitable partner in this work. However,
these geologists, scheduled in the Treaty for 1966–67, have not yet become
effective.

In 1966, NDC began to establish the Tanzania Diamond Cutting Company
at Iringa. By the end of 1967 it was employing 250 Tanzanian operatives.
No performance data are published so far. Most of the stones cut at Iringa
are small diamonds for industrial use at the present time.

Gold

Table 64. *Gold Exports, 1961–1967*

	1961	1962	1963	1964	1965	1966	1967
Weight '000 troy oz.	99.5	101.5	102.5	93.0	90.8	56.0	18.5
Value Shs. mn.	25	25	26	23	23	15	5

Source: Background to the Budget 1967–1968 and 1968–1969.

Gold until recently ranked second to diamonds among Tanzania's mineral
exports, but production has been declining in recent years, and is now under
2% of all mineral sales. It was mined by small-scale operators in the inter-
war period, reaching a peak export level of £1.2 mn. in 1940 when its war
value and small claim on shipping or air space gave it priority, but after that

14 R. H. GREEN and Ann SEIDMAN: *Unity or Poverty? The Economics of Pan-
   Africanism,* Penguin African Library, 1968.
15 N.D.C.: *Annual Report and Accounts, 1966* (pub. 1967).
16 *Background to the Budget 1967–1968 and 1968–1969.*

year growing difficulties due to shortages and rising costs caused many operators to quit the business. Since the war, the gradual easing of transport problems and other monetary or non-monetary costs associated with working in remote areas has caused output to rise, but known deposits of economic value have been successively worked out until at the present time only one mine is working. Although grains of alluvial gold can be found by panning in many streams draining the igneous and metamorphic rock formations, what is required for economic exploitation is large ore bodies capable of some degree of mechanisation in the mining technique. These need not necessarily be high-grade ores and for that reason may have been passed over unsuspected by earlier prospectors.

The gold is found either in alluvial form or in the rock. In the latter case it is usually in a quartz reef impregnated with auriferous sulphide, though pyritic and siliceous ores are also common. A considerable investment is needed for crushing the quartz and reducing it to a concentrate or to mine bullion. Even for alluvial gold, in which with simple panning nuggets of up to 1,025 ozs. have been found, more investment is required in Tanzania than in more favoured locations, since there is a drought or scarcity of water during much of the year, and the separation of the heavy gold grains must be done by forced draught of air instead of water.

The gold is exported as mine bullion by air for refining in London. The weights given in Table 64 are the weights of the gold content only, and the prices have been presumably those of the London market, less the cost of refining. Since the separation of the official and free market price for gold, it seems likely that Tanzania will in future recover a higher price per ounce. Under these circumstances, extensive surveying by modern methods, and intensive searches for the origins of alluvial streaks (most of which are as yet undiscovered) will probably be undertaken, and the industry may be saved from the decline into which, prior to the world gold crisis, it had apparently entered.

Minor minerals

A large number of other minerals have been exported, in small quantities, at one time or another from Tanzania and could, given appropriate price and transportation conditions, be exported again. Some of these are briefly mentioned below.

Asbestos

This is found in several places among the igneous and metamorphic rocks but mostly in a form (amphibole) in which the fibres are too weak to be spun. Such material is of some value as a filler in building materials. All known pockets are however very small, and mostly inconveniently located; no commercial production is undertaken.

126

Bentonite

This porous absorbent clay, somewhat inferior to Wyoming bentonite, has been exported in very small quantities. It is thought likely to exist in the neighbourhood of Dar es Salaam.

Cement

A layer of coral limestone amounting to about 20 million tons lies on Wazo Hill, outside Dar es Salaam. A small cement factory has been erected on this site using this limestone and local gypsum. The cement is largely import-substituting; the existing capacity supplies all of Tanzania's requirements of standard portland cement except for the northern areas which are more cheaply supplied from Mombasa. However, in order to assist Zambia in reducing her dependence on the south, Wazo Hill cement has been despatched to Zambia, worth Shs. 1 million in 1966. This was made good by increased supplies from Kenya, but the Wazo Hill capacity is expected to double with the erection of a second kiln. It is controlled by N.D.C.

A further 10 million tons of limestone is to be found just outside Tanga.

Coal

There is no large-scale coal mining in Tanzania, nor large imports (imports in 1967 were Shs. 60,000). Oil is the chief source of energy. Should coal deposits be worked it would be import-substituting against oil and possibly petrochemicals.

Post-war drilling investigations by the Colonial Development Corporation found coal in the Ruhuhu Depression near Lake Nyasa; at Mchuchuma 187 mn. tons were proved, of which 124 mn. were believed to be mineable under reasonable cost conditions. This does not include coal of less than 3 ft. in seam depth, nor with an ash content of over 25%. The average quality is typical of African coals but differs (in having a higher ash content) from the typical British coals on which coal-using technology has come to be chiefly based. A gross tonnage of 400 mn. tons was estimated to exist in the whole Ruhuhu Depression. Smaller quantities, with poorer qualities, have been located elsewhere; none are conveniently located except one very small field of low calorific-value coal on the shore of Lake Nyasa.

Garnets

Large deposits of garnet exist, some in very accessible places, both as rock and as sand. As an industrial abrasive the sand tends to be too soft and too fine, but as ornaments (semi-precious stones for cutting) the higher quality hand-picked stones have a definite export market. Most of the actual exports (some Shs. 800,000 in 1966) come from a reactivated deposit worked by the Germans, the "Luisenfeld". From 1928 to 1955 this field was overlooked. Other areas, in which one can literally walk upon fields of garnets, have now been located, but the world market is a very limited one. The techniques necessary to enlarge this market appear to be

- direct contact with leading market operators, and
- production of a unique Tanzania semi-precious ornament by local cutting.

Steps are proceeding with these aims. This is a very interesting prospect for Tanzania which has not received the attention it deserves.

Iron

Traditional local smelting is of a good quality ore which, though widespread, is not found in sufficient quantities for European-style smelting, though the Chinese methods might be appropriate. There is on the other hand a large quantity of titaniferous magnetite in the Njombe District, possibly around 50 mn. tons, containing around 48% of iron. The titanium oxide content (around 13%), while too low for economic extraction of titanium for its own sake, is too high to permit normal smelting methods under which the titanium creates a hard clinker and becomes inseparable from the iron. Ores containing more than a few tenths per cent of titanium cannot be smelted by normal methods. There is a suitable method, the Krupp-Renn process, but an extra cost is unavoidable.

Probably the main problem is the location of the deposit. Njombe is a very small town, cut off during the rainy season by bad roads. It is not far distant from the coalfields, which are also inaccessible. If the demand for steel were present in that area both would almost certainly be viable. There are possibilities here linked with the long-term development of the southern half of Tanzania and the potential export of steel and steel products to Zambia, but it is to be feared that by the time this is feasible, many of the uses of steel will have been taken over by new synthetic materials, which will be imported rather than exported. However, viability is now being reassessed by Chinese experts.

Kaolin

No kaolin has been exported for some years, but large areas of river valley in Njombe District are blanketed with kaolin 20–50 feet thick, suitable for making pottery and stoneware which could substitute against imported ware. The deposit, however, is difficult of access (from either Mbeya or Njombe).

Magnesite

Good quality magnesite is fairly common in Tanzania but in its crude form commands too low a price to be economically transported over large distances. Some magnesite from Lake Natron (in the north) has been sold to Kenya for use as chippings in terrazzo work. Otherwise, occurrences merely await the expansion of local demand (or the prior arrival of substitutes). Many deposits are conveniently located.

128

Meerschaum

Meerschaum is a hydrous aluminium silicate used in making smoking pipes, giving a cool smoke. Tanzania and Turkey are the only producers. It was discovered near Lake Amboseli in 1953 and the Tanzania meerschaum pipes have in the last few years established an international reputation and indeed a lead over Turkey. Reserves of the material are unknown. The pipe manufacture is carried out by the Tanganyika Meerschaum Corporation at Arusha, 100 miles from the mine; formerly it was manufactured in Kenya. The Corporation is a subsidiary of the N.D.C. and from its 1966 Report appeared to be unprofitable, with fixed assets costing Shs. 3.2 mn. and stocks worth Shs. $2^{1}/_{4}$ mn. Exports of pipes in 1966 fetched Shs. $1^{1}/_{2}$ mn. (mostly U.S.A., U.K. and Australia).

Mica

Mica has been mined in Tanzania since 1902, on a small scale, unmechanised, rarely worked to any depth except in following a particular strike down from the surface. In the 1945–61 period there were some large European-managed concerns, as distinct from African individuals or co-operatives, but the techniques were similar. A peak of exports was reached in 1952 with about Shs. 2.8 mn. worth; in 1966, exports of Shs. 1.8 mn. were realised, mostly to the U.K., but the industry is said to be developing. The quality of the mica varies widely in the various deposits, some being green, ruby and brown as well as clear, with associated minerals including beryllium, uranium, garnet, tourmaline and apatite. The extraction continues to be by individuals or small groups with very little capital and is mostly in the Morogoro Region.

Salt

Commercial extraction of salt occurs at the Nyanza Salt Mines, using a saline spring at Uvinza, on the Kigoma railway line. Exports in 1966 were worth Shs. 3.0 mn., going mainly to Burundi and Congo (Kinshasa). Salt imports in the same year were Shs. 0.8 mn. mostly from U.K. The Nyanza works are operated by Nyanza Salt Mines (Tanganyika) Ltd., a subsidiary of N.D.C., which of late has suffered from ageing machinery and an inheritance of inadequate depreciation. Profit is being ploughed back at present for modernisation in the form of a vacuum extraction plant.

Tin

Tin worth Shs. 7.0 mn. was exported in 1966, as ore concentrate (cassiterite). The source is the Karagwe tinfield near Bukoba. Part of the concentrate is recoverable by panning from surface detritus; vein mining to about 45 feet, or open-cast mining, requiring greater capitalisation, probably requires a high price for tin (estimated by the researches in 1951/53 at £800/ton). The same area has produced some tungsten in the form of wolframite running about 18–26 lbs of concentrate per ton from opencast mining or 26–31 lbs from underground mining.

General comments on minor minerals

Some of these minerals are "minor" only because exports have been very small or even nil. In reserve quantities, some are very large; limestone, magnesite, garnets, kaolin and by African standards coal.

Some appear to be prevented from appearing on the export market in significant quantities by transport costs (within Tanzania): kaolin, probably iron and coal (or their manufactured derivatives), possibly some garnet and mica. In these cases there is hope for expansion in the future as the long-run comparative cost advantages emerge. The growth of synthetics, and the centripetal tendencies of purchasing power, may make that emergence a mirage, but in a static and absolute sense the "comparative advantage" of Tanzania may well be found in its Ubendian and Karroo system minerals.

Several appear to be prevented from developing into local industries by lack of effective local demand: a whole coal/iron complex, the limestone of Tanga, kaolin, magnesite, further brine springs; also asbestos and tin, deposits of which are all small but could probably be profitably worked for local requirements.

Many appear to be under-capitalised in their operation, perhaps because of the preponderance of alluvial and dispersed strikes which has facilitated small-scale working by individuals and small groups, thereby incidentally avoiding the development of economic "enclaves". Diamond mining has become an enclave in a physical sense (with a fence around it) but the profits (to NDC) and royalties are siphoned off into the rest of the economy.

4. Exports of Manufactured Goods

The only manufactured item exported in large quantity is meat and meat products, mostly from a single factory, Tanganyika Packers Ltd.

Table 65. *Exports of Meat and Meat Products, 1961–1967*

	1961	1962	1963	1964	1965	1966	1967
Weight '000 tons	6.1	6.9	4.9	5.6	5.6	8.0	6.4
Value Shs. mn.	41	46	39	43	38	57	48

Source: Background to the Budget 1967–1968 and 1968–1969.

This is a factory just outside Dar es Salaam which takes cattle from various areas of Tanzania (broadly speaking, from the lines of rail) and converts those which pass the veterinary inspection into stewed steak, corned beef, steak and kidney, (all in cans supplied by Metal Box Co. Ltd.) and Oxo concentrate. Tanganyika Packers is now a subsidiary of NDC (1966 payoff: Shs. 1.7 mn.) but the minority shareholder, Liebig's Extract of Beef Ltd. handles the marketing. Liebig's is an old-established, international, canned beef company which formerly took the Tanganyika cattle offtake through its factory in Kenya. It controls the "Oxo" brand concentrate and several brand names including Fray Bentos without which, it is alleged, Tanzania would find it difficult to market its meat, or could not do so at present prices. This unsatisfactory position is of course under active review.

Another serious problem is the input of sufficient cattle of satisfactory quality. There is a high incidence of tuberculosis, and occasionally outbreaks of foot-and-mouth disease have closed the factory down for several weeks. Many die, and others lose weight, between delivery to railway station vicinities and arrival at the factory, due mainly to lack of water both on and off the trains. The East African Railways & Harbours do not accept responsibility for the wellbeing of the animals consigned by rail. Finally, railways are subject to annual washaways in the rainy season.

In the long run a further limiting factor must be the numbers of cattle available. The present stock is estimated at 10 million, but many of these are inaccessibly located; others are held as wealth or status symbols by the Masai and other herdsmen and are in general not on sale commercially. Most are in any case of low weight, being a hardy but small breed which is almost self-supporting so far as fodder is concerned. The acquisition of exotic stock (Friesland, Jersey, Angus, Charollais for instance) which provides some excellent crossbreeds is limited both by the unavailability of heifers in Kenya and by the long breeding cycle. This applies both to the dairy industry and to beef cattle. Efforts are being made to import heifers from Europe. It seems likely that within a few years a modern cattle industry will be established (with NDC ranches at its core) which will serve two or three "Tanganyika Packers"-type factories.

This is a case where rising local effective demand is helping to break through the scale barriers which impede export development.

Cattle is also a likely alternative to sisal in certain areas.

Other exports of manufactured goods are very small and take advantage of geography by exporting inland, going mostly to Zambia, Congo, Burundi. With the closure of the Suez Canal, Somalia and Mauritius also become easier markets. In nearly every case there is competition against a Kenya product having slightly lower production cost due to larger-scale production.

5. Geographical Direction of Exports

The following table shows changes in the direction of Tanzania's export trade since 1961.

Table 66. *Direction of Exports, 1961–1967*
(Millions of Shs.)

Area	1961	1962	1963	1964	1965	1966	1967
Kenya	43	56	62	87	94	81	68
Uganda	7	9	10	20	27	17	15
Sub-total	(50)	(65)	(72)	(107)	(121)	(98)	(83)
U.K.	354	373	418	436	382	486	473
India	62	85	70	101	107	129	108
Hong Kong	68	78	96	97	103	141	113
Other Sterling Area	68	73	93	91	91	61	193
Whole Sterling Area	(602)	(674)	(749)	(832)	(804)	(915)	(970)
E.E.C.	225	239	258	312	241	224	250
Japan	47	43	41	56	35	97	67
N. America	116	113	138	167	117	169	117
C.M.E.A.	7	3	29	33	22	36	56
China	–	–	75	47	95	69	59
Others	87	69	87	116	120	256	209
World	1,084	1,141	1,377	1,563	1,434	1,766	1,728

Source: Background to the Budget 1967–1968 and *1968–1969.*
Zanzibar is included; re-exports are not.

For purposes of analysis these sums may be presented as percentages of the total exports for each successive year.

It emerges, first, that the sterling area takes over half Tanzania's exports. The U.K. is the biggest consignee[17], with about a third of the total, though its share has fallen since 1964 to under 30%. If we assume, what is believed to be approximately correct, that all except the trade with North America and the E.E.C. is invoiced in sterling, we arrive at a figure for sterling export trade of 65%–80% of the whole. The proportion appears to have been rising: 68%, 69%, 65%, 69%, 75%, 77%, 78%. This is evidently because the effort of recent years to diversify into new markets has led to new outlets in China, Eastern Europe, and some peripheral sterling area countries, which on the whole deal in sterling. From the point of view of the sterling area this shift has been unfortunate in that a smaller proportion of Tanzania's exports goes to earn dollars and other convertible currencies. From the point of view of the national interest, however, the exploration of new

---

17 According to calculations made by G. K. HELLEINER on the basis of Customs figures and U.K. tariff rates, the cash value of Commonwealth preference on Tanzanian exports in 1966 was as little as £721,514. Presumably the incidence of this accruing in favour of Tanzania was even less.

Table 67. *Direction of Exports 1961–1967, as Percentages* [a]
(Percent of Total)

Area	1961	1962	1963	1964	1965	1966	1967
Kenya	4	5	5	6	7	5	4
Uganda	1	1	1	1	2	1	1
Sub-total	(4)	(6)	(6)	(7)	(8)	(5)	(5)
U.K.	33	33	37	28	27	28	27
India	6	8	6	6	7	7	6
Hong Kong	6	7	8	6	7	8	7
Other Sterling Area	6	7	8	6	6	4	11
Whole Sterling Area	(56)	(59)	(66)	(53)	(56)	(52)	(56)
E.E.C.	21	21	23	20	17	13	15
Japan	4	4	4	4	2	5	4
N. America	11	10	12	11	8	10	7
C.M.E.A.	1	–	2	2	2	2	3
China	–	–	7	3	7	4	3
Others	8	6	8	7	8	14	12
World	100	100	100	100	100	100	100

[a] Items may not add to totals or sub-totals because of decimal rounding.
Source: See Table 66.

markets has been of prime importance, particularly in view of the coffee quota position and the weakness of the European sisal market.

The second point is that China and the member countries of the Council for Mutual Economic Assistance now take around 6% of exports. Though the figure was negligible in 1961–62, this still does not represent a large growth. In view of the importance of those countries on capital account, i.e. in giving capital to Tanzania, the co-operation in commercial trade is remarkably small. In general those countries aim at bilaterally balanced trade, and the bottleneck is on the import side, where they have difficulty in competing against old-established agency lines, and sometimes in meeting the requirements of the market as to quality and presentation. Extended shipment periods and irregular sailings are a further problem for those countries.

Third, it is noticeable that exports to Kenya and Uganda are very small. The three East African economies continue to be broadly competitive rather than complementary. It is to be expected that the East African Development Bank will make a contribution in this field.

Exports go, for obvious reasons, predominantly to advanced industrial countries. The U.K., the E.E.C., Japan and North America now take rather more than half (53% in 1967). This figure was higher in the earlier years, before the decline of the U.K. share. There has been, in 1966 and 1967, a rise in the share of small countries (those treated as residuals in Table 67), but this does not provide evidence of structural economic change, since it may be argued that exporters were induced to seek new markets, without change of product, chiefly by deflation and import restrictions in the United Kingdom rather than for any developmental reason.

It should be borne in mind that official trade figures do not always show the country of first origin, or the country of final destination, where entrepôt activities are involved. The necessary data are not always available to the customs authorities. Some remarks on the divergence between declared and actual commodity movements will be found elsewhere in this volume.

IV. MERCHANDISE IMPORTS

The evolution of imports, and especially their rapid growth since independence, has been traced in some detail in the historical narrative; and the general pattern is discussed in the overall survey. The purpose of this chapter is to provide some more detail by giving particular attention to certain leading categories of goods and to certain factors affecting prices.

1. Imports of Machinery

The rise in the ratio of capital goods imports to total imports since independence has already been noted[1] with the remark that the classification of capital goods was necessarily arbitrary. If we exclude objects whose economic function is insufficiently indicated by their Customs Entry, and concentrate our attention upon machinery and implements, we will have what may be considered the leading element of capital goods imports. This analysis has been made for the years 1964 to 1967.

Machinery, equipment and implements for use in agriculture were imported as follows.

Table 68. *Agricultural Equipment Imports, 1964–1967*
(Thousands of Shs.)

	1964	1965	1966	1967
Tractors	16,490	15,340	11,175	17,443
Other mechanical equipment	7,240	6,583	8,272	6,476
Hand-operated implements	6,581	6,513	10,126	10,601
Total	30,311	28,436	29,573	34,520

Source: E.A. Customs and Excise: *Annual Trade Reports.*

The slight decline in all categories in the bad-weather year of 1965, and the remarkable rise in all categories except tractors in the excellent weather of 1966, show a high degree of short-term volatility on a rising growth trend.

---

1 In the historical section, Chapter 2.

This volatility in making investment decisions where the goods are likely to last for many years is presumably due to the volatility of investible cash surpluses which constitute formidable bottlenecks especially for the poorer smallholder.

The volatility of tractor imports is a special feature. The most popular makes are the robust Massey-Ferguson, and International Harvester; the principal sources are the U.K., and (for tracked vehicles) the U.S.A. But in 1964 a special consignment of 79 tractors worth Shs. 3.6 mn. was imported from Yugoslavia by a parastatal body as an attempt at diversification; this explains the high total for that year. The necessary spare parts were not imported, and as these tractors are of metric specification, they fell idle in increasing numbers and became unpopular. This, together with increasing realisation of the significance of the heavy burden of interest charges on mechanised settlement schemes, and of the dangers of soil disturbance in areas formerly ploughed less deeply than is the case with tractors, have made tractors in general increasingly suspect in Tanzania. The figure recorded in 1967 of tractor imports worth Shs. 17.4 mn. is an exaggeration; Shs. 6.9 mn. of these were Caterpiller or crawler-type tractors, some of which may have been wrongly classed as agricultural. Nevertheless, a recovery does seem to have taken place in 1967, contrary to official policy[2] which seeks to emphasize capital-saving forms of agricultural development.

The above relates to equipment used in the primary stage of agricultural production as distinct from the processing of the produce.

Table 69. *Imports of Machinery for Processing Agricultural Outputs, 1964–1967*
(Thousands of Shs.)

Branch	1964	1965	1966	1967
Textiles & leather	9,705	15,645	22,458	49,438
Sugar	2,675	1,558	5,438	2,489
Grain milling	1,198	1,083	3,031	962
Other food	602	4,074	6,402	2,806
Paper (incl. print)	2,498	2,008	4,017	3,049
Sisal	4,842	1,353	337	269
Tea	1,235	622	956	1,529
Coffee	401	908	886	491
Vegetable oils	599	729	2,166	3,266
Other	752	4,504	6,469	2,958
Total	24,507	32,484	52,160	67,257

Source: E.A. Customs and Excise: *Annual Trade Reports.*

2 *Socialism and Rural Development,* pp. 29–30 (Dar es Salaam, Govt. Printer, 1967).

From these totals one might again perceive a rising trend with some weakness in 1965, but from the details it is clear that this outcome is the result of very mixed experience in different branches. Sisal shows a dramatic decline, for obvious reasons, and this investment, like that of the tractors mentioned above, might be regarded as a misplaced investment, to be written off. It is to be hoped that the proportion of such mistakes will fall as the economy moves forward, thereby reducing the effective capital-output ratio. Textiles and leather machinery shows a remarkable growth which, since there is still no tannery, should continue in subsequent years. The large investments in sugar machinery reflect the "lumpy" projects of the factories at Arusha Chini and, in 1966, Kilombero; these imports may fall back to a low level for subsequent years, as the country is now roughly self-sufficient in sugar and in any case the world free market price is below Tanzania's production costs. Tea, coffee and vegetable oil processing machinery are still in some respects experimental so far as commercial viability is concerned and it is not yet possible to predict how this class of imports will behave in the future. Paper-making, printing and binding machinery is likely to rise further with the Government support of institutions producing educational books; the increase in 1966 was probably due to the erection of a commercial bookprinting works at Arusha. Nothing can be known about the category "other food" equipment since it is not further described in the trade statistics.

Commenting on the imports of processing machinery as a group, one would say that they reflect very clearly the general investment climate though they are on a strong growth trend.

Table 70. *Imports of Machinery for Construction, Mining and Mineral Processing,*
1964–1967

(Thousands of Shs.)

Branch	1964	1965	1966	1967
Construction, mining	9,441	9,117	17,935	32,143
Mineral processing	1,928	8,245	1,733	2,305
Glassworking	96	25	162	444
Metalworking	3,394	5,104	4,550	3,493
Total	14,859	22,491	18,380	38,385

Source: E. A. Customs and Excise, *Annual Trade Reports.*

This reflects above all the flow of soft loans for road building. One cannot regard the rest of this sector as sufficiently integrated into the economy as a whole to share in its basic trends.

Tanzania's known exploitable mineral resources are scanty, and barring any rise in the world price of gold, rather limited imports of equipment in connection with diamonds and semi-precious stones and another cement factory, are all that can be expected. Moreover, the establishment in Tanzania of enterprises using imported mineral inputs (apart from its apparent costliness) is likely to be forestalled by the relatively rapid move in that direction by neighbouring countries (Kenya and Zambia). Kenya in 1966, for example, imported Shs. 8 mn. of machine tools for metalworking (Tanzania Shs. 3$\frac{1}{2}$ mn.).

Another important category of imports, mechanical in nature, but not capable of being broken down by industry, is machinery parts.

Table 71. *Imports of Major Categories of Machinery Parts, 1964–1967*
(Thousands of Shs.)

	1964	1965	1966	1967
Pumps and centrifuges	4,401	6,177	6,675	6,267
Valves, cocks, taps	971	4,078	3,228	3,025
Bearings	853	1,210	1,144	1,431
Shafts, pulleys, etc.	435	536	518	431
Mechanical handling equipment	3,172	10,600	10,080	15,346
Parts n.e.s.	633	958	1,012	1,301
Total	10,465	23,559	22,657	27,801

Source: E. A. Customs and Excise, *Annual Trade Reports.*

This shows the impact of the TIPER oil refinery which was built in 1965–66, and probably (under "mechanical handling equipment") extension to the breweries and some equipment for the docks. None of these except dock equipment seems like to recur on the basis of investment projects now scheduled, so this category may fall in future years.

The rise in 1965 (higher than 1964 or 1966) which is the opposite pattern to agriculture-based investments gives some further explanation of the remarkable buoyancy of the economy in that year, already remarked upon in the historical narrative. The same phenomenon can be seen in the type of imports listed in Table 70.

There seems also to have been a spurt of activity in the electric power sector.

This very impressive development is, like that of road building, closely linked with the availability of sufficient finance on terms that are found reasonable in view of the lengthy periods of recoupment required for these types of investment. In any case the growth rate has been very satisfactory, and this seems likely to continue, as TANESCO (the responsible parastatal organisation) is under a standing instruction not to allow a shortage of electricity to impede economic development; up to now this has been faithfully observed.

Table 72. *Imports of Electrical Equipment, 1964–1967*
(Thousands of Shs.)

	1964	1965	1966	1967
Boiler-room plant	572	830	2,481	663
Generators, transformers, etc.	5,645	5,545	4,758	10,611
Switchgear	3,942	5,100	5,644	7,783
Motors	1,264	2,066	1,728	1,855
Cable, insulation	3,568	5,723	5,364	5,474
Telephone, lines, etc.	1,807	1,840	2,461	15,728
Instruments	491	651	1,128	1,467
Apparatus n.e.s.	927	1,495	1,249	1,501
Total	18,216	23,250	24,813	45,082

Source: E. A. Customs and Excise, *Annual Trade Reports.*

It is clear that, while a trend of imports can be discerned after aggregation, the disaggregated figures show considerable lumpiness; to what extent the smooth movement of the aggregate is due to careful Government planning and to what extent to chance it is difficult to judge.

A similar situation exists with imports of transport equipment.

Table 73. *Imports of Transport Equipment, 1964–1967*
(Millions of Shs.)

	1964	1965	1966	1967
Passenger cars	27.2	23.7	33.5	26.1
Buses, lorries, vans, etc.	44.4	60.0	97.4	84.3
Railway rolling stock	3.5	2.0	1.2	2.4
Bicycles	7.6	4.2	5.6	5.3
Other	32.0	38.0	58.0	93.3
Total	114.7	127.9	195.7	211.4

Source: Bank of Tanzania (but derived from monthly customs statistics).

Whilst the totals show the familiar trend (generally upward but affected by poor weather in 1965 and very good weather in 1966), the individual items by no means all conform to this; motor-car imports in 1967 were affected by the anti-Mercedes campaign and austere Budget of 1967; commercial vehicles were imported at very high levels between August, 1966 and March, 1967 mainly for the Zambia transit trade (a reaction to Rhodesian

139

independence); railway imports, after rising for the construction of the Ruvu-Mnyusi line, have fallen to a very low level since 1964 and seem unlikely to revive until the Tanzania-Zambia railway is built; bicycles probably are strongly influenced by weather conditions (via export earnings) but may also have been influenced by changes in buying procedures. "Other transport equipment" includes detached parts and its rise may also be attributed to the Zambian operation with its attendant repair needs. This may in fact fall when the road concerned is reconstructed, but this is doubtful since the number of vehicles using it is likely to rise.

There is at present no project under construction of the magnitude of the oil refinery. The next large project appears to be the railway to Zambia, which however will spread its imports over several years. A steel-rolling mill has been mooted but is by no means definite at the present time. Consequently there is a possibility that capital goods imports will drop in the early years of the Second Five-Year Plan until a series of important new projects are implemented.

2. Imports of Articles of Mass-Consumption

Two leading commodities in the consumer goods field have been selected for special study: textiles and tinned milk. The latter raises interesting problems of brand-preference.

a) Textiles

Textiles occupied an important place among imports already in the time of German East Africa, as cottons gradually replaced hides and skins as articles of clothing. Thus in 1897, textiles and clothing accounted for 52% of the colony's imports; by 1911, owing to the importation of quantities of rice (a major foodstuff along the lines of rail) and equipment, this had fallen to 31%. By 1930 the proportion was down to 20%; in 1940 (when total imports, under war-time conditions, were at three-quarters of their 1930 level and development imports were minimal), it was up slightly at $22^1/_2$%, but in 1950 it was further down at $17^1/_2$% and in 1960 still lower at $15^1/_2$%[3]. The absolute value, of course, was rising; the 1960 figure was £5.8 mn. as compared with £0.8 mn. in 1930, a greater difference than could be

---

3 There are small differences in the coverage at these various dates, but for the 1930, 1950 and 1960 figures the error is negligible.

accounted for by rising prices. Meanwhile a special vogue has been established in the mass market for black rayon (worn by Muslim women), printed cotton khangas, and khaki drill.

It should be borne in mind that the secular decline in the textile ratio was not due (until very recently) to local production; the latter, whether by cottage industry or mill methods, was negligible until after independence. In 1964, when local production of cotton cloth reached 8.9 million square yards, importation reached 191.1 millions[4]. In 1965 local production was 12.1 mn. sq. yards, in 1966 17.1 mn. and in the year ending October, 1967 18.4 mn., but considerable new capacity is expected to be brought on stream in 1968 by the Mwanza and Friendship textile mills (estimated production 24 mn. sq. yards each) and it is estimated that by 1970, most of the country's textile requirements will be met by local production.

In connection with the secular decline it is interesting to note Mr. I. Östby's calculation[5] based on an expenditure survey in Dar es Salaam covering an income range of Shs. 150 to Shs. 300 per month in 1965, that as family expenditure increases by 1⁰/o, expenditure on clothing increases by only 0.55⁰/o.

Mr. Östby contrasts this figure with that of 1.55⁰/o for Nairobi, which is based on a sample covering an income range of Shs. 335 to Shs. 1,305; clearly clothing is an article of ostentatious consumption in Nairobi to a degree which does not obtain in Dar es Salaam. This difference must work in favour of Tanzania in the sense of saving foreign exchange and other resources but will presumably create a particular problem in that large-scale garment-manufacturing industry will have a strong preference for locating in Kenya; this is particularly so while many Tanzanian women dress in the simple un-made-up khanga, and as the fashion changes with rising incomes, importation of garments from Kenya is likely to be the result. Tanzania regularly imports more clothing from Kenya than Kenya does from Tanzania. Even in 1967 when Tanzania's imports were depressed, the figures were Shs. 1.6 mn. and Shs. 0.9 mn. respectively.

The making up of garments is an important local small-scale industry, and as a result of the possible fashion changes mentioned above, it may later become an important cottage industry, thereby filling a need in Tanzania, which is remarkably lacking in rural non-agricultural employment opportunities. This industry boomed in 1966 but like the large-scale industries, it did not expand greatly in 1967:

---

4 Sources: for local production, *Monthly Statistical Bulletin;* for imports E.A. Customs and Excise, *Annual Trade Reports.*
5 "An Econometric Study of Demand Patterns in Dar es Salaam", E.R.B. Paper No. 68/5, University College, Dar es Salaam. Preliminary review by Ivar Östby.

Table 74. *Sewing Machine Imports, 1966 and 1967*
(Thousands of Shs.)

	Tanzania		Kenya		Uganda	
	1966	1967	1966	1967	1966	1967
Domestic machines	1,807	555	38	1,404	1,705	590
Industrial machines	2,218	342	668	1,086	817	357
Parts and accessories	739	474	2,620	622	560	558
Total	4,764	1,371	3,326	3,112	3,082	1,505

Source: E. A. Customs and Excise, *Annual Trade Reports.*

The main categories of textiles imported in recent years have been as follows.

Table 75. *Major Textile Imports, 1964–1967*
(Thousands of Shs.)

	1964	1965	1966	1967
Cotton cloth, grey				
India	5,524	9,085	4,156	704
Pakistan	2,350	1,132	302	–
Uganda	1,687	843	1,730	932
China	4	206	–	–
Others	199	73	78	404
Total	9,764	11,339	6,266	2,040
Cotton cloth, bleached				
U.K.	292	376	577	169
Hong Kong	27	155	633	128
India	817	942	257	84
Pakistan	99	79	21	–
China	53	830	4,180	557
Japan	2,818	3,042	1,689	312
Uganda	1,238	1,228	2,124	703
Others	452	1,327	737	276
Total	5,479	6,979	10,218	2,229
Cotton cloth, woven of coloured yarns				
India	2,082	1,780	885	525
Japan	2,123	225	127	40
China	–	–	83	56
Uganda	–	41	163	169
Others	531	138	164	119
Total	4,736	2,184	1,422	909

	1964	1965	1966	1967
Cotton cloth, dyed in the piece, including khaki drill				
Uganda	16,382	20,689	27,356	14,631
China	41	3,524	9,537	4,201
India	9,214	10,030	8,380	4,913
Japan	13,902	8,586	5,527	4,317
Hong Kong	326	1,665	3,977	1,002
U.K.	3,145	2,543	3,134	1,141
East Germany	90	277	1,530	631
Poland	13	169	883	643
Others	4,080	1,362	1,408	3,121
Total	47,193	48,845	61,732	34,600
Khangas				
India	418	1,956	6,176	106
Japan	20,006	6,412	6,087	4,992
Hong Kong	2	–	3,451	2,788
China	–	473	3,617	3,938
Netherlands	1,727	2,097	2,086	1,279
Others	11	–	–	–
Total	22,164	10,938	21,417	13,103
Other printed cotton including kitenge				
Hong Kong	421	264	4,897	3,303
India	4,302	8,133	8,913	1,925
China	34	1,740	8,449	3,635
Japan	12,381	5,975	9,595	3,026
Netherlands	842	1,836	3,248	3,085
West Germany	494	1.061	2,485	664
Others	965	1,763	3,352	1,886
Total	19,439	20,772	40,939	17,524
Synthetics, woven, dyed in the piece				
Japan	16,088	10,065	9,286	5,591
China	13	419	2,646	1,444
India	170	135	1,441	575
U.K.	374	732	875	137
Others	1,126	355	5,212	2.841
Total	17,771	11,706	19,460	10,588
Synthetics, printed				
China	36	1,983	8,643	1,114
Japan	14,853	8,991	4,354	600
India	292	352	3.511	245
Others	262	677	3,863	1,616
Total	15 443	12,003	20,371	3,575

Source: E. A. Customs and Excise, *Annual Trade Reports.*

Taking the results of leading country suppliers throughout the range of these 8 categories we have:

Table 76. *Imports of Major Textile Categories, by Origin, 1964–1967*
(Thousands of Shs.)

	1964	1965	1966	1967
China	185	9,175	37,155	14,945
Japan	82,205	43,326	36,664	18,878
India	22,819	32,413	33,720	9,077
Uganda	19,307	22,801	31,480	16,630
Hongkong	831	2,087	13,058	7,262
U.K.	4,412	5,035	6,465	2,492
Netherlands	2,607	4,168	5,604	5,113
Poland	97	833	3,216	823
East Germany	107	409	3,032	1,428
Pakistan	2,683	1,349	589	199
Others	6,736	3,200	10,832	7,721
Total	141,989	124,796	181,815	84,568

These results are tabulated in order of their values in 1966. A number of conclusions can be drawn.

There was a fall of over 12⁰/₀ between 1964 and 1965; this was when textile imports were confined to the parastatal organisation COSATA before the organisation was fully equipped to handle the business.

Going through the categories, we find the fall occurred in khangas and synthetics, but not in cottons (other than khangas); the former category corresponds to fabrics which COSATA imported in its own name through a merchanting department and the latter corresponds to fabrics for which COSATA acted merely as agent, through an indent department, importing at the request of wholesalers. It was therefore in the merchanting department that the weakness lay.

The trouble can be pinpointed further as a weakness in buying from the Far East; imports from Hongkong and China were too slow to materialise, and imports from Japan fell sharply. Total textile imports from Japan fell from 82 to 43 million shillings; this was before a restrictive import licensing system was imposed against Japanese goods in 1966 which reduced the imports only a little further to 37 million shillings.

In 1964 Japan supplied 58⁰/₀ of the total; in 1966 only 20⁰/₀; in 1967 22⁰/₀. The main beneficiaries of the import licensing appear to have been China, which came up to first place; Uganda and Hongkong. The rises of China and Hongkong were however delayed through 1965 for COSATA internal reasons. To a lesser extent, room was also made for imports from Eastern Europe.

In the case of khangas, Japan and India remained well ahead of China. The non-importation of Indian khangas in 1967 was due to a price increase following devaluation of the rupee, paradoxically enough, which was not acceptable to the State Trading Corporation.

A most interesting figure is the change from 1966 to 1967 in all 8 categories of textiles, a drop of 53% in value. The heaviest falls were those where local mills were coming on stream: simple cotton cloths and khaki drill; also printed synthetics, which are mainly in demand among the Asian communities (Asian emigration was unusually heavy in January and February of 1967). The entire trade, however, was depressed until the closing months of the year, in consequence of the bad rains, the political impact of the nationalisations, the emigrations, and the over-stocking of 1966 which stood revealed in the ensuing liquidity crisis of the wholesale textile trade.

At the time of writing (March, 1969) the institutional pattern of importation remains basically the same: COSATA, now the Textile Division of the State Trading Corporation, still has the confinement of textiles. Khangas, vitenge, suitings and synthetics (including nylon) in the piece are imported on a merchanting (though mostly back-to-back) basis, while other cottons, e.g. khaki drill, brocades and other miscellaneous small orders are placed through the indent department on a commission basis.

The profit margin of the merchanting department and the commission rate of the indent department were originally fixed at fairly high levels (which cannot be disclosed here) as a source of financial strength for the newly-formed COSATA; since the foundation of the State Trading Corporation, a reduction of these margins has been the subject of controversial discussion. It is also claimed by the private sector that the merchanting department, quite apart from its profit margin, actually buys the textiles at higher prices than the private wholesalers could achieve themselves by direct importation. In fact, considering the prices of Indian and Netherlands khangas as representative, these have risen on a foreign exchange cost basis by 1.1% and 7% per annum respectively between 1964 and 1966, and given the tendency towards more colours per khanga, this performance can scarcely be considered unsatisfactory. On the other hand there is no evidence that the bulk-buying policy has produced significant benefits so far. This may be because the business was conducted largely on a back-to-back basis, which precludes genuine bulk-buying in fact.

Some further evidence as to the performance of this buying system can be found in the price changes which followed the devaluation of sterling in November, 1967. The Tanzanian shilling rose against the pound by 16.7% and the S.T.C. endeavoured to minimise the concomitant sterling price rises so as so maximise the price reduction in shilling terms. Of those U.K. textile suppliers who increased their sterling prices, those three which supplied suitings (purchased by the S.T.C. on a merchanting basis) raised their sterling price tariffs by 4%/o to 6%/o, 2¹/₂%/o and 5%/o to 5¹/₂%/o respectively, thus giving the majority of the benefit to Tanzania, while the ten others on whom indent orders are placed increased their sterling price lists as follows: 5%/o to 9%/o; 3%/o to 28%/o; 2¹/₂%/o to 3%/o; 30%/o; 20%/o; 10%/o to 34%/o; 5%/o; 7¹/₂%/o to 10%/o; 7¹/₂%/o to 20%/o; 9%/o to 10%/o; in short, behaved with much more freedom, to the detriment of Tanzania. The popular khaki drills went up by more than the extent of the devaluation, by 30%/o and 20%/o according to the two suppliers involved. This is certainly an argument for transferring some types of textiles from the indenting to the merchanting system.

Table 77. *Textile Imports and Monetary Private Consumption, 1961–1966*

	Textile Imports Shs. mn.	Consumption Shs. mn.	%
1961	146	1,754	*8.3*
1962	160	2,009	*8.0*
1963	166	2,118	*7.8*
1964	190	2,266	*8.4*
1965	184	2,351	*7.8*
1966	286	n. a.	*n. a.*
(1961–1965)	(846)	(10,498)	*(8.06)*

Source: Textile Imports from E. A. Customs and Excise, *Annual Trade Reports.* Private monetary consumption: H. E. DAHL: *The Economy of Tanzania* (Christian-Michelsen Institute, Bergen, 1967). DAHL's time series is based on primary sources supplied by the Central Statistical Bureau, Dar es Salaam.

Table 78. *Expected Import Substitution in Textiles*

		1969	1970	1971
Consumption (mn. Shs.)				
	(i)	2,761	2,874	2,992
	(ii)	3,047	3,251	3,469
Potential textile imports (mn. Shs.)				
	(i)	221	230	239
	(ii)	244	260	278
Domestic production				
(mn. sq. yards)		58	70	82
(mn. Shs.)		116	140	164
Textile imports				
	(i)	105	90	75
	(ii)	128	120	114

Assumptions: (i) Growth rate of 4.1%/o p.a. (corresponds to performance from 1960/62 to 1966).
(ii) Growth rate of 6.7%/o p.a. (corresponds to planned performance).

146

Considering the market for textiles more broadly defined, i.e. SITC Division 65 with the exception of industrial textiles such as conveyor belting (655), we find imports from all sources into mainland Tanzania have behaved in the following way with respect to estimated private consumption expenditure.

A considerable import substitution programme is under way for cloth, and a rough idea of the effects of this programme may be obtained, for future years, by making certain assumptions.

Potential textile imports are set at 8% of monetary consumer expenditure. Domestic production estimates are based on commercial enquiries. Value is foreign exchange value at Shs. 2.0 per square yard, a realistic figure.

Thus by 1970 import substitution is likely to satisfy between 50% and 60% of textile requirements, and actual imports can be expected to fall absolutely.

b) Tinned Milk: a Case of Consumers' Brand Preferences

Among the imported goods which are sold under brand names are some for which a noticeable consumer preference exists without rational basis in terms of objective product quality. Nestlé tinned milk may be cited as an example. Specifications of tinned milk quality have been laid down by international convention and in terms of these specifications several other brands of tinned milk are available on the world market which are equally good, including Nestlé's own "yellow dog" product, Teapot Milk, at lower prices. There is no doubt that consumers are willing to pay a premium for milk bearing the brand name "Nestlé". This is by its nature a product whose quality cannot be tested by the consumer except at risk to himself, and it is not irrational to prefer a brand which has proved satisfactory in the past, given the consumers' state of knowledge. The old-established brand therefore has an advantage, quite apart from any advantages which might be derived from a long history of brand advertising or from the national affiliations of the leading importing houses. There are also slight differences in taste and colour, and it is reasonable to suppose that the consumer typically acquires habits in these respects.

The question therefore arises, is it possible to save foreign exchange by improving consumer rationality (or consumer knowledge), i.e. can arrangements be made to induce consumers to buy a comparable product from a cheaper source?

Nestlé milk is sold under the "Milkmaid" label, on which the name "Nestlé" is prominently displayed, and the identical milk is available under the "Teapot" label on which the name "Nestlé" is not mentioned. The c.i.f. prices are Shs. 58/75 for Milkmaid and Shs. 49/75 for Teapot, per carton of 48 tins of 14 ozs each. Sales in Tanzania during the twelve months September,

1966 — August, 1967 (as indicated by import licences issued[6]) were 3,025 cartons of Milkmaid and 9,745 cartons of Teapot. The total c.i.f. value of Nestlé milk was thus Shs. 662,532/50, of which Shs. 27,225/- or 4.1% would have been saved if only Teapot milk had been bought.

Attempts have been made (by Messrs. Cosata) to import tinned milk in bulk from sources cheaper than Nestlé (Teapot) including the U.S.S.R., but these attempts are reported to have foundered despite the "substantial" price advantage at the wholesale level, against the rock of habitual brand preference.

Three possible solutions have been explored by the writer.

The first is for a parastatal body such as the Grocery Supply Division of the State Trading Corporation to import all milk by regulation and to buy from the cheapest available source or sources[7]. This would require the setting up of a central organisation to stock the milk and to control its physical movement inwards and outwards. A considerable personnel would be required including highly-paid experts (since tinned milk, especially condensed, deteriorates in storage). At parastatal wage-rates and with the appropriate staff amenities the overhead costs would be in excess of those met by the small businesses which at present handle the milk[8] and are staffed largely by family labour. Consequently the retail price of milk might actually rise, which would conflict with the official policy of price stabilisation. This might be viewed as a worthwhile price to pay for savings in foreign exchange but it seems unlikely that the organisation concerned would be willing to undertake the necessary capital outlay in order to enter into a situation in which political considerations would exert a strong downward pressure upon the profits.

The second possibility is to refuse to give import licences to those importers who make no attempt to depress, by negotiation, the import price, or who appear to be paying significantly above the average import price for a particular type of milk. Applications for licences do have to be accompanied by a copy of the indent in which quality, packaging and c.i.f. price are stated. However, c.i.f. prices vary with freight charges even between the same two ports. Moreover the independent importers (which, as has been said, are mostly small businessmen) are not in a suitable bargaining position to negotiate the prices anyway.

The third possibility is to control prices, by regulation. Such price controls as now exist (tinned milk is not among them) operate at the retail level,

---

6 The licensing system does not appear to be evaded to any significant extent.

7 A plurality of sources would retain some degree of consumer choice, unless all the milk were marketed under the same label.

8 For this reason, the large foreign-owned importing houses have in recent years progressively ceased to handle tinned milk and other staple articles exhibiting rapid turnover and low mark-up.

from which the political pressure for stabilisation arises. Retail price controls are designed primarily to protect the consumer budget, not the balance of payments. In order to ensure a continuing supply of the product despite rising prices in the world market it is necessary that:

- distribution margins be compressible; or
- importers are able to switch to cheaper sources; or
- importers are able to hold down c.i.f. prices by negotiation (which implies that manufactures' margins are compressible); or
- distributors are willing, or can be compelled, to distribute milk at less than "normal profit" (in the Marshallian sense) alongside other, uncontrolled, lines, which give them more than normal profit; or
- some combination of these.

The compressibility of distributors' profits in general can be doubted on the evidence of the distribution survey which found that Tanzania had, broadly speaking, "a low-cost distribution system", and in the specific case of tinned milk the fact that its distribution has passed partly into the hands of low-overhead family businesses indicates that margins have already been compressed. It is conceivable, certainly, that further compression is possible.

As regards the possibility of obtaining lower c.i.f. prices, it is relevant that most of the tinned milk is imported by appointed agents of the manufacturers[9], who are neither able to switch to a cheaper source nor to negotiate prices, though they may in some cases be able to press for more of the cheaper-label types of milk. This raises the question of the desirability of such agencies.

Agency agreements typically may be terminated by 3 months' notice on either side. The agent receives, say, 5% commission on either c.i.f. or the f.o.b. value and undertakes to carry the stocks, to handle no competing products, to assist in promotional activity (most of which is, however, undertaken by the manufacturers) and to give the manufacturer complete control over the whole price structure from the ex-factory price down to the retail price, including the various types of discount. The "principal" does not normally discuss prices with his agent. A popular-brand agency is a sought-after prize, not lightly given up; for many one-agency importers, it is the rock on which their livelihood is built. To do away with the agency system would seemingly involve:

- no guarantee of adequate availability of stocks, unless a parastatal body undertook some importing (but see above for the difficulties of this);
- probably more demand by importers for the most popular brands, irrespective of price, to which they did not formerly have access; unless

---

9 One of them, Riley Trading Co., imports about half of it. This is a Netherlands agency (Co-op. Cond. Friesland).

the pre-eminence of price were reinforced by an appropriate form of price control: a point which is picked up below.

Retail price control involves many difficulties in a country with poor and expensive transport facilities. Regional differences clearly must be permitted[10], but as regional centres (wholesale depots) are not necessarily in the centre of their regions, it would be possible for retailers to buy from outside their regions. Then between wholesaler and retailer distribution costs vary considerably. One retailer may use a van; another may rely on the local bus driver. One may be able to use a weekly delivery service, another may have to buy 3 months' supply to see him through the rainy season when roads are impassable, or he may pay for head porterage. In such circumstances, the fixing of uniform retail prices is extremely difficult. Nevertheless it can be done if:

a) reliable wholesalers are appointed who undertake to bear all the costs of distribution initially;

b) these costs, receipted, are passed to the supervisory agency and loaded on to the average price charged to the wholesaler through an equalisation account;

c) small inequities in costs at the retail level are borne without complaint by the retailers because the controlled products are only a part of their business;

d) imports are undertaken solely by, or strictly controlled by, supervisory body.

Point d) raises difficulties. If a government or parastatal body actually does the importing it incurs extra costs (as described above). If it merely issues licences to independent importers the problems will be:

1. if these are appointed agents, each manufacturer will have an inducement to flood the market and raise the c.i.f. price, knowing that his agent will be protected from losses by the equalisation account. The c.i.f. prices will tend to rise and eventually control over retail prices will prove a forlorn hope;

2. if these are really independent importers they will be able to find suppliers willing to over-invoice the merchandise in order to transfer wealth abroad (evading Exchange Control) and to improve the importers' tax position.

The solution to these difficulties would appear to be to have a central buying agency (parastatal) and a number of appointed stockists (private). This would minimise both foreign exchange costs and distribution expenses.

Once such a system had been set up, the switchover to cheaper sources of

---

10 If a parastatal body could do the importing, freight charges could be refunded by that body to the buyers on production of freight receipts and charged against the overall mark-up through an equalisation account, as is done for one domestically produced commodity, sugar.

supply would meet with greatly reduced problems of consumer conservatism. The old, "undesirable" brand could be either cleared, withheld, priced-up or withdrawn from promotional activities without legal complications with the manufacturers.

To which types of product would such a policy recommendation refer? In view of the high-level expertise required to set up and to operate such schemes it would be impracticable to extend it to more than a few commodities.

- They should be commodities of which the import price could probably be substantially reduced. Brand-preference is an indicator (though not a good one) of this; price-variety at the c.i.f. level is another.
- They should be articles of great importance, i.e. articles of mass consumption, or crucial for nation-building.
- They should not be articles which can be dealt with more easily by other methods; bicycles, for example, most of which are already sold by the S.T.C., could be cut in price by switching to another source or by putting pressure on the manufacturers without fear of competition from other importers. Textiles, similarly, are already institutionally under control.

The articles of mass consumption are listed in the survey of distribution as:

a) piece-goods and cheap clothing
b) maize meal
c) rice
d) beans
e) sugar
f) salt
g) cigarettes
h) soap
i) kerosene
j) tea
k) tinned milk
l) cooking oils
m) matches
n) various patent medicines
o) razor blades
p) aluminium & enamel ware
q) biscuits
r) beads in certain areas
s) cotton thread
t) writing materials
u) wheat flour
v) sembe
w) dagaa

and various vegetables together with coffee, tinned baby food a "small section of imported tinned foods". Also mentioned are shoes, hoes, bicycles and spare parts, corrugated iron sheets, sewing machines, radios, cheap crockery and cutlery, padlocks, hurricane lamps, watches and radio batteries.

Technically the most difficult area in which to bring pressure to bear on import prices may be the myriad of items imported in very small quantities. These are as a rule goods in which import substitution is not possible. One revealing example on which research has been done is electric lamps for film and slide projectors used in schools. The 29 schools with projection equipment were found to require 22 different types of lamp. It was calculated that if the future (growing) demand were standardised, a project could be organised to supply 640 lamps per year at Shs. 12,000. The price payable by schools for the same lamps under existing arrangements (indenting individually through agencies) was Shs. 60,000 [11]. As purchasing power rises and such items as this are successively placed on a bulked basis, the foreign exchange cost per item must fall, but to accelerate this process is a formidable task.

3. Import Substitution and Protection

Since primary products make up a very large part — about 87% — of what is produced in Tanzania, it is still largely true that any form of manufacturing can be regarded as import substitution: either a substitution against existing imports, or a substitution against future import demand as projected from present trends. Thus the Government's "import substitution policy" is largely the same as its "industrial policy". Those projects which might be included in the latter but not in the former would be projects designed primarily to process local produce for the export market — cashew nut processing, castor oil manufacture and instant coffee-powder making, sisal rope and twine, fruit juices, etc., and even these have to be tied in with the import substitution programme at the policy-making stage because they create greater demands for imports and because their location has to be considered together with the location of import substituting projects in order to avoid inequitable areal benefits.

Since there is a constant shortage of manpower in both private and public sectors at the project preparation stages there cannot be a fully rational process of reviewing and ranking all projects possible at any one time. In the private sector, of course, projects are not ranked but considered individually by entrepreneurs on a yes-no basis, broadly speaking; but they may be put forward to the Industrial Studies and Development Centre for feasibility study; in which case the staff of that organisation may advise the entrepreneur that it would be more profitable to concentrate more or less on a certain aspect of the project. Also, the entrepreneur normally makes a request through the Ministry of Commerce & Industries for tariff protection (or for a customs rebate against the tariff on imported inputs) in which case the Ministry will assess the project on the basis of a questionnaire and will refuse to grant protection if the project fails to meet certain requirements.

11 C. A. PRATT: *Projection Lamp Supply Service,* Institute of Education, University College, Dar es Salaam, 1967, mimeographed. The figure of Shs. 60,000 is inflated by a 30% import tariff which is not included in the figure of Shs. 12,000. Nevertheless, the ratio is nearly 4:1.

152

What those requirements are, and whether a consistent policy of applied criteria is followed, is not known: no policy has been published[12]. Certainly the process of investigation is a protracted one. It may be presumed that roughly the same criteria are applied to these projects as are applied in the public and parastatal sectors; at present these are as described in Appendix VIII.

Import substitution in Tanzania is likely to be based on domestic inputs to a very large extent if it is to be viable. But the processing of domestic inputs brings Tanzania into direct competition with neighbouring countries with similar agricultural characteristics. Imports from the south (Mozambique) are nil; imports from the west (Zambia, Malawi, Congo-Kinshasa) are negligible; imports from Uganda in *processed* form are very small; imports from *Kenya* are inevitably therefore the chief target. The competition between Kenya processed products and domestic processed products will be now mainly in the field of *temperate-climate products,* since neither country has substantial processing facilities for sisal or nuts, substitution in textiles is well under way, and substitution against products made from oilseeds is (with the exception of margarine) relatively unimportant.

Among the temperate-climate products imported from Kenya are:

Table 79. *Temperate Climate Imports from Kenya, 1966–1967*
(Thousands of Shs.)

	1966	1967
Meat, meat preparations	3,235	2,706
Milk, cream; fresh	1,262	1,919
Butter, ghee, cheese	5,932	5,700
Wheat, unmilled	2,694	1,568
Malt	2,269	950

Source: E. A. Customs and Excise, *Annual Trade Reports.*

In addition there were substantial imports of industrial products from Kenya; since the beginning of 1968 these have been affected by transfer taxes, a new system of special customs duties levied within the East African Community, to which further reference will be made.

---

12 One criterion is well-known, having been established since the 1920's: anxiety to avoid loss of public revenue. It is also known that up to 1967 the emphasis was on import substitution as distinct from export promotion; this passively reflected the balance of applications for protection coming forward, which may be an indication of market realities. In 1967 there was a deliberate shift of emphasis towards export promotion with special attention to the Zambian market.

The restrictive system.

Although Tanzania has a State Trading Corporation, this is not to be thought of as a foreign trade monopoly of the Eastern European type; only some 20% of Tanzania's imports pass through the S.T.C., and it adds virtually nothing to the impact of the general restrictive system, which consists of customs duties and import licences. Nor is there any difficulty in obtaining foreign exchange, once the importer has got his import licence. Tanzania is a member of the General Agreement on Tariffs and Trade (GATT).

A General Notice of import regulations is gazetted every December. At present this provides a list of goods for which specific import licences are required (broken down into one list for goods of Kenya or Uganda origin, and one list for other goods) and, apart from these, provides an open general licence for the importation of all other goods so long as they originate in the following countries:

- all Commonwealth countries
- all GATT member countries, except Japan
- all countries with which bilateral Trade Agreements have been ratified, viz. Poland, Yugoslavia, U.S.S.R., Burundi, Bulgaria, Federal Republic of Germany, Czechoslovakia, People's Republic of China, Hungary, Democratic People's Republic of Korea.

The effect of this is to place on the specific licensing basis Japan and those few other countries not mentioned, such as the G.D.R., Rumania, Cuba, etc.

Imports from Portugal, South Africa and South-West Africa, and Rhodesia, are specifically prohibited and this is backed up by foreign exchange controls.

The discrimination against Japan was imposed in 1965/66 in order to be able to carry out a policy of restricting imports from Japan to the level of exports to Japan. A loan agreement with Japan was also concluded in 1966, the disbursement of which is presumably impeded by this restriction.

The transfer tax system was introduced on 1st January, 1968, under the terms of the Treaty for East African Co-operation[13].

Where goods are subject to transfer tax, as for instance Kenyan goods entering Uganda, the manufacturer is liable to pay the tax to the Customs and Excise authorities as the goods cross the border. These authorities then credit Ugandan Treasury with the amount of tax collected. Annex IV of the Treaty sets out the schedule of manufactured goods on which the new tax may, in certain circumstances, be imposed. It includes, beside factory products as normally understood, bacon, ham, tinned milk, cheese, butter, ghee, flour, roasted coffee and other processed foods, and petroleum products, cigarettes

---

13 The provisions of this Treaty are discussed in Chapter X.

and textiles. A Partner State which is in deficit in its trade with the other two states in manufactured goods, so defined, may impose a transfer tax on selected manufactured goods, provided that the value of the goods selected for taxation shall not exceed the deficit, in respect of either of the other states taken separately. Thus, using 1966 figures, Tanzania has a deficit with Kenya of Shs. 196 million and may impose transfer tax on selected Kenya goods up to that value; and Tanzania has a deficit with Uganda of Shs. 42 million. Uganda has a deficit with Kenya of Shs. 148 million but no deficit with Tanzania. Kenya has no deficit and so may not impose any transfer taxes at all. However, Article 20 further provides that transfer taxes may not be imposed for *revenue* purposes only; they may only be imposed where there is also a *protectionist* motive, i.e. where there is, or is likely to be within three months, a domestic industry (producing similar goods) to be protected. Nor may this domestic production be merely nominal; it must account for at least 15% of the domestic consumption of the goods in question, or have an ex-factory value of at least Shs. 2 million. This, of course, drastically reduces the range of goods on which a transfer tax may be imposed.

The effect of this special provision (leaving revenual considerations aside for the moment) should be as follows. If the East African market is large enough for only one factory of a given type, and if there is only one, it can enjoy the full market without paying any transfer tax. If subsequently it is found that there is room for two, the second factory may be built in another member State and, by virtue of a transfer tax which may be imposed against the first four up to eight years, may enjoy a degree of protection (not only in its own domestic market) while it struggles to establish itself. However, if the proposed second factory is to be built by the company which already owns the first, the threat of transfer tax would probably make it preferable to invest in the further expansion of the first, instead; this, moreover, is less risky. So Article 20 cannot have its full intended effect unless there is a plurality of willing investors in each industry.

The transfer tax is payable by the manufacturing company concerned, when its goods cross the border into another member state, to the East African Customs and Excise Department, and from that Department to the importing state. The transfer tax is thus conceptually, if not explicitly, an internal customs duty. The maximum rate applied to any commodity is 50% of the external tariff rate, so that the East African producer still has a measure of protection against the overseas producer, except in cases where the external tariff is zero. Suppose there are two producers, one in Uganda and one in Kenya, and a transfer tax of 10% is applied against the latter, the external tariff being 20%; and suppose that the 20% tariff gives just sufficient protection to enable the Uganda industry to compete against overseas imports but that the Kenya industry requires only 5%. Then the Kenya producer (paying let us suppose, only 4% for transport costs into Uganda) can still undercut the Ugandan producer in Uganda — as well as in Kenya and Tanzania. Where the external tariff is very high, and where the hypothetical Ugandan producer is very inefficient, such a situation could arise. Where the external tariff is low, and the difference in efficiency is slight, the transport costs will effectively protect the Ugandan producer.

With the exception of cigarettes and pipe tobacco, all goods subject to transfer taxes are subject to specific import licensing as well as external tariffs. This does not mean, however, that the transfer taxes are considered ineffective, since in most cases, where goods are subject to transfer tax, the import licence is not required if they originate in East Africa. The only exceptions, where the transfer tax is reinforced by intra-East African licensing, are sugar, bicycle tyres, cotton (other than printed) and rayon fabrics, louvre-windows and components, and matches. Of these, only louvres and matches are in this category for protectionist reasons; the rest are treated in this manner either for revenue reasons or to secure orderly marketing (it is interesting to note that all six commodities are marketed by the S.T.C.).

Cigarettes and pipe tobacco are subject to a 50% transfer tax (external duty 55/- per lb) but not to specific import licensing; the high rates of duty probably make licensing unnecessary.

It is interesting to note that, of 37 tariff categories on which transfer taxes have been imposed, in only 19 cases was the tax imposed up to the full permissible level, namely 50% of the external tariff. The distinction between these 19 and the other 18 does not appear to be one of articles of mass consumption versus articles for the high income market, which would have implied a fear of inflation on the part of the Treasury, but it seems rather to be between industries which for various reasons are in need of greater protection, such as milling, textiles, biscuits and matches (still technically backward) and those which have progressed to a point where less protection is required, e.g. ghee, cigarettes, suitcases and metal furniture.

The Treasury thereby demonstrates its justifiable concern to reduce tariff protection at the earliest practicable stage. To what extent the Ministry of Commerce and Industries follows the same policy through its import licensing is not known, since the circumstances governing the refusal of import licences are not made public. It is known, however, that when licences are applied for, there is consultation between the Ministry and the domestic producer.

External rates of duty vary widely; effective rates by S.I.T.C. section were tabulated in the introductory survey, Table 8. The basic or modal protective tariff inherited from the colonial period was 30%, but since independence so many upward modifications have been made that the 30% mode is scarcely discernible.

Mr. D. KESSEL has made estimates of the effective rate of protection as a percentage of the "value added under free trade conditions" [14], following the work of H. G. JOHNSON and W. M. CORDEN [15], in an Economic Research Bureau Paper. Mr. KESSEL found *inter alia:*

"In most industries, the effective protection rates are considerably greater than the nominal rates ... Compared with most Latin American countries, nominal tariff rates in Tanzania are low ... However, the difference in effective rates (between Argentina and Tanzania) is not so striking. In both countries about half the listed industries were estimated to have protection rates greater than 100%. Effective protection rates in Tanzania are generally highest for import substitute industries producing non-durable consumer goods ... Clearly the protection offered to "import substitute" industries is much greater than that given to processing industries using domestically produced primary products. One notable exception is the textile industry ..."

Mr. KESSEL studied 35 industries, using two alternative methods of calculation; 15 of these were found to have "real" protection rates of over 120% by the first method, and the second method produced the same result for 14 of these 15. The doubtful case was biscuits, and the 14 "definites" were cigarettes, matches, paints, bicycle tyres and tubes, textiles, cosmetics, dairy products, sugar refining, beer, canning of fruit and vegetables, soap, clothing, leatherwork and footwear.

It is noticeable that all but three of these very highly tariff-protected activities are further protected by import licensing.

There is no indication that Tanzanian manufacturing industry is generally under-protected; few cases have been reported of below-capacity operation (except for short-term special reasons such as cattle disease). There is, on the contrary, some evidence of over-protection in certain cases, especially matches. Mr. KESSEL remarks that "the frequent complaints about the

---

14 The rate of effective protection is:

$$E_i = \frac{t_i - \Sigma a'_{ij} t_j}{v'_i}$$

where t_i is the tariff rate on the product of industry i,

t_j is the tariff rate on the input j of industry i,

a'_{ij} is the input coefficient for input j of industry i under "free trade" conditions, i.e. where there are no tariffs, and

v'_i is the value added under free trade conditions.

See Dudley KESSEL: *Effective Protection of Industry in Tanzania*, ERB Paper 67/8, University College, Dar es Salaam.

15 Harry G. JOHNSON: "The Theory of Tariff Structure, with special reference to World Trade and Development", in *Trade and Development*, Etudes et Travaux de l'Institut Universitaire de Hautes Etudes Internationales, No. 4. Geneva, 1965; and W. M. CORDEN: "The Structure of a Tariff System and the Effective Protection Rôle", *The Journal of Political Economy*, Vol. LXXIV, No. 3 (June 1966).

quality of domestically produced matches seem to indicate that the high level of effective protection is cushioning inefficiency if not profits as well". This is a case where extremely high protection has led to the sheltering of an extremely poor quality product. Recently, however, the management has been changed. Other cases mentioned by Mr. KESSEL are sugar, aluminium working and cashew nut processing: certain factories in these industries have been incurring losses despite high effective protection. Again, inefficiency rather than high profit seems to be the outcome, but this is slightly dubious, since a portion of the profit may be concealed. Finally, mention may be made of the general rise in prices in the second quarter of 1967, when the retail price (wage-earners') index rose by 11%. There was at this time a scarcity of imported goods due to banking and shipping difficulties, and the prices of imported goods generally rose. Local products were also put up in price to take advantage of the situation and have not subsequently fallen back. If they were not under-protected before, they are over-protected now. This is, however, a generalisation which must be treated with reserve in view of the slight evidence available.

Before leaving the topic of imports it is necessary to mention the average or marginal propensity to import.

Dr. I. RESNICK [16] of the University College, Dar es Salaam, has attempted to establish the coefficients of the average and marginal propensity to import by comparing changes in imports (calculated in several alternative ways) with changes in monetary GDP over the period 1960—1965. His chief figures are as follows.

Table 80. *The Propensity to Import*

Year	Private monetary GDP and private imports [a]		Total monetary GDP and retained imports [b]	
	APM [c]	MPM [d]	APM	MPM
1960	0.45		0.37	
1961	0.47	0.08	0.38	0.86
1962	0.45	0.20	0.36	0.02
1963	0.43	0.18	0.34	0.19
1964	0.44	0.50	0.34	0.38
1965	0.50	3.05	0.38	3.89

[a] "Private imports" are net imports plus inter-territorial imports minus Government imports minus re-exports. Mainland only.
[b] "Retained imports" are private imports plus Government imports.
[c] APM = average propensity to import.
[d] MPM = marginal propensity to import.

It is fairly clear that on a year-to-year basis the marginal propensity to import is so unstable as to be unusable. The average figures appear to be more usable except for the 1964–1965 change which was exceptional (and

16 Ms. written for a textbook on the economy of Tanzania, forthcoming, entitled *Economic Problems of Tanzania*.

has already been discussed above). Even so it is not clear whether there is a persistent downtrend in the APM because the 1964 figure as well that of 1965 suggests an upturn. When one bears in mind the many institutional changes which have been described in the historical narrative, the changes in tariff and licensing protection, the lumpy changes in import-substituting capacity, and especially the severe climatic changes which affect GDP more than imports, it is obvious that no stable relationship can be expected between GDP and imports. It should be noted furthermore that, for statistical reasons, any observed stable relationship is likely to be partly fictitious, because the figures on capital formation — which go into the GDP estimates — are based largely on observations of capital goods imports. Nor is it possible to rely on the relationship between *consumption* and imports, since consumption is calculated in the social accounts as a *residual*, and is therefore affected by the weakness of the capital formation estimates mentioned above.

Because of all these factors, the concept of a propensity to import must be judged suspect, and applied, if at all, with reservations. In particular, because of the rapidly changing economic structure, the propensity to import ought to be viewed purely as an *ex post* relationship, and therefore not really as a propensity, or *vis*, at all. With this in mind, the fluctuating ratios and the odd rise at the end of the time series, noted by RESNICK, are not surprising.

The further calculations which may be made, after RESNICK completed his work, by using the new 1966 data, confirm RESNICK's results.

Table 81. *Imports as Percentage of GDP, 1960–1966*
(Millions of Shs.)

	1960—1962	1962—1964	1964—1966
1. Commodity Imports	1,051	1,168	1,461
2. Monetary GDP (factor cost)	2,258	3,038	3,637
3. (1) as % of (2)	41.1%	38.4%	40.2%

Sources: Budget Surveys, Annual Trade Reports and E.A.S.D. balance of payments data. "Commodity Imports" here are mainland imports from all sources plus a valuation adjustment for goods arriving via Mombasa.

We may eliminate the effects of price changes:

	Monetary GDP at 1960 prices Shs. mn. (1)	Commodity Imports at 1960 prices Shs. mn. (2)	(2) as % of (1) (3)
1960–1962 average	2,475	1,084	43.8
1963	2,700	1,135	42.0
1964	2,920	1,170	40.1
1965	3,050	1,234	40.5
1966	3,312	1,456	44.0

Again we find the disturbing rise in 1965 and especially 1966. One can only speculate as to the reasons. In 1965 GDP was depressed by bad crop weather, while imports remained buoyant as the result of a nascent investment boom; business confidence rose further in 1966 which was a year of stockbuilding. If these explanations are sufficient, the 1967 results should show a lower ratio, perhaps under 40%. However, there has been a sharp rise in money incomes also at work (discussed in our historical narrative) which continued into 1967. Finally, there are the pessimistic explanations which arise from a too rapid or misguided policy of import substitution, postulating that such was the case. In years to come, data will no doubt be available which will permit the authorities to keep a closer scrutiny upon this changing coefficient, which becomes increasingly important in the context of an official policy of "self-reliance".

V. ENTREPÔT ACTIVITIES IN TANZANIA'S FOREIGN TRADE

A high proportion of the goods entering into Tanzania's external trade are not sold directly from the Tanzanian producer to the foreign importer, or from the foreign exporter to the Tanzanian importer, but are sold in the first instance to a merchant in another foreign country who acts as intermediary.

The most important thread in this pattern is the import of goods via Mombasa, Kenya. Tanzania, with its 12.3 million population and an average income per head of around Shs. 440, is still too small a market to be attractive to the stockists of certain goods unless a way can be found to avoid the overhead costs of complete, independent, sales organisation. That way is, in many cases, to maintain a base (usually in Nairobi) covering the whole of East Africa in its operations, with a minimum of effective representation elsewhere in the region. East Africa as a whole appears to be about the right size which many world-wide selling organisations choose for a local unit; and this method of organisation has been facilitated by the history of common rule in the past (British rule), by the absence of internal customs barriers, by common framework mercantile law and taxation, and by the complete absence of exchange controls within the region (until the Zanzibar revolution in 1964, and the introduction of capital account restriction with current account vetting by Tanzania mainland in February-June, 1967). Kenya was the natural centre to choose for such a base, having the wealthiest market itself, an attractive climate for private investment, and by far the best harbour facilities in East Africa (Mombasa); it also has the most efficient railway system and is the best served by international airlines.

It should also be mentioned that, as Mombasa is near the south of Kenya's coastline and close to Tanzania, while Dar es Salaam lies much further south, the northern part of Tanzania can be most cheaply served through Mombasa. Tanzania has a seaport in the north, Tanga, but this is a small lighterage port and many vessels have insufficient inducement to call there. It is mainly used for produce exports; in 1967 the tonnage exported through Tanga was 256,000 tons while only 90,000 tons were imported[1].

As a result of these factors it has been a common practice in many lines of business for goods to be consigned in bulk to Kenya, later to be distributed

---

1 Monthly Bulletin of Statistics, December, 1967.

to sub-agents in Kenya, Tanzania and Uganda according to minor changes in local inventories which were not known at the time the goods were originally ordered. In 1965, out of £50 million of goods reaching Tanzania from outside East Africa ("net imports"), £24 million entered via Kenya ("indirect imports"). How much of this £24 million passed through the hands of Kenyan principals as distinct from Kenyan agents is not known but it has been estimated that between arrival at Mombasa and arrival in Tanzania some 15%, or £3.6 million, was added to its price, owing to transportation, demurrage, breaking bulk, a small amount of repackaging and processing, and profit.

The estimate of 15% value added on indirect imports was arrived at by the East African Statistical Department on the basis of an exercise carried out in 1965 by the Customs and Excise, checking back to the original import "entries". It covers indirect imports to Uganda as well as to Tanzania; and in fact the true percentage may be a little higher for Uganda and a little lower for Tanzania.

These indirect imports are recorded by customs entries, and are deducted from the total of original entries for imports into Kenya to give the net imports into Kenya; likewise they are added to the direct imports entries for Tanzania and Uganda to give the net imports to those countries. However, the overseas countries from which the goods were originally exported are not notified of the transfer (unless it was decided originally that the goods were en route for Tanzania or Uganda) and so their trade figures show the goods as being sent to Kenya. The result is that Kenya's imports

Table 82. *Kenya Imports from Chief Suppliers, 1961–1966*
(Million U.S.$)

Country of Origin [a]	1961	1962	1963	1964	1965	1966
United Kingdom	85.4	84.7	84.7	65.9	70.4	105.7
	(81.6)	(83.6)	(85.7)	(93.5)	(97.2)	(122.5)
Japan	23.7	26.9	34.4	19.9	25.4	(7.5)
	(22.9)	(27.8)	(29.3)	(31.6)	(25.7)	(7.3)
West Germany	12.0	14.0	17.0	19.6	17.2	22.6
	(15.2)	(15.9)	(20.2)	(25.8)	(18.6)	(23.6)
India	11.2	9.9	11.1	6.6	6.1	9.8
	(12.3)	(10.5)	(12.0)	(11.0)	(10.6)	(10.9)

[a] The USA which should come fourth on the list is omitted because of the inaccuracy of the US data. Other important supplying countries show the same point but data are not reproduced here.

Sources used for all tables in this section are, for East African figures, E. A. Customs and Excise, *Annual Trade Reports,* and for foreign figures IMF/IBRD, *Direction of Trade,* published monthly. At the time of writing, some few foreign data were available for 1967; not reproduced here, they confirm the argument of the text.

according to foreign trade statistics appear larger than according to Kenyan trade statistics.

The figures in brackets are data from the foreign sources and in most cases will be seen to be larger than the corresponding Kenya data; *in all cases,* in fact, if an allowance of 10% is deducted from Kenya data to bring them from c.i.f. to a f.o.b. basis.

For the same reason, Tanzanian and Ugandan figures tend to be understated by the foreign data, by comparison with East African data.

It will be noted that Japanese trade in 1966 appears to depart from the common pattern, which is encouraging.

Table 83a. *Tanzania Imports from Major Suppliers, 1961–1966*
(Million U.S.$)

Country of Origin	1961	1962	1963	1964	1965	1966
United Kingdom	33.3	29.1	30.4	40.8	45.5	56.1
	(29.1)	(26.7)	(28.1)	(26.7)	(31.0)	(42.0)
Japan	8.8	9.2	10.8	20.5	13.0	(11.7)
	(8.2)	(9.2)	(10.1)	(14.7)	(9.2)	(11.7)
West Germany	4.2	4.4	5.2	7.9	11.6	15.4
	(3.6)	(3.5)	(4.5)	(5.0)	(8.0)	(10.4)
India	6.0	6.3	5.8	7.3	9.6	9.3
	(5.7)	(6.2)	(5.5)	(5.4)	(8.0)	(7.8)

Table 83b. *Uganda Imports from Major Suppliers, 1961–1966*
(Million U.S.$)

Country of Origin	1961	1962	1963	1964	1965	1966
United Kingdom	15.6	14.3	16.4	31.2	43.9	43.4
	(14.0)	(12.6)	(13.9)	(15.8)	(12.2)	(25.1)
Japan	6.0	5.5	7.9	13.7	11.6	6.5
	(5.6)	(5.2)	(7.4)	(6.8)	(6.4)	(6.4)
West Germany	4.0	3.5	5.5	10.4	10.7	13.4
	(–)	(–)	(–)	(–)	(7.0)	(9.3)
India	1.9	1.8	2.4	4.0	5.5	5.5
	(1.6)	(1.0)	(1.5)	(1.8)	(2.1)	(2.7)

Other major countries of origin, which have been tested, are U.S.A., France, Belgium/Luxembourg, Italy and Holland. All show the same tendency[2].

A similar error occurs in the export figures, because there are companies in Kenya which buy up Ugandan and Tanzanian produce for export. In order

---

2 In connection with these figures, there is a problem which will be reverted to under the heading of capital movements, that the East African statistics may have been deliberately (and illegally) inflated. There is, in fact, some evidence for this. However, taking the Kenyan figures into consideration with the others, the hypothesis of entrepôt trade is well supported.

to study the trading patterns further it is therefore necessary to "net out" this East African entrepôt trade by adding together the Kenya, Uganda and Tanzania figures; we may then compare these East African totals with the foreign data for East Africa, and thus focus on the second stage of entrepôt patterns, that which takes place outside East Africa. This can best be done for East African *exports,* which we will consider first.

In the following tables it is necessary to bear in mind that the foreign data (in brackets) are c.i.f. and therefore something like 10% too large:

Table 84. *East African Exports to Major Destinations, 1961–1966*
(Million U.S.$)

Destination	1961	1962	1963	1964	1965	1966
Belgium/Lux.	10.2	7.2	9.7	17.4	27.2	11.5
	(5.5)	(6.2)	(8.9)	(12.2)	(15.0)	(11.3)
Italy	10.9	10.5	15.0	11.7	9.3	15.0
	(9.9)	(10.3)	(14.2)	(10.2)	(8.3)	(12.9)
Netherlands	17.7	15.4	19.2	23.9	17.0	23.2
	(12.8)	(11.2)	(14.1)	(13.4)	(12.8)	(14.1)

For clarity of exposition we shall consider these three recipients first. In every case the foreign data substantially understate the values as compared to East African data. This cannot be explained by exchange control evasion, since that would have the opposite effect. The hypothesis is that these countries are serving as entrepôts, passing on the East African goods to other countries.

Most countries in compiling their trade statistics, endeavour to ascertain the true origin and the ultimate destination of the merchandise, as far as possible, but it seems reasonable to suppose that the entrepôt country itself will be the best informed of the transitory nature of the trade, while the other countries involved will be less well informed. Suppose goods are sent from Kenya to West Germany via Rotterdam (Holland). Exports from Kenya to West Germany will be understated, and exports to Holland overstated in the Kenyan statistics; imports from Kenya will be understated, and from Holland overstated, in the West German statistics; but the Dutch statistics are more likely to be correct.

Hence the hypothesis that Belgium, Italy and Holland are acting as entrepôts. The question, to which countries they are re-exporting the goods, will be looked at later.

We may now refocus on the trade statistics of Kenya, Uganda and Tanzania individually with respect to these three countries.

And from this it is clear that Uganda is the country on whose behalf the entrepôt method of distribution is chiefly carried out. This gives rise to a subsidiary hypothesis, namely, that countries at a relatively early stage of

164

Table 85. *Exports to Belgium/Luxemburg from East Africa, 1961–1966*
(Million U.S.$)

Source	1961	1962	1963	1964	1965	1966
Uganda	4.5	1.6	1.6	7.1	19.7	3.7
	(–)	(–)	(–)	(–)	(7.5)	(2.1)
Kenya	1.3	0.1	1.7	1.7	1.4	1.4
	(1.7)	(1.3)	(2.5)	(2.7)	(1.1)	(0.8)
Tanzania	4.4	5.5	6.4	8.6	6.1	6.3
	(3.8)	(4.9)	(6.4)	(9.5)	(6.4)	(8.4)

economic and political development are forced to rely more on entrepôt distribution. There are indivisibilities in marketing. Kenya is at a more advanced stage, and can do more business direct with principals. This is not simply a matter of larger turnovers, since Kenya's exports to Europe are smaller than those of Uganda; it is a matter of greater commercial expertise, bargaining strength, and better communications[3].

We may apply the same analysis to Italy:

Table 86. *Exports to Italy from East Africa, 1961–1966*
(Million U.S.$)

Source	1961	1962	1963	1964	1965	1966
Uganda	3.9	3.6	4.6	3.7	2.7	5.5
	(1.9)	(1.2)	(4.3)	(1.5)	(1.2)	(4.7)
Kenya	3.5	3.6	5.3	3.2	3.4	4.6
	(4.4)	(4.5)	(5.2)	(3.8)	(3.8)	(3.8)
Tanzania	3.5	4.3	5.1	4.8	3.2	4.8
	(3.6)	(4.6)	(4.7)	(4.9)	(3.3)	(4.4)

Again we find that Uganda is the country for which Italy is consistently acting as entrepôt.

A slightly different picture emerges for Holland.

Table 87. *Exports to Holland from East Africa, 1961–1966*
(Million U.S.$)

Source	1961	1962	1963	1964	1965	1966
Uganda	5.5	2.4	4.3	7.5	3.0	5.1
	(–)	(–)	(–)	(–)	(0.7)	(2.2)
Kenya	3.8	4.6	5.9	5.9	5.8	9.6
	(4.9)	(5.1)	(8.0)	(5.4)	(5.7)	(5.5)
Tanzania	8.4	4.8	9.0	10.5	8.2	8.5
	(7.9)	(6.1)	(6.1)	(8.0)	(6.4)	(6.4)

---

3 Communications from Uganda and Tanzania — whether by airmail, telephone, etc. — go via Kenya and are therefore slower and more costly.

Here we find that both Uganda and Tanzania are giving entrepôt business to Holland, and in the period 1964–66 possibly Kenya also.

The rise of this Dutch entrepôt business may be tentatively ascribed to the following factors:

- The keen interest of Dutch traders in East Africa following the loss of their business in South-East Asia.
- The competitive expansion of Holland's harbour facilities and the development of the Dutch economy towards increased reliance on earnings from external trade.
- The existence of Dutch banks in East Africa.
- The development of a close political-commercial relationship between Tanzania and Holland.
- The establishment of Holland as a distribution point for certain major commodities from East Africa, including some sisal.
- The decline of Britain as an entrepôt centre, following the sterling devaluation scare in 1965–66. We can see this later in the British trade data.
- The greater attraction of the European Common Market.

These, in a sense, random influences show the weakness of a simple, sweeping hypothesis such as was stated above. That poor, underdeveloped countries tend to use entrepôts is an oversimplification, but nevertheless one that may stand as a basic tendency.

The decline of the U.K. as a distribution centre is revealed in the following figures.

Table 88a. *East Africa's Exports to the U.K., 1961–1966*
(Million U.S.$)

Source	1961	1962	1963	1964	1965	1966
East Africa	93.4	106.1	119.8	114.5	114.3	136.8
	(83.1)	(95.8)	(113.9)	(131.2)	(122.9)	(149.9)

From this it is clear that up to 1963 the U.K. was a major entrepôt of East African goods but from 1964 to 1966 received about as much from other entrepôts she herself handled on an entrepôt basis. The breakdown by source-country is:

Table 88b. *East Africa's Exports to the U.K., 1961–1966*
(breakdown by source-country)
(Million U.S.$)

Source	1961	1962	1963	1964	1965	1966
Uganda	18.1	21.3	28.1	22.6	30.1	34.4
	(15.1)	(18.1)	(17.9)	(15.4)	(24.2)	(31.2)
Kenya	26.1	32.6	33.7	31.6	31.0	37.8
	(34.8)	(42.6)	(52.0)	(54.3)	(45.4)	(55.4)
Tanzania	49.2	52.2	58.0	60.3	53.2	64.6
	(33.2)	(35.1)	(44.0)	(51.5)	(53.3)	(63.3)

166

And from this it is quite clear that Tanzania was responsible for the change. After 1963, therefore, the U.K. was one of the major countries to which goods were sent via entrepôts. Other indirect recipients throughout the period from 1961 were, probably, France and West Germany:

Table 89. *Exports to France and West Germany, 1961–1966*
(Million U.S.$)

	1961	1962	1963	1964	1965	1966
To France	4.5	4.4	6.9	7.4	6.8	5.3
	(–)	(6.3)	(11.0)	(10.1)	(13.0)	(10.7)
To W. Germany	38.3	39.1	44.1	48.7	39.5	45.6
	(52.1)	(41.5)	(53.5)	(51.8)	(54.3)	(59.9)

So far as can be ascertained, this pattern holds true for Kenya, Uganda and Tanzania.

Exports to the U.S.A. indicate, if anything, direct trading, as do the figures for exports to India. Exports to Japan also show a normal pattern, being 11.0% higher over the period according to Japanese data than according to East African data, which is fully in line with a normal difference between f.o.b. and c.i.f. prices.

Table 90. *East Africa's Exports to Japan, 1961–1966*
(Million U.S.$)

Source	1961	1962	1963	1964	1965	1966
East Africa	13.5	10.9	13.4	17.1	14.1	27.6
	(16.4)	(13.3)	(14.4)	(19.9)	(15.6)	(27.1)

So much for entrepôt patterns on the export side. There appear to be no significant overseas entrepôts on the import side [4], and this is not surprising, since East Africa does not import significant amounts of primary products of the kind which go through commodity markets. The only significant import entrepôt for Tanzania is, therefore, Kenya, which is because of special reasons outlined above.

---

4 The comparison of domestic and foreign data for imports, in the fashion performed for exports, is not reproduced here, since no "entrepôt patterns" emerge.

VI. SERVICES

1. Services Accounts

The following tables (91–96) show the services accounts of the balance of payments as drawn up by the East African Statistical Department. The Roman numerals alongside each table show the numbering of the tables according to standard I.M.F. practice.

Before proceeding to a discussion of the major items in the services accounts, some annotations to the following tables may be in order.

The freight and insurance account, together with an entry in the "other services" account, is criticised below, in discussing Insurance.

Passenger fares are receipts (from non-residents) by East African Airways attributable to Tanzania. The strong upward trend reflects the growth of the airline.

Port earnings are ascertained from harbour authorities in Tanzania, together with the number of visiting crew members, which is multiplied by a "guesstimate" of expenditure per head to give crews' local expenditures.

Tourist receipts are analysed in detail, below.

Passenger fares, debit, official are ascertained from Treasury vouchers. Private fare payments are known from carriers' annual returns. Shipboard expenses are a "guesstimate".

Miscellaneous expenses of local carriers outside Tanzania are ascertained from EAA and the East African National Shipping Line, apportioned to Tanzania on a one third basis.

Numbers of persons proceeding abroad on official leave are ascertained from Government, and figures for persons in the private sector are estimated from total numbers of expatriates in the country. The assumption is 3 months' leave every two years, which is customary. Similar methods are used for business travel. Students' expenses are grants by the Ministry of Education, omitting the private subsidies by parents.

Figures for rents, profits and dividends ("international investment income", discussed in detail below) are obtained every April by an EASD questionnaire of companies. The number of companies on the mailing list has been enlarged in recent years but the unincorporated enterprise, typical of the Asian family business, is unfortunately omitted.

Table 91 (EASD Tables IIIA and IIIB). *Freight and Insurance on International Shipments*
(Millions of Shs.)

Credits	1961	1962	1963	1964	1965
Freight earnings of local shipping companies and air-lines	2.6	3.2	4.8	6.2	7.9
Net premiums on marine insurance	0.6	0.7	0.9	1.7	1.5
Insurance services rendered by Kenya	1.5	1.7	1.8	1.5	2.0
Total	4.7	5.6	7.5	9.4	11.4

Debits	1961	1962	1963	1964	1965
Freight paid to international shipping companies	3.4	3.2	3.1	3.1	3.2
Net claims on marine insurance	0.3	0.3	0.3	1.0	1.2
Insurance services rendered by Kenya	0.6	0.7	1.0	0.6	0.5
Total	4.3	4.2	4.4	4.7	4.9

Source: East African Statistical Department, balance of payments tabulations.

Table 92 (EASD Tables IV and V). *Foreign Travel and Other Transportation*
(Millions of Shs.)

Credits	1961	1962	1963	1964	1965
Passenger fares	7.9	9.6	17.8	25.9	37.6
Port earnings					
a) Sale of fuel and stores	0.6	3.6	4.7	4.2	1.9
b) Repairs and servicing	6.5	7.5	8.1	8.6	9.2
c) Port dues	5.7	5.7	7.3	7.4	8.4
d) Crew expenditure	2.3	3.1	2.0	2.3	1.8
e) Sundries	3.6	3.6	2.7	2.8	2.9
Visitors and tourism					
a) Visitors	27.8	35.7	43.9	43.6	37.2
b) Transients	3.4	4.6	2.7	2.7	2.1
c) Students	—	0.2	0.4	1.0	1.1
Total	57.8	73.6	89.6	98.5	102.2

Debits	1961	1962	1963	1964	1965
Passenger fares					
a) Official	8.7	8.9	7.7	3.5	3.0
b) Private	23.4	22.2	24.0	28.1	28.8
c) Shipboard expenses	1.5	1.4	1.3	1.4	1.4
Miscellaneous expenses of local carriers outside Tanzania	6.3	8.3	18.6	16.1	17.0
Overseas Holidays					
a) Official leave	13.9	15.2	8.3	4.8	5.3
b) Private	17.3	16.8	14.5	11.1	10.7
Business Travel					
a) Govt. officials	0.5	0.9	0.9	1.0	1.6
b) Others	0.6	0.8	1.0	1.3	1.4
Students	14.8	17.0	20.3	22.6	24.3
Total	87.0	91.5	96.6	89.9	93.5

Source: East African Statistical Department, balance of payments tabulations.

Table 93 (EASD Table VI). *International Investment Income*
(Millions of Shs.)

Credits	1961	1962	1963	1964	1965
1. Central Govt.	6.2	7.7	7.4	8.4	7.1
2. EACSO	0.3	0.3	0.5	0.9	1.1
3. Local Govt.	0.3	0.7	0.6	0.7	0.7
4. Govt. enterprises (EAR & H, EAP & T)	5.3	5.7	5.6	5.4	4.1
5. *Private*					
Statutory Boards	1.4	1.4	1.3	1.2	–
Companies	–	–	1.4	2.9	3.1
Individuals	–	–	1.9	2.3	3.2
Unspecified	1.5	1.6	0.4	0.3	0.4
6. E. A. Currency Board	18.1	17.3	16.0	19.4	19.6
7. Commercial Banks	2.1	2.4	2.1	3.8	3.8
8. P. O. Savings Bank	0.9	0.9	0.9	0.9	1.0
Total	36.1	38.0	38.1	46.2	44.1

Debits	1961	1962	1963	1964	1965
1. Central Govt. Interest to					
EACB on fiduciary issue	3.6	2.5	2.5	2.3	–
Other	7.1	16.7	16.2	21.7	18.7
2. EACSO	–	–	–	–	0.1
3. Govt. enterprises (EAR & H, EAP & T, EAAC)	16.9	20.0	21.1	22.4	18.5
4. *Private* (companies)					
Undistributed profit	2.4	9.7	46.7	21.5 Cr.	8.1
Distributed profit	45.3	45.0	37.9	32.0	39.1
Interest	2.8	2.5	10.3	10.6	13.8
Dividends	19.5	14.9	27.0	27.4	63.8
5. Commercial Banks (interest and rent)	1.4	1.1	1.1	1.3	1.4
Total	99.0	112.4	162.8	139.2	147.3

Source: East African Statistical Department, balance of payments tabulations.

Table 94 (EASD Table VII). *Government Transactions not Included Elsewhere* (Millions of Shs.)

Credits	1961	1962	1963	1964	1965
1. Local personal expenditure by foreign troops	14.0	3.2	3.2	3.0	8.4
2. Local expenditure by diplomats	9.0	16.0	26.1	28.7	29.7
3. Miscellaneous Govt. receipts	1.7	1.6	0.3	0.5	0.1
4. Net benefit of EACSO's services	2.0	2.0	2.0	2.0	2.0
Total	26.7	22.8	31.6	34.2	40.2

Debits	1961	1962	1963	1964	1965
1. Diplomatic expenditure abroad	–	1.4	3.7	6.7	8.0
2. Services under aid programmes	1.8	5.0	5.9	6.2	9.9
3. Agents' fees and commissions	1.6	0.8	0.7	0.8	0.8
4. Overseas expenditure by EACSO	1.8	1.8	1.9	1.8	2.5
5. Miscellaneous	0.8	0.8	1.2	0.7	0.8
Total	6.0	9.8	13.4	16.2	22.0

Source: East African Statistical Department, balance of payments tabulations.

Table 95 (EASD Table VIII). *Other Services*
(Millions of Shs.)

Credits	1961	1962	1963	1964	1965
1. Insurance claims on reinsurance outside E. Africa	2.3	1.8	1.3	2.8	2.9
2. Communications	1.4	1.4	1.3	1.2	1.5
3. Office expenses	2.4	2.4	2.3	2.0	1.8
4. Pensions, fees, etc.	0.7	0.8	0.9	0.9	1.0
5. Local expenditure of technical assistance staff	1.4	3.7	4.4	2.7	7.5
Total	8.2	10.1	10.2	9.6	14.7

Debits	1961	1962	1963	1964	1965
1. Insurance premiums on reinsurance outside E. Africa	3.3	4.6	3.0	5.4	7.0
2. Communications	4.1	4.5	4.0	2.3	4.2
3. Office expenses	16.6	16.6	16.2	15.5	13.7
4. Film rentals	12.0	12.9	13.0	13.1	13.2
5. Construction activity	–	3.0	2.4	1.0	–
6. Miscellaneous	0.4	0.3	0.3	0.2	0.4
Total	36.4	41.9	38.9	37.5	38.5

Source: East African Statistical Department, balance of payments tabulations.

173

The following table summarises the foregoing EASD data for 1961–65 together with Bank of Tanzania data for 1966 and (estimated) 1967.

Table 96. *Summary of Invisibles, 1961–1965*
(Millions of Shs.)

Account	Credits							Debits						
	1961	1962	1963	1964	1965	1966	1967	1961	1962	1963	1964	1965	1966	1967
Freight, insurance, etc. on international shipments	4.7	5.6	7.5	9.4	11.4	38.4	74.0	4.3	4.2	4.4	4.7	4.9	2.7	0.7
Other transportation and foreign travel	57.9	73.6	89.6	98.6	102.1	149.4	186.1	87.1	91.5	96.6	89.9	95.6	91.8	129.5
International investment income	36.3	38.0	38.1	46.2	44.2	54.6	39.6	99.0	112.5	162.8	139.3	147.3	192.0	156.8
Other Govt. transactions	16.7	22.8	31.6	34.1	40.2	41.6	37.0	6.1	9.8	13.4	16.2	22.0	18.9	17.1
Other services	8.2	10.1	10.4	11.6	14.6	12.6	12.0	36.5	41.8	39.0	37.6	38.5	52.7	26.0
Total	123.8	150.1	177.2	199.9	212.5	296.6	348.7	233.0	259.8	316.2	287.7	308.3	358.1	330.1

Source: East African Statistical Department, balance of payments tabulations.

Diplomatic expenditure abroad is ascertained from the Ministry of Foreign Affairs, and in Tanzania by a questionnaire sent to all embassies. This questionnaire also asks the value of imports which is credited to the import side of the merchandise account, since embassy staff are not regarded as residents of Tanzania.

The net benefit of EACSO's services is worked out by a complex enquiry into the financing and expenditure patterns of EACSO[1].

Communications expenses are ascertained from EAP&T and the Post Office.

Local expenditure of technical assistance staff is that part of their salaries which is payable in Tanzania under technical assistance agreements. Its contra-entry is part of the technical assistance received, on the credit side of the official transfer account.

Film rentals are hire charges levied (and reported) by Nairobi film distributors. For the future this item will be more reliably reported by the Tanzanian agent, the NDC, which has a monopoly of commercial film hire since 1968.

a) Insurance

In estimating the effect on the balance of payments of insurance transactions it is necessary to distinguish between the insurance of import and export freight on the one hand, and all other classes of insurance on the other.

In Tanzania's balance of payments, exports are valued f.o.b. while imports are valued c.i.f.: this is tantamount to assuming that all freight insurance is carried out by foreign insurers and the cost of insurance is therefore included in the import (c.i.f.) charge and deducted in the export (f.o.b.) receipts. If in fact any such insurance is performed by Tanzanian resident insurers, the error is corrected by a credit entry in the accounts. This is standard I.M.F. procedure.

What is unusual in the EASD procedure is the treatment of the Tanzania-Kenya relationship. The reader is referred to Table 91 of the services

---

1 EASD: *The Territorial Incidence of the EACSO General Fund Services, 1960 1965*, Nairobi, mimeographed, 1966. There is some disagreement on the best treatment of the East African Organisations. For national income accounting purposes their local activities are best regarded as domestic. For balance of payments statistics it is more informative to treat them as non-residents. The former view has generally prevailed. For a detailed analysis, see A. R. ROE: *The Impact of the East African Treaty on the Distribution of EACSO Benefits*, ERB Paper 67/15, Dar es Salaam, 1967 (mimeographed); and A. HAZLEWOOD: "The Territorial Incidence of the East African Common Services", *Bulletin of the Oxford University Institute of Statistics*", August 1965, on which the EASD paper (op. cit.) is largely based. Further references may be found in ROE's paper.

account (EASD Table IIIB) in which the item "insurance services rendered by Kenya" appears. This is, in the opinion of the present writer, indefensible. The actual premium on marine insurance paid *in Tanzania* in 1961 was Shs. 0.6 mn. This seems a very small sum, as does the corresponding figure for Uganda. Consequently, the EASD, acting on IMF advice, added a further Shs. 1,5 mn. under the heading of "insurance services rendered by Kenya". The new total of Shs. 2,1 mn. was obtained by taking premia in East Africa and dividing it among the three countries on the basis of their respective shares of merchandise exports from East Africa. This procedure overlooks the important fact that the insurers were in Kenya and not in Tanzania, or Uganda, for the most part. A similar entry was made on the debit side[2].

Secondly, insurance in Tanzania laid off with reinsurance offices in Kenya is omitted. Table 95 of the service accounts (EASD Table VIII) shows that only insurance business placed outside East Africa has been included in the statistics.

Consequently the EASD figures give a misleading impression of the foreign exchange outflow on insurance account. This does not necessarily mean a wrong figure for the whole of the services account since an estimate of insurance profits was included in the investment income account, with some compensating effect[3].

In the following discussion an attempt is made to deal with the payment flows in a more informative manner.

Insurance of Freight

Prior to 1967 all but one insurer in Tanzania were agents of companies incorporated elsewhere; either in Nairobi or outside East Africa (mostly U.K. and India). The one local firm, the National Insurance Corporation, handled only a very small amount of business until the legal changes of 1967[4].

The residential status of such foreign-owned insurance agents for balance of payments purposes is debatable[5] but since in practice those agents remitted their takings to Nairobi (and drew on Nairobi for claims) it is considered best here to regard them as non-residents. Accordingly no credit entry should be made for premiums in this category. Similarly no debit entry need be made for claims paid out by them, since such claims represented short-falls in quality or quantity of physical merchandise imported, and are notionally

---

2 EASD correspondence with the author, 1641/13/874/1178.

3 EASD correspondence with the author, 1641/13/879/1367.

4 These facts are widely known in the trade though no statistics on the subject have been published. The N.I.C. was established in 1964 and by 1967 had about a one-sixth share of insurance in Tanzania.

5 The EASD has been in correspondence on this both with an IMF expert (Dr. BADGER) and with the author.

offset by the difference between the actual goods received and the import figures taken from Customs entries based on invoice values. Local expenditures by such agents should however be entered as a credit entry, and these are known for two years, 1963 and 1964 namely Shs. 638,160 and Shs. 753,869 respectively[6]. We can estimate the figures for 1965 and 1966 by taking a roughly constant proportion of GDP generated in commerce, and we get Shs. 820 and 954 thousands respectively.

Other Insurance

For other classes of insurance it seems rational, following analogous reasoning, to regard all local premiums as remitted outside Tanzania, therefore debit entries; all claims and local expenses are credit entries. A considerable amount of transactions are also entered into directly between local policyholders and foreign insurers, especially in respect of expatriate life assurance schemes, but no data are available on these.

Local non-freight insurance figures are:

Table 97. *Estimated Outflow for Insurance (Other than Freight)*
(Shs. '000)

	1963	1964	1965 est.	1966 est.
Premiums (debits)	50,679	54,679	58,540	62,431
Claims (credits)	20,125	21,311	22,590	23,945
Local expenses (credits)	12,071	15,664	17,857	20,393
Net debits	18,483	17,704	18,093	18,093

Source: EASD, East African Insurance Statistics 1963 and 1964. For 1965 and 1966 claims rise at constant rate (6%); local expenses rise at same rate as annual wage bill in commerce (14% and 14.2%); net debits constant at 1963–1964 average level; premiums by summation.

Finally, an attempt may be made to estimate the non-freight transactions carried out directly with insurers outside Tanzania. As mentioned before, no data are collected on this, but we may take it that the most important category is payments by employers on behalf of expatriate employees as a condition of the work contracts. Such payments represent pension contributions rather than insurance premia but it is convenient to treat the two together.

A small sample of companies employing altogether 1,600 employees was found to be paying Shs. 145,380 p.a. in this form in 1967[7]. If we reduce this figure by 15% per annum[8] to go back to a 1964 estimate and apply the

---

6 These figures include the N.I.C. (treated here as negligible) and Zanzibar agencies. Source: EASD: *East African Insurance Statistics*, 1963 and 1964.

7 Confidential data in the possession of the author.

8 This was the average annual salary increment given to expatriates in recent years. Insurance contributions are usually linked to salaries.

result to the total labour force outside agriculture (187,668 in 1964) but assuming that expatriate control covered only 70⁰/o of this labour force[9] we arrive at an annual payment of Shs. 7,85 mn. for 1964. By 1966 this would be around the ten million mark. Offsetting claims are negligible. Evidently this is quite a significant item, but the poor quality of the data — especially the smallness of the sample — make it impossible to include it in the accounts. It is therefore to be borne in mind as a significant omission.

In 1967 the situation was completely changed by a statute (Act No. 4 of 1967) which vested in the National Insurance Corporation the sole right to carry on life insurance in mainland Tanzania as of 12th February, 1967, and all other classes of insurance, as of 1st January, 1968.

The effect of this was that during 1967 all other insurers (except a small number which decided to withdraw from Tanzania) made arrangements to operate as agents of the N.I.C.

As of 1968 it is therefore appropriate to credit the balance of payments with premiums received by the N.I.C. in respect of international freight, partially offset by a debit entry for claims. However, a part of the risk will be laid off with reinsurers abroad; this should be debited, with a credit for claims.

For other classes of insurance, only reinsurance should enter the balance of payments accounts, but it is understood that the N.I.C. is attempting to cover any necessary reinsurance as far as possible with reciprocal incoming business. Unless and until the relevant statistics are made available no estimate of the effects can be produced except to say that this should largely wipe out both the credits for local expenses in respect of freight cover and the net debits arising from other types of cover, thus:

Table 98. *Estimated Outflow for Insurance (All Classes)*
(Thousands of Shs.)

	1963	1964	1965	1966	1967	1968
Freight						
Cr. Local Expenses	638	754	820	954	?	nil
Dr. Reinsurance gross profit	–	–	–	–	–?	–little
Other						
Net debits	–18,483	–17,704	–18,093	–18,093	–?	–little

The overall effect should be therefore an improvement of 10 to 15 million shillings per year[10].

9 Expatriates covered 70⁰/o of the company capital in 1964. See MARLIN, op. cit.
10 The payments direct to foreign insurers will, of course, continue, though on a reduced scale because some of the firms concerned have been nationalised and are in principle opposed to such payments in respect of newly-recruited expatriate staff.

There is another aspect involved, which is where the insurer invests his funds. This does not enter into the invisible accounts of the balance of payments (it goes into the capital account) but it is appropriate to note at this point that the N.I.C. is seeking as far as possible to invest its funds in Tanzania [11].

b) Tourism

The basis of tourism in Tanzania is twofold: wildlife reserves, and the beaches and aquatic sports of the Indian Ocean. The latter is, however, still in a very early stage of exploitation.

The most popular game reserves are in northern Tanzania, and together with Nairobi and certain other areas of Kenya form the "northern circuit", a series of sightseeing spots linked by motor transport beginning and ending predominantly in Nairobi. This circuit includes three large National Parks: Serengeti, created in 1940 with an area of over 11,500 km², in the north; Ngorongoro, created in 1959, 6,500 km², in the north-east, including the Crater Highlands; and Lake Manyara, created in 1957 with about 1,000 km² in the north-east including the northern part of the Lake itself. There is also a smaller area, including Momella lakes and Ngurdoto Crater, which is to be constituted the New Arusha National Park, and several smaller wildlife reserves in which hunting is permitted on a limited scale. Mount Kilimanjaro is also in the northern circuit.

In the south there are two large reserves where hunting is permitted, the Ruaha and the Selous, with about 20,000 and 30,000 km² of area respectively; these reserves were established in German times and reactivated in 1951. These are the scenes of the "serious" hunting safaris. There is also a smaller reserve at Mikumi, the only one within easy reach of Dar es Salaam.

The "southern area" — one can scarcely speak of an integrated "southern circuit" — also includes Dar es Salaam itself, Zanzibar (of great historical interest to the visitor), and the island of Mafia which specialises in the catch of big fish in the ocean.

Whilst the beaches offer plenty of development potential, with their clean, light-coloured sand, coral outcrops and palm trees, the game areas are of unique interest with their large numbers of large and small wild animals, especially perhaps the Craters where the game is highly concentrated, offering a satisfactory level of experience to the motorised visitor.

The institutions responsible for tourism are headed by the Ministry for Information and Tourism; since January, 1965 the Ministry has been assisted by an advisory body, the Tourist Promotion Committee. The Ministry has

---

11 This will result in no loss of foreign exchange earnings since these earnings did not accrue to Tanzania anyway.

also now appointed a Director of Tourism. More on the executive side is the National Tourist Board, established by Act of Parliament in July, 1962, which operates tourist promotion offices in Nairobi, Frankfurt and London; a further office is projected in New York. In the hotel field the biggest operator is the N.D.C., which has moreover a considerable expansion programme; and there are a number of travel agents and excursion operators, mostly foreign-owned.

Total tourist arrivals are calculated from frontier data and multiplied by estimated expenditure per head (based on surveys made by Treasury and E.A.S.D. officials) to give foreign exchange receipts as follows:

Table 99. *Tourists Receipts 1960–1966*

Year	Visitors numbers	Average Expenditure per Head £EA	Total Shs. mn.
1960	9,847	129	25.4
1961	12,218	128	31.2
1962	15,666	128	40.3
1963	20,350	114	46.6
1964	20,257	114	46.3
1965	21,500	91	39.3
1966	31,000	86	53.3

Sources: Numbers of visitors: Ministry of Information & Tourism. Total expenditure: EASD balance of payments tables. Average expenditure per head, obtained by division (originally obtained by direct survey but not published in that form).

The decline in per capita spending is officially attributed to the opening of cheap package tours to East Africa based on chartered aircraft; these tours bring visitors of lower-income groups and at the same time reduce the fares below the normal level at which the cost of travel cannot seem justified except by a prolonged stay. It is reported that in Kenya too the same phenomenon was noticed: average expenditure decreased from £EA144 in 1964 to £EA134 in 1965 and £EA131 in 1966. Those figures however show a more gentle decline (from 144 to 131 is 9% compared with 25% in Tanzania between 1964 and 1966) and from a higher initial level; the two differences require separate explanation.

The severe decline in per capita spending by tourists in Tanzania cannot, in the present state of knowledge, be definitely explained, but certain possibilities suggest themselves. It may be that, given the rapid growth in external trade, the ratio of holiday to business travellers has fallen, and the latter tend to spend less[12]. It may be that more successful advertising by Kenya

12 Of all visitors arriving from outside East Africa in 1958 for holiday or on business, 25% stated they were on business; in 1964 the proportion was 44%. (Source: *Statistical Abstract*, 1965.) One reason why the latter may spend less is that hospitality is frequently provided by the local businessman free of charge.

180

has caused tourists on the northern circuit to spend a smaller proportion of their time (and money) in the Tanzanian part. It may be that social changes in Tanzania have reduced the emotional appeal of this country to the wealthy big-game hunter[13] (who may spend a month with a large retinue) and enhanced its appeal to others with smaller resources[14]. Finally, the expenditure figures may be declining partly, as the result of inaccuracy in the estimates.

Secondly, the higher level of tourist expenditure in Kenya even before this decline is largely due to the attraction of Nairobi as the beginning and end-place of the off-plane tourist circuit which takes in part of Tanzania. The majority of visitors to Tanzania have been in Kenya first, and if businessmen (who generally fly directly to the town of their choice) are excluded, only a very few tourists (those interested in the southern attractions) come to Tanzania first. Consequently their rest after the air journey is taken in a Nairobi hotel, and their kitting-out is supplemented in Nairobi. The small buses which carry them into Tanzania and back to Nairobi do not visit any attractive shopping centres en route.

The location of Nairobi airport — to the *north* of Tanzania — gives it a natural advantage over Dar es Salaam for European visitors[15] but clearly from the point of view of mere distances, Moshi and Arusha have even more natural advantages. The central position of Nairobi is due not to geographical but to historical and political reasons. In order to have tours starting in the Tanzanian part of the northern circuit it is necessary:

- to construct modern hotels and specialised shopping and entertainment facilities either in Arusha or in Moshi;
- to improve the airport in Arusha or Moshi;
- to have Tanzanian tourist authorities or hotel-owners negotiate directly with EAA and other airlines to arrange charter flights;
- to develop tour operators, with vehicles, based in Tanzania;
- to develop promotional services abroad, working specifically for Tanzania, and co-operating with a central booking centre in Arusha or Moshi (a Tanzanian travel agent);
- to arrange, from Moshi or Arusha, southward tours and open up sub-circuits not easily accessible from Nairobi;
- to have incoming regular-schedule flights to Arusha (or Moshi) as far as possible direct from Europe or at least without the necessity for passengers to change planes at Nairobi.

---

13 Hunting safaris average 28 days at Shs. 1,200 per day.

14 In this connection it is relevant to note that, of all visitors arriving from outside East Africa in 1958, 71% were Europeans, but in 1964 only 61%. Source: *Statistical Abstract*, 1965.

15 All airports in mainland Tanzania lying north of Dar es Salaam (and served by regular scheduled EAA flights) are closer to Nairobi than to Dar, and this is reflected in fares.

And in order to establish a southern circuit it would be necessary to establish a strong centre, possibly Dar es Salaam, with outward radial excursions by air or by sea, with its own special promotional image.

Whilst the entrepreneurial drive appears to come mainly from hoteliers and charter flight operators, local travel agents could play a significant rôle in guiding tourists into excursions or sub-circuits. The question arises, however, "What is a 'local' travel agent?". Since commission rates tend to be cartelised, the travel agent has no interest in promoting any particular tourist place (such as Tanzania without Kenya) but rather in promoting extended tours (such as the nothern circuit including Kenya). Dar es Salaam has only one genuinely local travel agent — that is Dalgety's (nationalised) travel service, with four branches in Tanzania.

Aircraft Booking Agents

	Travel Agents	Expatriate	IATA Agents	Cargo Agents
Dar	7	6	7	4
Nairobi	22	19 or 20	17	4
Mombasa	8	8	6	2
Entebbe	1	0	0	0
Kampala	7	6	6	2

Source: IATA handbook.

It follows from all this that to break away from being an adjunct of Kenya's tourist traffic, Tanzania would have to make considerable organisational changes and find considerable finance for new hotels and infrastructure. It should also be borne in mind that the artificial bisection of the present northern circuit might make East Africa as a whole less attractive to tourists. It would therefore be preferable first to provide the new facilities and then to promote the Tanzania based circuits on their positive merits rather than by imposing any administrative restraints on the present arrangements.

The present facilities in Tanzania[16], according to returns processed by the Central Statistical Bureau, provide 2,960 beds or 1,080,040 bed-nights per year if all were 100% occupied. However, if we exclude those hotels which are too humble to cater for international tourists, we are left with four to five hundred thousand bed-nights per year depending on classification. In 1966 there were 31,000 visitors from outside East Africa, and the number of bed-nights (estimated on a 9-month basis) was 207,500[17] implying an average stay of 7 days and an occupancy rate of only 45–55%.

---

16 End of 1966.
17 Central Statistical Bureau.

This low occupancy rate implies two things:

- the strategy of first building hotels and then marketing them is misconceived;
- the geographical strategy should be aimed at ironing out seasonal fluctuations by providing all-season attractions.

It is to be hoped that the increasing separation of Tanzania-based and Nairobi-based holidays will create two distinct seasonal peaks in demand instead of one large one.

The extension of tourism will of course create additional employment. It has been calculated[18] that there are about 1,800 permanent jobs in hotels (1966). To expand this up to the Kenya (1966) level would be a five-fold increase or 7,200 additional jobs.

The investment required to complement this employment is difficult to calculate in vacuo. But according to a study made elsewhere[19] the investment per man might be of the order of Shs. 85,000 or Shs. 600 million in all. This is based on an observation of B.W.I.$20,000 per job (British West Indies Dollars). Another study (Puerto Rico) found an investment was required of B.W.I.$25,000–30,000 per hotel room[20]. This would mean, in the given case, Shs. 475–640 million. Of course, these are standards of capital intensity appropriate to capital rich countries; but insofar as Tanzania relies upon foreign hoteliers, such standards are likely to be applied. Another point is that Tanzania may specialise in relatively primitive "lodges" rather than top-grade hotels; even so, a projection of under Shs. 400 mn. for the necessary hotel investment would seem to be on the optimistic side.

On the revenue side this should increase the tourists' expenditure from Shs. 60 mn. to Shs. 300 mn., an additional Shs. 240 mn. per year. According to a 1963 study[21] about 3.2% of this or Shs. 7.67 mn. is available to the hotelier for depreciation, profits, interest and taxes which would scarcely seem an adequate return on Shs. 400–600 million of investment.

The foreign exchange aspect is more difficult to calculate since the investment in hotels is only a part of the total investment needed to provide facilities for an extra Shs. 240 mn. of tourist expenditure. Assuming, however, that Shs. 500 mn. is sufficient to cover all initial outlay and that Shs. 200 mn. of this is the import component with an annual return of 20% (Shs. 40 mn.), while the import component of the tourists' expenditure is generally agreed to be 40–50% in the Tanzanian case leaving a revenue of Shs. 120–144 mn., there is probably a net gain. Only "probably" because the indirect effects have yet to be taken into account. The Shs. 120–144 mn. injected into the economy will have a multiplier effect up to, say, Shs. 300–500 mn., and

---

18 Ministry of Information & Tourism.
19 Report of the Tripartite Economic Survey of the East Caribbean, HMSO, 1967.
20 Quoted in 19.
21 East Africa Tourist and Travel Association.

if we apply a 25% marginal propensity to import we have indirect imports of Shs. 75–125 mn., which brings the net foreign exchange effect very low indeed. This of course is not an argument against the tourism, since the indirectly-generated imports are the real net benefit. It will be clear, however, that if the hotels are of the latest capital-intensive type, if their import component is unsupervised, if the yield on foreign investment is over 20%, and if the multiplier effects are significant, the whole scheme will cause trouble for the balance of payments. Unfortunately, under pressure for development, one may find oneself very much in the hands of the foreign investor in these matters.

2. International Investment Income

a) Private Account

The payment of rent, interest, dividends and profits abroad has been surveyed each year by the East African Statistical Department. For East Africa as a whole figures from 1959 to 1961 are published, and for Tanzania mainland from 1961 up to the first estimates for 1966. The overlap in 1961 enables us to extrapolate for Tanzania back to 1959 [22]. Using only the data for *private* investment income and juxtaposing figures for net private capital inflow (taken in the same manner) we have:

Table 100. *Outflow of Private International Investment Income (Gross) and Inflow of Private Long-Term Capital (Net), 1959–1966*

Year	Profit Outflow Shs. mn.	Capital Inflow Shs. mn.	Notes		
1959	(—) 79.44	(+) 79.38			
1960	(—) 89.60	(+)153.36	$\dfrac{Profit}{Capital} = \dfrac{240.46}{282.28} = \underline{0.852}$		
1961	(—) 71.42	(+) 49.54			
			Independence		
1962	(—) 73.28	(+) 58.12			
1963	(—)123.00	(+)155.18			
1964	(—) 92.74	(+) 78.52	$\dfrac{Profit}{Capital} = \dfrac{512.64}{422.14} = \underline{1.214}$		
1965	(—)110.04	(—) 5.68			
1966	(—)113.58	(+)136.00			

22 Assuming that in 1959 and 1960, as in 1961, Tanzania accounted for 33.45% of the East African share of outward private investment income and 36.2% of net long-term private capital inflow. The latter figure seems suspiciously high so that no "trend" conclusions are to be drawn. Primary data source: East African Statistical Department.

From this it can be seen that, in the years before independence, the net private capital inflow exceeded the outflow of profit, etc. In the years 1959–61, on the assumptions made here, profit outflow was only 85% of investment inflow; and it is likely that the figures for earlier years were similar (80%–90%) since 1959 was the last in a series of quasi-stagnation years. From 1962 to 1966, however, profit outflow was 120% of investment inflow. The growth of profit outflow is to be attributed to:

1. Growth of GDP;
2. Reduction in provisions for depreciation after independence (affecting net profits in 1963);
3. Rise in private investment from new sources after independence (1963) affecting profits in subsequent years.

The second of these points may be illustrated as follows:

Year	Profit Outflow Shs. mn.	GDP at factor cost Shs. mn.	Profit as % of GDP
1961	70.00	3,870	1.81
1962	72.14	4,189	1.72
1963	121.88	4,547	2.27
1964	91.46	4,837	1.89
1965	108.68	4,880	2.22
1966	110.00	5,455	2.02

It will be noted that profit remittances exceed 2% of GDP in 1963, 1965 and (barely) in 1966. Bearing in mind that most companies close their accounts on December 31st[23] and profit remittances follow soon afterwards, these 1963, 1965 and 1966 remittances represent decisions taken in previous years, or at any rate, decisions made in the light of data and within the impact of the business climate of the previous years, viz. 1962, 1964, and to a lesser extent 1965. These were the great periods of capital flight from Tanzania, and it is logical to suppose that profit-taking should be higher in such periods[24].

These relationships cannot be used for forecasting purposes because of the nationalisations of 1967. It would be reasonable to expect:

• A decline in new private capital inflow in 1967;
• Compensation payments beginning in 1967;
• Retention in Tanzania of profits from nationalised companies, beginning in 1968;

23 See *Surveys of Industries*, 1965, Table 12.
24 This hypothesis may be checked by studying the behaviour of profit remittances in 1968, a year after the Arusha Declaration; this material should become available in 1969 (May–June).

- Rise in profit outflow of non-nationalised companies, both in 1967 (better 1966 results) and in 1968 (run-down of inner reserves).

Whilst the rate of profit on capital employed must by its nature vary, it is reasonable to suppose that, in order to attract private foreign investment, a minimum *anticipated* yield must exist at any time in the minds of potential investors, i.e. a minimum supply price, depending on long-term yields else-where, the degree of risk and uncertainty ascribed to the project in Tanzania, and the attitudes of investors to risk and uncertainty. All of these factors no doubt vary over time, and the project-risk is certainly very variable since some projects involve experiments in the processing of tropical products, e.g. cashew nuts, which have not been mechanically processed before, or disease risk (sugar's "yellow wilt", for example) while other projects are of a standardised and familiar character. Some forms of investment, especially such services as banking, importing and insurance have been highly profitable with extremely little initial investment; a large source of capital for these expatriate enterprises has been the growth of commercial bank deposits[25]. Other investments — especially in agriculture — have required heavy initial outlays and have in many cases, but especially in sisal, been showing losses or very small profits in recent years and it is clear that the actual yields obtained from these various long-standing enterprises cannot be used as a basis for estimating the minimum yield required by suppliers of fresh capital.

ARRIGHI[26] puts the latter figure at 15%–20% for Tropical Africa; possibly with the more troubled conditions of the 'sixties, and the hardening of yields in Europe, 20%–25% would be more accurate. This, is, however, a matter for negotiation with the Treasury (or other Ministry responsible) in each individual case.

It should be noted that this yield takes hidden forms which are not included in the remittances shown in balance of payments figures. Among these are:

- Profits on the importation of machinery;

- Over-invoicing of other imports, bought from or through affiliated companies or branches;

- Under-invoicing of exports, sold to or through affiliated companies or branches;

- Remittances of payments to overseas Head Offices for management fees, royalties, agency fees, etc.

---

25 Deposits of commercial banks in mainland Tanzania rose from Shs. 401 mn. at the end of 1958 to Shs. 887 mn. at the end of 1966, an increase of Shs. 486 mn. Paid-up capital at end-1966 was only Shs. 16 mn. Net foreign private long-term capital inflow over this period was Shs. 704 mn.

26 G. ARRIGHI: op. cit.

For example, prior to nationalisation, one expatriate trading company paid its overseas parent company an agency fee of $2^{1/2}$% on the f.o.b. value of all its imports and exports (although only about 30% of this business was handled in any way by the parent company), and in addition certain supplies of imports paid secret commissions to the parent company which reached 9% in one established case. Allowing, for example, a profit of 10% on capital goods and $2^{1/2}$% on all other imports would provide (in 1966) an additional Shs 75 mn. to add to the declared Shs. 110 mn. It might be more correct, therefore, to regard the outflow as being equal to 3 or more per cent, rather than 2 per cent, of GDP, prior to the nationalisations of 1967. This would represent 15%–20% of gross fixed capital formation, a substantially higher percentage of net fixed capital formation, and therefore a considerable drag (however necessary it may be thought) on growth. This is, of course, merely the price of capital, measured from a zero price base which is certainly not normative. Nevertheless it is a "high" price to pay in the sense that:

- The yield required on private investment — estimated at 20%–25% — is not so attractive to Tanzania as intergovernmental aid or aid from international institutions. Even at $6^{1/2}$% interest, which is now the price of "hard" aid, and even supposing that the aid is tied to a supplier who takes 25% of the aid away [27], the annual servicing cost (including amortisation) of the latter type will still be less than that of private capital at 20% or more effective annually, except during the redemption period if the latter is under 5 years with no period of grace.

- With an effective yield of 20%–25% on private foreign capital it is obvious that the number of projects which would, in the long run, improve rather than worsen the balance of payments must be very limited indeed. This problem might be overcome by assuming a constant increase in the inflow of fresh capital to bolster up the balance of payments, but this would have to be an increase *ad infinitum* — otherwise, when it stopped, a balance of payments crisis would occur; moreover, it would have to be a remarkably high rate of increase [28].

The only other way out of the impasse into which the economy would be brought by heavy reliance on foreign private capital on such terms is by ultimate confiscation.

---

27 Dr. HELLEINER has suggested that the goods bought by Tanzania under tied aid agreements are at least 20% more expensive than they would be on the world market. See G. K. HELLEINER: "Trade and Aid in Tanzania", *East Africa Journal*, April, 1967; also R. H. GREEN: *Some Problems of National Development Planning and Foreign Financing*, Lecture to the Economic Society of Tanzania, January, 1967.

28 ARRIGHI (op. cit.) estimates that 10% to 11% per annum would be the minimum rate of growth, which is unlikely to be attained since it is well above the trend growth rate of exports, which make up 45–50% of monetary GDP.

Given this situation, the measures adopted by Tanzania have been:

- Nationalisation, with compensation, of major foreign private assets, especially those with high yields on foreign capital invested (banks, insurance, trade);
- Determination to rely more upon domestic sources of finance, especially through taxation and the public Development Budget ("socialism and self-reliance");
- Government or parastatal participation in new ventures together with foreign private capital, thereby presumably reducing the risk premium element;
- Participation in the East African Development Bank, which is also designed to bring in foreign capital with the risk premium reduced.

b) Government Account

In addition to investment income outflows, analysed above, from the private sector, similar payments are made by the Tanzania Government and the "Tanganyika share" of East African public organisations. (Other parastatals such as NDC are included in the private sector for this purpose.) These are all actually contractual interest payments:

Table 101. *Interest Payments: Public Sector (Debits)*
(Shs. mn.)

Paid by	1961	1962	1963	1964	1965	1966
Central Govt. and						
EACSO	10.68	19.22	18.68	24.08	18.82	29.10
EAR & H	14.10	17.00	18.20	19.14	15.66	16.44
EAP & T	2.00	1.98	2.00	2.44	2.16	2.08
EAAC	0.84	0.98	0.90	0.86	0.66	0.38
Total	27.62	39.18	39.78	46.52	37.30	48.00

Central Govt. and EACSO   1961–1963 average: 16.19
1964–1966 average: 24.00
Difference represents growth at 14.0% p.a.

Central Government payments have been estimated ahead up to 1980 on the basis of external loans contracted as of 13th December, 1966; the Chinese commodity credits are excluded, plus one U.K. loan, and so too is interest on short-term debt.

188

Table 102. *Tanzania Estimated Contractual Service Payments on External Medium-
and Long-Term Public Debt Outstanding Including Undisbursed as of
June 30th, 1966*

Year	Debt Outstanding (Beginning of period) including Undisbursed	Payments during Period (Thousands of Shillings)		
		Amortization	Interest	Total
1966	1,027,021 [a]	15,993	26,236	42,229
1967	1,016,100	18,929	29,814	48,743
1968	994,229	16,079	30,257	46,336
1969	974,957	22,171	30,529	52,700
1970	949,600	24,371	29,893	54,264
1971	921,914	27,536	29,200	56,736
1972	890,800	85,400	26,179	111,179
1973	802,193	66,107	23,179	89,286
1974	733,307	28,864	19,450	48,314
1975	702,950	40,721	18,500	59,221
1976	660,607	41,550	17,793	59,343
1977	617,286	39,979	16,757	56,736
1978	575,393	40,436	15,693	56,129
1979	532,879	36,671	14,607	51,278
1980	493,964	37,114	13,636	50,750

[a] Amount outstanding is as of June 30, 1966; payments are for entire year 1966.

Source: Background to the Budget 1967/68, Table 71. Prepared in the Accounts
Department of the Treasury. The Chinese credit is excluded because the cash
value is not known; the U.K. loan is excluded because interest is calculated
from dates of bills of lading, which cannot be forecasted.

As appears from the record of Central Government payments 1961–66, the
interest payments appear to have been rising at a growth rate of something
like 14% p.a. Applying growth rates of this order (12%, 14%, 16%) to the
interest charges predicted by the Treasury on the basis of the debts contracted as at December, 1966, we find:

Table 103. *Central Government External Interest Payments Projections*
(Shs. mn.)

	1970	1975	1980
Assuming growth rate of:			
12% p.a.	41.3	72.8	128.2
14% p.a.	44.3	85.3	164.3
16% p.a.	47.5	99.8	209.6

Total GDP in 1966 was Shs. 5,455 mn. (provisional estimate) and assuming
this to grow at 6–8 per cent per annum, the above interest payments will
represent the following percentages of GDP:

Table 104. *Central Government External Interest Payments Projected as % of GDP*

	1970	1975	1980
Assuming growth rate of:			
12% p.a.	0.6	0.7–0.8	0.8–1.0
14% p.a.	0.6	0.8–0.9	1.0–1.3
16% p.a.	0.6–0.7	0.9–1.1	1.3–1.7

To these must be added the interest payments on Roads and Harbours, Posts and Telecommunications, and East African Airways; these have shown no clear trend over the period 1961–66, but clearly must increase following the purchase of Super-VC10 aircraft, the major harbour extensions at Dar es Salaam and Mtwara, and the erection of a ground station for satellite tele-communications. Further details are given in the capital account section and in Appendix II.

c) Summary of Debits

The total of the investment income debits, at about Shs. 240 mn. (estimate) in 1966 or 4.4% of GDP [29] could well have risen, but for the nationalisations, to 4.7% in 1970 and 5,7% in 1980 [30] at the least, and possibly considerably more. What will be the effect of nationalisations is not known (i.e. the proportion of profit-potential taken over, and the effect on new investments) but on certain reasonable assumptions [31] the investment income outflow can be expected to rise (see Table 105 on page 191). As shown in the table, it rises from about 4% of GDP to a little over 5%. In 1966, before the nationalisations (1967) it was about 4.4%; thus, in terms of the importance of investment income outflows, the effects of the Arusha Declaration will be wiped out by the powers of the compound interest table some time in the mid-1970's.

---

29 Shs. 5,455 mn. including subsistence. At factor cost.

30 Applying the favourable assumption of a 10% growth rate in investment income and an 8% growth rate in GDP. Using the unfavourable assumptions of 14% and 6% (respectively) we get 5.9% (1970) and 12.2% (1980).

31 According to the East African Statistical Department, quoted in Peter v. Mar-LIN, *The Impact of External Economic Relations on the Economic Development of East Africa* (mimeo., IFO-Institute, 1966), the proportion of equity and loan capital of Tanzania-registered companies, held by owners outside East Africa, was about 70%. Assuming that the proportion of foreign ownership in future will be 20% to 25% as a matter of policy and assuming that the pro-fitability of concerns selected for nationalisation is typical, outflows should go down by 65–70%. This is applied to the 1966 private outflow of Shs. 240 mn. (estimated) and the balance is projected at 7%. Government and parastatal debits grow at 14%, GDP at 6.8% (as in the First Five Year Plan).

Table 105. *Outflow of International Investment Income: Projected*
(Shs. mn.)

		1970	1975	1980
Private sector	(1)	204–220	287–309	402–433
Public sector	(2)	81	156	301
Total (1 + 2) =	(3)	285–301	443–465	703–734
GDP	(4)	7,097	9,861	13,702
(3) as % of (4)	(5)	*4.0–4.2*	*4.5–4.7*	*5.1–5.4*

d) Inflows of Investment Income

There is no significant offset, so far as the private sector is concerned, of a credit entry in the account. Such private inward earnings have been very small: Shs. 3.6 mn. in 1961 rising to Shs. 9.3 mn. in 1964 and Shs. 10.5 mn. in 1965 [32].

Public sector earnings are a little larger, the main elements being interest on overseas reserves (held by EACB, Tanzania Government and later Bank of Tanzania) and on official Sinking Funds (British securities).

Table 106. *Inflows of Investment Income 1961–1966*
(Shs. mn.)

	1961	1962	1963	1964	1965	1966
Private sector	3.6	4.0	5.8	9.3	10.5	n.a.
Public sector	32.7	34.0	32.3	36.9	33.7	n.a.
Total	36.3	38.0	38.1	46.2	44.2	49.4 (est.)

It can be seen that whereas public sector earnings fluctuate slightly around Shs. 33.9 mn., depending on the level and yield of external reserves and on the state of sterling liquidity of E.A.R. & H. and E.A.P. & T., the private earnings figure has rapidly and steadily risen. This is not likely to continue, for two reasons. First, a large part of these earnings were from assets in the U.K. and other sterling countries outside East Africa: Shs. 3,1 mn. in 1965. These assets are not permitted to increase further, under the Exchange Control regulations of June, 1965. Second, another large part was earnings of commercial banks in Tanzania — formerly privately-owned — from their external assets: Shs. 3.8 mn. in 1965. This too is not likely to rise further, since such assets are now held at minimum working levels as a matter of policy.

32 This is no estimate yet for 1966. Note: these figures correspond to EASD figures for private investment income (credits), Statutory Boards excepted.

The private assets in Kenya and Uganda, owned by non-bank private Tanzania residents, which earned Shs. 3,6 mn. in 1965, may however be expected to continue to grow [33], reaching possibly Shs. 10 mn. in 1980.

e) Summary

Assuming the other credits are constant we can offset these projected credits against the projected debits of investment income up to 1980, and we find:

Table 107. *Investment Income (Net): Projections*
(Shs. mn.)

	1970	1975	1980
Debits	285–301	443–465	703–734
Credits	46	48	51
Net Debits	239–255	395–417	652–683
As % of GDP	*3.4–3.6*	*4.0–4.2*	*4.8–5.0*

The rise in outflow as a percentage of GDP (which, as remarked earlier, can be seen as a serious problem when regarded as a percentage of net capital formation) may be caused merely by the spurious projection up to 1980 of trends which in fact will not outlast the 1970's; in particular, the sharp rise in Government external borrowing, twice as fast as the rise in GDP. Why does this borrowing not raise incomes *pro rata?* One possibility is that there has been, in recent years, a temporary rise in the value of capital projects held in gestation, so that, when this phase is completed, the relationship between borrowing and income will improve. There is, however, no evidence on this. Another suggestion is that there has been a rise in the prices of imported capital goods, so that a given level of income requires the incurring of more and more external debt. Certainly the import price index has risen remarkably since 1962. In this case there may be an improvement in future years and the 14% rate of growth noticed in central Government external interest payments should not be necessary in order to sustain a 6–8% growth rate in GDP.

Shipping

Tanzania has made considerable efforts to reduce foreign exchange losses connected with shipping; these may be considered briefly under two heads, the extension of national ownership (or chartering) of the actual ships, and the nationalising of shipping agencies.

---

33 At a rate, we may assume, similar to that of Kenya GDP: say, 7% p.a.

Shipping lines

The East Africa National Shipping Line was set up in mid-1966 by the
Governments of Tanzania, Uganda, Kenya and Zambia. It bought one ship
in early 1967 at about Shs. 7$^{1}/_{2}$ mn., and another early in 1968; the two
together cost Shs. 17,786,300[34]. In addition, 8 vessels were hired in 1967.
Owing to the terms of the charter, the hiring charges were not fixed at the
time of the closure of the Suez Canal, and the rise of the charges at that time
(well above the rise in operating costs for shipowners) involved the EANSL
in a loss on three voyages.

Also, in 1967, Tanzania began a new shipping line, jointly with China. This
has two vessels, of which one began work in 1967. The first vessel belongs to
Tanzania but was purchased with an interest-free long-term loan from China.
The second remains Chinese. The combined cargo capacity of these two
vessels, the "Ushirika" and the "Asia-Africa" is given as 31,124 tons.

In normal times, much depends on the efficiency factor. Hypothetically, a
ship bought for Shs. 7.5 mn. with repayments (say) over 8 years at 6%,
assuming the net current gain to the balance of payments is constant at (say)
25% of the gross freight earnings, will help the balance of payments if it has
a capital-output ratio of 1.8:1, but damage it at 2:1. The following table
may make this clear.

Table 108. *Hypothetical Example of Foreign Exchange Gains from Purchase of
Foreign Ships*
(in Shs.)

	A	B	C	D
1. Capital cost of ship	7,500,000	7,500,000	7,500,000	7,500,000
2. Gross capital/output ratio	1.5:1	1.8:1	1.94:1	2:1
3. Gross freight earnings	5,000,000	4,166,666	3,862,500	3,750,000
4. Net current gain to balance of payments, assuming 25% of 3.	1,250,000	1,041,666	965,625	937,500
5. Debt servicing, annual for 8 instalments at 6%	965,625	965,625	965,625	965,625
6. Annual overall balance of payments gain	+284,374	+76,041	breakeven	−28,121

Source: This table and its methodology are based on Paper TD/26/Supp. 1 dated
November, 1967, written for the UNCTAD Conference in New Delhi,
1968, *Establishment or Expansion of Merchant Marines in Developing
Countries* (preliminary report by the UNCTAD secretariat).

34 Parliamentary reply, *Tanzania Standard*, 19. 8. 68.

If operating costs may be taken as given (though, as we have seen, this was not the case when the Suez Canal closed), the main determinant is success in securing cargo, which in turn depends on:

- relationships with overseas buyers (in East Africa trade it is predominantly the *buyer* who has the right to nominate vessel or line, as regards exports);
- relationships with exporters in Tanzania (in cases where the buyer does not nominate);
- quality of service especially timing of calls.

Relationships with overseas buyers are particularly difficult for a small, struggling national line to establish. Such relationships, whether gentlemanly or pecuniary, are difficult to change. The lines with headquarters in Europe have the advantage.

As regards timing of calls, with so few ships the EANSL has little room to manoeuvre. The most advantageous timings are at the beginning of the month[35] or at the end of a month[36]. Where the exporter is free to choose his carrier, this is overriding, but even if an EANSL berths at the month-end it is likely that a rival line with which the exporter has an ongoing (not to say bibulous) relationship, will have a berthing at the same time.

Expansion by normal accumulation of profit, for a line like EANSL, is therefore a slow business.

Shipping agencies

Until the establishment of the State Trading Corporation in February, 1967, most of the shipping agencies were subsidiaries of foreign private companies. The STC inherited about half of them. The shipping agency canvasses for cargo, supervises loading or unloading, and sorts out difficulties. It takes a commission which varies according to line, freight and duties but in Tanzania averages about 1% of the net freight charge on imports and about 4 1/2% on exports. The following table, using rough orders of magnitude and making some conservative assumptions, will serve to establish the orders of magnitude involved.

As the capital required (and therefore the compensation payments) for shipping agency work is extremely small, nationalisation of shipping agencies is clearly an attractive proposition. At the present time (mid-1968) about half the business seems to have been nationalised, as the above table shows.

Services and "Self-Reliance"

The Arusha Declaration of 1967 announced for Tanzania an official policy of "socialism and self-reliance". Even before, the policy had of course been

---

35 So that the exporter, whose contract calls for shipment during a stated calendar month, can draw payment as soon as possible.

36 To cater for exporters whose goods are likely to be delayed (possibly by overland transport problems) but who are bound to ship during a stated calendar month.

194

Table 109. *Shipping Agency Commissions*
(Shs. mn.)

	1966	1967	1968 forecast
Imports, c.i.f.			
Kenya & Uganda excluded	1,359	1,345	1,500
Freight at 10%	136	134	150
Commission at 1%	1.4	1.3	1.5
Exports, f.o.b.			
Kenya & Uganda excluded	1,780	1,677	1,600
Freight at 10%	178	168	160
Commission at 4^1/$_2$%	8.0	7.6	7.2
Total commissions	9.4	8.9	8.7
STC share, approx.	–	3.6	4.3
less import elements	–	0.2	0.2
Foreign exchange saving	–	3.4	4.1

Sources: Customs returns and State Trading Corporation. The STC data are the author's estimates based on STC accounts and budget estimates. The 10% freight rate is a conservative assumption.

one of increasing economic independence and the breaking of the ties of what is often referred to as neo-colonialism.

These terms, vague as they often are in popular usage, may take on very specific meanings in relation to balance of payments problems; and in Tanzania, the changes are taking place, not primarily in the trade account as the economic textbooks would lead one to suppose, but in the services account. Import substitution, it is true, is taking place with impressive rapidity; but its effects in terms of economic independence are limited. Import content of investments is believed to be too high, and repayment terms too hard, for the future current balance of payments to be improved, generally speaking, and the spectre of Latin American debt experience is haunting Tanzania. New projects moreover bring with them new charges on account of patents, agency fees, commissions and expatriates' personal remittances.

It is import substitution in services, and in some cases the cutting out of unnecessary services or reduction of their costs, that constitutes the most dramatic change. The major changes are:

- cutting out of debits for bank commissions and profits;
- reduction of debits for insurance;
- reduction or cutting out of confirmation or buying commissions on imports;
- extension of national shipping and aircraft services.

It will be noticed that these are all connected with state ownership and all have a bearing on services which are adjuncts to merchandise trade.

On any given merchandise import, these improvements are likely to reduce foreign exchange costs, where they are applied, by between 5% and 16%.

(The wide spread is chiefly because of the diversity of secret commissions found to have been operated by unscrupulous confirming houses.) A rather smaller, but still significant, margin improvement is obtainable on exports. It is not yet possible to calculate an average for the whole of Tanzania's foreign trade, but the magnitudes involved are clearly of enormous economic importance. This is without taking into account possible gains from reorganising the *pattern* of trade such as by bulk buying, nor does it take into account the saving of profits on nationalised *manufacturing* concerns. This is purely to do with ordinary trade. It is clear that an overseas tax (in effect) of upwards of 5% on all imports and possibly 3% or 4% on all exports will amount to such a large burden on GDP as to account for most of the gap between the level of savings required for economic stagnation and the level necessary for a take-off into self-sustained growth, to use Rostow's terminology. These simple institutional-commercial factors largely account, in other words, for the phenomenon of economic dependency or *neo-colonialism*. Much additional research, however, needs to be done and is in progress.

It is worth noting that the administrative capacity required to bring about these changes is enormous. Nationalisation in itself can improve only the international investment income account. It is possible to have control over the institutions concerned without knowing how to use it; and, indeed, the mainstream of economic literature is unhelpful in this field [37].

Much remains to be done, because of the problem of administrative capacity, to take the full gains which are there to be taken. But it is in this field (services relating to trade) that the key to economic independence for Tanzania will be found [38].

---

37 The political literature on neo-colonialism is equally unhelpful on these technical points.

38 This conclusion has repeatedly impressed itself on the writer during two years of analysis of Tanzania's external payments. No claim is made to draw conclusions for developing countries other than Tanzania. Especially this conclusion may not be relevant for countries in which imports and exports are less important relative to GDP, or which the former Colonial Power was not Britain (because Britain's balance of payments has been exceptionally dependent on its services account). Furthermore there are many developing countries in which the problem of debt-servicing — not serious in Tanzania — has assumed overriding proportions. The author does not wish to underrate the complexity of the *general* problem of underdevelopment.

VII. TRANSFER PAYMENTS

1. Private Transfer Payments

The biggest source of foreign exchange on private transfer account has been, so far as is known, donations received by missions and churches in Tanzania. According to a postal questionnaire directed to these institutions by the East African Statistical Department, receipts were:

Table 110. *Receipts by Missions and Churches 1961–1965*

	1961	1962	1963	1964	1965
Shs. mn.	33.4	30.7	35.5	36.0	37.0

Source: East African Statistical Department.

This inflow does not appear to be correlated with any obvious explanatory factor of an economic or political nature. It is worth noting that it mostly comes from non-sterling sources (80% in 1965).

Second in importance comes educational grants received by Tanzanian students. These have behaved as follows:

Table 111. *Student Grant Receipts*
(Shs. mn.)

	1961	1962	1963	1964	1965
From foreign governments	5.0	5.4	6.0	6.2	6.5
From private institutions	2.0	3.0	4.0	5.0	5.5
Total	7.0	8.4	10.0	11.2	12.0

Primary source: Ministry of Education. Data collected by Central Statistical Bureau and presented by E.A.S.D. in their balance of payments tabulations.

These are grants given to assist Tanzanian students studying abroad. In some cases, accommodation is provided free or at a subsidized price, and the cash value has to be estimated. However, this does not generate error in the overall balance of payments because the same figures are entered in the debit side of the foreign travel account. This foreign exchange never actually enters Tanzania, and could logically be "netted out" of the accounts completely, but is put in to comply with standard international practice[1].

The other sources of private transfer income are personal remittances and immigrants' transfers. These are "guesstimates". Personal transfers have gone down in recent years since southern Tanzania no longer provides a pool of migrant labour to South Africa. Immigrants' transfers are related to recorded "new permanent immigration" at about Shs. 1,600 per person.

Table 112. *Inward Personal Remittances and Immigrants' Transfers*
(Shs. mn.)

	1961	1962	1963	1964	1965	1966
Personal remittances	1.3	1.4	1.6	1.8	1.1	1.0
Immigrants' transfers	6.3	5.5	3.6	2.8	3.3	3.7
Number of immigrants	3,979	3,354	2,237	1,766	2,050	2,341

Source: East African Statistical Department for 1961–1965. Immigrants remittances for 1965 and 1966 however are estimated by multiplying Shs. 1,600 by the number of new permanent immigrants taken from *Statistical Abstract, 1965,* and *Monthly Bulletin of Statistics,* May, 1968.

Private inward remittances cannot at present be systematically recorded. Immigrants' transfers in kind are declared to Customs, but consisting mostly of second-hand goods (duty-free) are only roughly evaluated. It seems likely that such imports will increase as expatriates in the public and private sectors are no longer to be provided with free cars, cookers, refrigerators, air-conditioners, etc. Many will import their own hardware under free travel allowances, as is already common among university staff.

On the debit side of the private transfers account, family remittances are the largest item. The figures in the following table are E.A.S.D. guesstimates, based on numbers of foreigners in Tanzania, but an exercise carried out by the author on exchange control approvals produced roughly similar results. Preliminary results of this exercise[2] indicated an outflow of about Shs. 25 mn. in 1966, of which Shs. 9 mn. were to support family members undergoing education abroad, Shs. 9 mn. were for other forms of maintenance, and Shs. 7 mn. were remitted by foreigners temporarily resident in Tanzania, chiefly as a form of saving but partly also to pay off old debts. The education remittances include sums of several hundreds of pounds to students in U.K. and U.S.A., but are mostly small postal orders of Shs. 40/- to schoolchildren in Malawi[3].

1 See I.M.F.: *Balance of Payments Manual.*
2 Published in Bank of Tanzania: *Economic Report, July–Dec. 1966,* page 26. Subsequent results are not yet published; the exercise continues, now on a permanent basis.
3 Shs. 40 is the maximum remittable under the Post Office scheme which is much simpler than the procedure for larger amounts.

198

Table 113. *Outward Family Remittances*

	1961	1962	1963	1964	1965
Shs. mn.	20.6	22.4	21.3	25.7	27.3

Source: East African Statistical Department.

There were also small outward remittances for football pools and lottery tickets, and emigrants' transfers (shown in Table 118).

The second important item in recent years on the debit side has been remittance of compensation for loss of office by civil servants. When independence was given to Tanzania in 1961, it was agreed as part of the "package deal" that the new Tanzanian Government would be responsible for the pension rights of the civil servants then in office. Mention has already been made, in the historical section of this book, of the way in which these liabilities grew to considerable proportions even in the nineteen-thirties. In the years 1961–68 many officials were replaced by Tanzanian civil servants before reaching retirement age, and received a lump sum, known as either commutation or compensation, in lieu of pension rights. Gratuities were also paid on leaving the service. Others reached retirement age and received pensions. There are therefore three elements of outflow : compensations, gratuities and pensions. The compensations, however, fall into two sub-divisions: some were paid out directly overseas, and are recorded under Government transfer payments in the balance of payments accounts, while others were paid out in local currency at the request of the officials concerned. Part of the latter were used to meet local commitments and the balance then remitted abroad, recorded in the private transfers account. In the following table they are all shown together.

Table 114. *Official Outward Payments of Pensions, Gratuities and Compensations*
(Millions of Shillings)

	1961	1962	1963	1964	1965	1966
Private						
Compensations	21.6	25.2	21.7	18.1	14.5	10.1
Government						
Compensations	18.4	28.1	31.5	35.0	34.9	30.8
Pensions	12.3	21.7	26.0	27.7	29.4	37.2
Gratuities	10.6	9.4	10.9	11.8	10.2	12.0
Unclassified	–	–	–	–	5.8	6.0
Total	41.3	59.2	68.5	74.6	80.3	86.0
Total	62.9	84.4	90.2	92.7	94.8	96.1

Source: East African Statistical Department.

Thus by the end of 1966 these payments, essentially to retired British civil servants, were running at the rate of around £5 million a year, a huge sum by Tanzanian standards. However, they were partly offset because the U.K. Government agreed to meet half the cost of the compensation payments (as distinct from commutation of pension rights payments). The U.K. Government also provided loans to postpone the foreign exchange cost of the commutations and the other half of the compensations. This will be described below in discussion of the capital account. The actual current outflows were therefore limited to pension and gratuity liabilities; as Table 114 shows, these reached Shs. 49.2 million in 1966 which was still a substantial figure by Tanzanian standards.

2. Government Transfer Payments

The entire debit side of the official transfers account has been shown in Table 114. It remains only to add that the payments shown were made not only by the Government of Tanzania but also, to a smaller extent, by the East African Common Services Organisation (EACSO), East African Roads & Harbours (EAR&H), and East African Posts & Telecommunications (EAP&T) in respect of expatriate officers serving in Tanzania. In 1968 the last 12 expatriates serving with the Central Government on civil service terms were compulsorily retired, but some continuing payments are still to be expected from the East African parastatals.

On the credit side, the account has benefited from the U.K's payment of half the compensations, as described above. These direct contributions from the U.K. Government to U.K. officers for the account of the Tanzania Government and the East African parastatals have run as follows.

Table 115. *U.K. Payments to Civil Servants*

	1961	1962	1963	1964	1965	1966
Shs. mn.	49.3	55.7	49.1	44.1	43.8	42.4

Source: East African Statistical Department.

Apart from this book entry, inward donations have been as follows (according to EASD).

In 1965 a British loan of £7½ million was suspended. This agreement had been initialled when Tanzania broke off diplomatic relations with the U.K. over the Rhodesian issue. At the same time U.K. transfer payments were

200

Table 116. *Official Donations Received in Tanzania*

	1961	1962	1963	1964	1965
Grants to the Tanzania Govt.					
Inter-governmental:					
Technical assistance	2.5	6.3	9.2	14.5	14.9
Famine relief	–	2.0	–	7.8	21.7
Military	–	3.2	–	–	–
Other	38.7	61.1	42.1	19.5	23.6
(of which: sterling)	(38.7)	(61.1)	(40.1)	(11.0)	(6.9)
From foundations:	–	1.8	–	2.8	1.4
Grants to EACSO					
From foreign govts	6.2	10.5	9.0	7.4	6.9
From foundations, etc.	–	0.1	0.2	0.2	0.4
Total	47.4	85.0	60.5	52.2	68.9

Source: East African Statistical Department. Figures available for Zanzibar show grants of Shs. 2.7 mn. in fiscal year 1964/65, Shs. 10.3 mn. (estimated) in 1965/66, and Shs. 4.0 mn. (estimated) in 1966/67. *Background to the Budget, 1967–1968*, Tables 84 and 87.

sharply reduced. However, the above table shows that sterling transfer inflows had been declining for some time since independence.

To a great extent China stepped into the breach in 1965 with a negotiated programme of cash donations, commodity donations, and loans. The donations appear in the Appropriation Accounts as follows:

Table 117. *Chinese Grant Fund*

Cash from Bank of China		
up to June 30, 1965	Shs. 5.3 mn.	
July 1, 1965 to June 30, 1966	Shs. 5.4 mn.	
		Shs. 10.7 mn.
Sale of donated Chinese goods		
up to June 30, 1965	Shs. 0.6 mn.	
July 1, 1965 to June 30, 1966	Shs. 7.8 mn.	
July 1, 1966 to June 30, 1967	Shs. 0.4 mn.	
unsold at July 1, 1967	Shs. 2.5 mn.	
		Shs. 11.3 mn.
	Total	Shs. 22.0 mn.

Source: *The Appropriation Accounts*, Revenue Statements, etc. for the years 1964/65, 1965/66, 1966/67. Government Printer, Dar es Salaam.

3. Summary of Transfers

The following table summarises the private and public transfer accounts together.

Table 118. *Transfer Payments Account*
(Millions of Shillings)

	Credits						Debits					
	1961	1962	1963	1964	1965	1966	1961	1962	1963	1964	1965	1966
Private												
1. Missions and Churches	33.4	30.7	35.5	36.0	37.0	—						
2. Students' grants	7.0	8.4	10.0	11.2	12.0	—						
3. Personal and family	1.3	1.4	1.6	1.8	1.1	—	20.6	22.4	21.3	24.7	27.3	—
4. Migrants' transfers	6.3	5.5	3.6	2.8	3.4	3.5	11.4	16.0	10.8	12.3	9.6	—
5. Football pools and lotteries							1.4	1.6	2.0	2.1	—	—
6. Officials' compensation							21.6	25.2	21.7	18.1	14.5	10.1
Public												
7. Compensations, gratuities, pensions	49.3	55.7	49.1	44.1	43.8	42.4	41.3	59.2	68.5	74.6	80.3	86.0
8. Aid donations	47.4	85.0	60.5	52.2	68.9	—						
Totals												
9. Gross	144.7	186.7	160.3	148.1	166.2	125.8	96.4	124.3	124.3	132.8	133.5	135.3
10. Net	48.5	62.3	36.2	15.4	32.6	—	—	—	—	—	—	9.5

Source: East African Statistical Department except for 1966 totals which are taken from a different source, namely *Background to the Budget, 1968/69* using primary data from Bank of Tanzania. The fall in credits in 1966 is mysterious even though the Bank of Tanzania may have omitted the Chinese Grant Fund. This would add about Shs. 7 mn. to the credits.

202

VIII. THE LONG-TERM CAPITAL ACCOUNT

The outstanding feature of the long-term capital account has been its weakness, i.e. the failure of the external sector to contribute to capital formation in Tanzania, until quite recently. It is convenient to illustrate this by comparing three sets of figures: planned investment (using figures derived from the first Five-Year Development Plan), actual investment, and the net balance of long-term capital in the balance of payments.

Table 119. *Net Foreign Investment and Gross Fixed Capital Formation*
(Millions of £ [a])

Calendar Year	"Planned" Gross Fixed Capital Formation	Actual Gross Fixed Capital Formation	Net Balance of Foreign Long-Term Capital	
1961		26.5	+ 3.4	
1962		24.4	— 0.1	
1963		24.3	+ 0.5	weak period
1964		28.5	— 7.9	
1965	39.7	38.2	+ 4.4	
1966	45.6	44.7	+17.1 prov.	improvement (largely due to NDC and Treasury)
1967	53.1	53.7 prov.	+20.0 [b] est.	
1968	60.7	--	.	
1969	. . .	--	—	
1970	65.0	—	—	

prov. = provisional
est. = rough estimate

[a] In working with Five-Year Plan figures it is inconvenient to depart from the old usage of "pounds". A "pound" was twenty East African (now Tanzanian) shillings. Pounds are also used elsewhere in this section where the original data was in pounds.

[b] See page 27, *Background to the Budget, 1968/69.* This is clearly only a rough estimate, and is indeed surprisingly high.

Sources: Actual figures: *Background to the Budget,* various issues. Foreign balance figures: EASD data, but see also I.M.F.: *Balance of Payments Manual.* Errors and omissions are dealt with, as in Table 12.

Before examining the figures of 1962–65, when the weakness was most apparent, it is worth noting that in 1965–66–67 the foreign contribution was apparently about £41.5 million or 30% of the actual capital formation,

which in turn at £136.6 mn. was a satisfactory performance, being 98.7%
of the figure implied in the Plan (£138.4 mn.). This calculation rests, however, upon several preliminary estimates and doubtful statistics including
that of the capital formation outturn itself.

In the last year before independence, the long-term balance of capital was
positive at £3.4 million. This was made up as follows[1]: private sector, net
outflow of £1,223,000; Government enterprises, net inflow of £2,002,000;
Local Government, net outflow of £105,000; and Central Government, net
inflow of £2,677,000; total £3,351,000. There was in 1961 a drawing by
East African Railways and Harbours on a sterling loan amounting to
£2,500,000 in respect of investment in Tanganyika, and there was a Central
Government loan which was drawn on to the extent of £3,035,000, connected
with the independence arrangements. Both of these were exceptional, certainly autonomous balance of payments flows rather than compensatory in
their nature. Without them, the fundamentally negative character of the
private account during this politically difficult period would have come to
the fore and indeed probably dominated the entire economy.

Why the private long-term capital account was weak is obscure. Such a weakness is not unusual at a period of political change, but one would expect it
to take the form of a reduction of the external liabilities of foreign-owned
enterprises in Tanganyika in the first place. In fact, according to the EASD
estimates, private long-term external liabilities of *companies* (there is a zero
estimate for the unincorporated sector) actually rose in 1961 by £2.5 mn.,
and continued to rise in 1962 and 1963 by a further £2.9 mn. and £7.8 mn.
respectively; even in the worst year, 1964, liabilities rose by a further
£3.9 mn. The peculiar form in which the private capital outflow took place,
according to EASD, is through the purchase by *individuals* resident in Tanganyika of foreign "securities and other long-term assets".

Table 120. *Net Purchase of Foreign Securities by Residents, 1961–1964*

	1961	1962	1963	1964
Increase of assets	£3,700,000	£4,300,000	£5,157,000	£8,763,000

Source: EASD.

In addition there is the debit entry of the residual item in the balance of
payments; in certain years, a part of this may be taken as private long-term
outflow, as explained in Table 12. This amounted to £1.5 million in 1963
and £6.3 mn. in 1964. Much of this may be presumed to have been due to
capital export by individuals and unincorporated enterprises, the typical
business form of the Asian sector.

---

1 Source: EASD.

We thus arrive at the interesting suggestion (conclusion would be too strong a word) that while capital continued to be pumped in through the corporate sector it was being pumped out by individuals[2]. It seems highly likely that the basic distinction here is an ethnic one, rather than one of legal form. From the European investor's point of view, the hand-over of Government by the British was orderly and peaceful. Similar changes elsewhere in the world had not been followed by expropriation. The Asian and Arab businessmen had no such comforting experience; and it is noticeable that the peak flight came in 1964, the year of the Zanzibar revolution and the Tanganyika-Zanzibar union, when the racial feelings of Africans against decades of oppression came sharply to the surface[3].

In 1962 there was a pause in overall economic activity, with gross fixed capital formation declining from £26.5 million to £24.4 million[4]. This was in both the private and the public sectors, though the new parastatal sector showed an increase. The reasons for the decline in Government investment in 1962 and 1963 have been analysed in the historical section. The private sector was affected by the political changes; by the relatively poor agricultural results (exports were barely higher than in 1961), and by the sluggish activities of the EAR & H, EAP & T and EAAC, which from 1962 onwards (until 1966) did not bring about any injection of capital into Tanzania.

The table below is constructed in the usual way with a minus sign to indicate outflow of capital (reduction of external liabilities or increase in external assets) and no sign to indicate an inflow. Particularly striking is the rise in assets, item 4. which shows that in the four years after independence these organisations invested £2,514,000 (attributable to Tanzania alone) in British securities. This indicates their lack of ability, or possibly unwillingness, to develop appropriate expenditure programmes in Tanzania. The Five-Year Plan called for an increase in their capital investment in Tanzania amounting to £18 million over the 5-year plan period. In fact, their early performance has been discouraging, the most significant single improvement being the purchase of 3 Super VC 10's by EAA in 1966/67, one of which is

---

2 This deduction does not rely entirely on the EASD's figures for security purchases by individuals, the derivation of which may be dubious. The reporting of the corporate sector was reasonably good, and there was certainly an overall capital flight in 1963 and 1964.

3 1964 was also the year of Kenya's independence, and it might be argued that this was a further unsettling factor for private capital in Tanganyika, since it had no longer a safe haven in Kenya. There is no evidence, however, to show the direction of capital flow as between Kenya and Tanganyika in 1961–1963. The EASD figures indicate a heavy flow towards Tanganyika, but this probably shows the omission from the figures of certain bank transfers. The whole of East Africa experienced substantial capital flight in 1962, 1963 and 1964.

4 *Background to the Budget, 1967–1968.*

Table 121. *East African Government Enterprises' Capital Account, 1961–1965*
(Thousands of Pounds)

	1961	1962	1963	1964	1965
1. *Loans raised on London market: change on register*					
a) EAR & H	− 39	− 91	52	− 46	180
b) EAP & T	− 71	− 67	− 27	27	− 6
c) EAAC	–	–	–	–	–
2. *Inter-official loans, from foreign governments*					
a) EAR & H:					
drawings	2,500	53	54	885	76
repayments	–	− 42	− 45	− 48	− 51
b) EAP & T:					
drawings	165	73	140	82	88
repayments	–	− 3	− 3	− 4	− 5
3. *Inter-official loans, from international sources*					
a) EAR & H:					
drawings	–	–	–	–	–
repayments	−166	−172	−216	−184	−193
b) EAP & T:					
drawings	–	–	–	51	–
repayments	–	–	–	–	− 4
c) EAAC:					
drawings	–	54	–	–	–
repayments	−145	–	−189	−371	−120
4. *Overseas assets (securities), change*					
a) EAR & H	− 62	−257	−127	−346	−1,112
b) EAP & T	−180	− 50	− 48	−314	−260
5. *Net Flow*	+2,002	−502	−409	−268	−1,407

Source: EASD.

in principle (if not in flying miles) attributable to Tanzania at a capital cost of Shs. 60 mn. Since 1965/66, however, there has also been a renewed growth of road and harbour development.

A further source of weakness in 1962, also probably deriving from inability to spend, was the Local Government Capital Account. Local authorities have had no external debts, but have held surplus funds in the form of sterling securities, and fluctuations in these have affected the balance of payments. Data from the Central Statistical Office, London, show that these holdings were run down in 1961, 1963, 1964, and 1965, but that in 1962 they rose by £¹/₂ million.

Table 122. *Local Government Foreign Assets (Securities)*
(Thousands of Pounds)

	1961	1962	1963	1964	1965
Increase (−) or Decrease (+)	+105	−466	+117	+15	+9

Source: Original data from CSO, London, quoted by EASD, Nairobi. Tanzania internal reporting is not yet adequate on this point.

This was not a specifically Tanzanian feature; long-term external assets of local authorities throughout East Africa rose by £864,000 during 1962[5]. Tanzania accounted for 54% of this. But in the following year, when the total fell, Tanzania accounted for only 4% of it. This indicates that inability to spend on local development was a more severe constraint in Tanzania than in the rest of East Africa.

1963 was also a better year for the private capital account. The EASD estimates show an increase in external liabilities of £7³/₄ million, as compared with under £3 million the year before. There was also a rise in external assets, but the net balance of private long-term capital showed a distinctly favourable shift[6].

The general improvement in economic conditions in 1963 was analysed at length in the historical section. Salient points were the rise in the price of sisal by 47%, the 13 point rise in the export price index and the 9 point rise in the import price index. It was clearly a year of relatively high profits. Table 123 shows the behaviour of profits accruing to foreign investors.

Table 123. *Distributed and Undistributed International Investment Income, Debits, 1961–1966*
(Millions of Shs.)

	1961	1962	1963	1964	1965	1966
Remitted rents, profits and dividends	96.6	102.8	116.1	117.8	110.6	..
Undistributed profits (retentions)	2.4	9.7	46.7	21.5	22.6	..
Total	99.0	112.5	162.8	139.3	133.2	192.0
Retentions as % of Total	2	9	29	15	17	..

Source: 1961–1965, EASD. 1966, Bank of Tanzania.

5 From £2,665,000 to £3,529,000. By the end of 1963 they had fallen to £861,000, a drop of £2,668,000, but only £117,000 of this drop was from Tanzania. Source: EASD.
6 To some extent the *recorded* improvement may have been due to changes in statistical technique, especially the extension of the mailing list of the annual company questionnaire.

It was in 1963 that retained profits reached their peak both absolutely and as a proportion of total profits. The Shs. 46.7 mn. recorded in that year as a debit on invisibles account was of course a *per contra* credit entry on the capital account. The importance of undistributed profit in the capital account is shown in Table 124.

Table 124. *Undistributed Profits in the Private Long-Term Capital Account,*
1961–1965
(Millions of Shs.)

	1961	1962	1963	1964	1965
Retentions	2.4	9.7	46.7	21.5	22.6
Other changes in liabilities/ assets	—26.5	—18.5	— 14.9	—258.1	— 43.6
Total — net balance of private long-term capital account	—24.5	—27.9	+ 31.8	—236.6	— 21.0
Rise in recorded liabilities only	+49.5	+58.1	+155.2	+ 78.5	+103.0
Retentions as %/o of rise in liabilities as recorded	5	17	30	27	22
Recorded liabilities net of retentions, change	+47.1	+48.4	+108.5	+ 57.0	+ 80.4

Source: 1961–1965, EASD. 1966, Bank of Tanzania. Capital flows include a part of the residual item, as explained above; see Table 12.

From the foregoing, we can make the following deductions about private capital movements:

- A rise of profitability induces an inflow of capital (rise in external liabilities) both in the form of enlarged retentions and in the form of new capital (loans and equities).
- This effect is stronger, proportionately, upon retentions than upon new capital, i.e. when new capital inflow accelerates, retentions accelerate faster, and rise in proportion to the new capital. At the same time a higher proportion of current profit is retained.
- The above effects occur independently of what is happening to the rest of the private long-term capital account; i.e. change in external assets and unidentified capital flight. A rise of liabilities may accompany a capital flight (1963 and 1964). This may be a difference between the corporate sector and the unincorporated or individual sector, or perhaps an ethnic difference, or both[7].

7 The reader may notice here a departure from conventional (Keynesian) investment theory which regards Government investment as "autonomous" and private investment as being for the most part of the "induced" variety. Here we have a large part of private (dis-)investment of an autonomous or "wildcat" nature and the remainder together with public capital is "induced". Of course,

The above deductions need to be taken with caution in view of the small number of observations.

This analysis may be considered together with a previous analysis to be found in the historical section dealing with public aid and the Currency Board fiduciary issue, which showed that public capital tended to be more readily available when export earnings were highest, i.e. when it was least needed. Broadly speaking, it seems that private borrowing behaves in the same perverse way, except the most volatile element of it (retentions) is a *per contra* entry in the balance of payments and operates partly by reducing the outflow of investment income in the current account when retentions rise as a proportion of total profits. The other side of the capital account (change in external assets) together with unidentified capital movements may not be related to economic factors at all. This is illustrated in the following table.

Table 125. *Hypothetical Illustration of Private Capital Movements*

	Bad Year	Good Year Before response	Good Year After response
1. *International Investment Income, Debits*			
Distributed profits	— 97	—194 (double)	—140
Retained profits	— 3 (= 3%)	— 6 (= 3%)	— 60 (= 30%)
Total profits	—100	—200 (double)	—200 (same)
2. Capital Account: Change in liabilities			
a) retentions	+ 3 (per contra)	+ 6 (per contra)	+ 60 (per contra)
b) new capital, net of repayments	+ 50	+100 (double)	+100 (same)
3. *Sub-total* (1 + 2)	— 47	— 94 (double)	— 40
4. *Change in assets, and un-recorded items*	? (random shock)	? (random shock)	? (random shock)
5. *Total*	?	?	?

Since the Arusha Declaration, the industries in which foreign (or domestic) private capital is welcomed have been limited.

---

we are dealing here only with external sources, which typically do not appear in Keynesian investment theory at all. Also we are dealing with a period prior to the emergence of a Government capable of exerting any strong countervailing force. The above model is not intended to relate to the post-Arusha period (1967 onwards).

Government Paper No. 4 (1967) states:

". . . Following the Arusha Declaration, it is the policy of Government to rely less upon foreign sources of capital for the achievement of its investment programme. Indeed, this shift to self-reliance had already taken place as a matter of necessity during the first three years of the Development Plan; whereas the Plan called for 78 per cent of planned public sector investment to come from abroad, foreign sources have in fact only made up 41 per cent of the total. This has resulted in considerable underachievement of the Plan's objectives and will result in more modest, but more realistic, investment objectives for the future. It is now essential that an investment policy be based primarily upon the possibilities for domestically financed investment, though we will continue to seek technical and financial co-operation from friendly countries. It is the policy of the Government to achieve the maximum domestic investment, public and private, which is consistent with the balance of Tanzania's foreign payments, domestic price stability, and the gradual improvement of incomes for the mass of the people of Tanzania. These maximum investment possibilities will be kept under constant review by the Government . . .

"Following the nationalisation of the banks, insurance, the eight food processing firms, and the eight external and wholesale trading firms in February, the Government has declared that no further nationalisations are to take place. Firms not already nationalised will not be taken into exclusive public ownership. Furthermore, all existing private firms other than those in which the Government has already expressed its intention to acquire majority, rather than exclusive, ownership are assured that they may continue with their present ownership.

". . . This position is summarised as follows:

Activities Reserved exclusively for the Public Sector	Activities normally requiring Public Sector Majority Ownership
Large-scale Processing of maize and paddy	Mining
External and wholesale trade	Oil
Banking	Steel
Insurance	Machine tools
Arms	Motor cars
Electricity	Fertilisers
Posts	Cement
Telecommunications	Breweries
Railways	Textiles
Radio	Cigarettes
Water	Shoes
	Metal containers
	Extracts

"Government may permit private majority ownership in those areas normally requiring public sector majority ownership in special circumstances. In those sectors in which private investment is to be encouraged, the Government will sympathetically consider minority participation if so requested."

The legal framework of foreign capital participation is given, principally, by the Foreign Investments (Protection) Act (No. 40 of 1963) which states that, for "approved" foreign investments, in the event of nationalisation, "full and fair"[8] compensation shall be ascertained and paid in foreign currency. This is generally believed to be the most important point covered by such Acts[9].

The value of such an undertaking depends partly on the terms of the Act and partly on the Government's reputation for honesty and fair dealing. Fortunately the Government of Tanzania is known throughout the world for its outstanding moral probity. The Act itself, however, is sometimes scoffed at, for being vague and "only a piece of paper". It is indeed brief, but its terms are no different (effectively), so far as this writer can see, from those of the corresponding Kenya Act (No. 35 of 1964). It is perhaps different in comparison with the many similar legislations in Africa — certainly those of the French-speaking states — in that it does not set out lists of industries of greater or lesser national importance, with different provisions ("regimes") for each, but this should not be a serious deterrent. A proposed investment either receives a certificate of approval or it does not.

The Act is like all other similar acts in that it does not lay down the method of determining what is a "full and fair" compensation, and this is sometimes pointed out as a weakness. However, the Tanzanian Government has made its methods clear since 1967. The expropriated investor is requested to make a claim, supported by audited accounts and other suitable evidence if "hidden reserves" or other intangibles are involved. The Tanzanian Government makes its own investigation, assisted by Messrs. Steen Hansen, a leading Danish auditing firm of first-class international standing, the costs of which are met by the Tanzania Government. Negotiation then begins, and in most cases an agreed settlement has been quickly reached, the only serious cause of delay having been in the initial auditing stage. However, the Tanzania Government has repeatedly made clear that one of the aims of nationalising is to divert the flow of future profit into the Treasury; hence it refused to compensate for loss of future profit, which is sometimes expressed in the original claim under the heading of "goodwill". Outstanding cases where large claims for goodwill have so far (July, 1968) prevented final settlement are those of Barclays Bank, D.C.O., and Standard Bank Ltd.

---

8 This phrase has been repeated in the legal instruments of nationalisation.
9 See *Investment Laws and Regulations in Africa,* U.N., 1965, Part I, para. 66–67.

On the whole, it cannot be argued that the weakness of foreign investors' protection has been a major factor in the weakness of the capital inflow.

Taxation is another factor. Profits are taxed at a rate of 40%. Investment allowances are moderately liberal (not as generous as in Zambia) [10]. Customs waivers and tariff or licensing protection are a matter of negotiation but on the whole are on the generous side [11].

Tanzania is not, then, particularly unattractive to capital so far as Government terms and conditions are concerned. Yet there has been very little private inflow.

When one examines existing enterprises with foreign participation, one finds that *either* they are sponsored by NDC with such favourable terms for the foreign investor that most of the risk is borne by NDC, *or* they are supported (if not entirely financed) by such official bodies as Commonwealth Development Corporation, International Finance Corporation, International Development Agency (World Bank), Deutsche Entwicklungsgesellschaft, and Netherlands Overseas Finance Company.

The private financiers which have *recently* been brought in by the NDC include Cementia Holding A.G. (Zurich), Associated Portland (London), Tegry Industrial and Development Corporation (Israel), Oltremare (Italy), L. Rose & Co (U.K.), Hallway Hotels Overseas, Ltd. (U.K.), Macmillan & Co (British publishers), Alfa-Laval and Tetrapak (Sweden), Amenital, Sodefra (Paris), Textilconsult (Vaduz), Ehrnbergs (Sweden); banks involved are Barclays, Standard, Algemene Bank Nederland, Mediobanca, Credit Lyonnais, and Banque Française du Commerce Extérieur. This is not a discreditable list for the few years of NDC's operations; it compares very favourably with the near-stagnation of earlier years, but it does not equal the achievements of Kenya, still less those of Zambia.

The basic problems have been twofold: the superior attractiveness (in general) of Kenya, and the superior attractiveness (in general) of advanced countries as recipients of investment. Tanzania has no oil, and only modest reserves of other workable minerals of economic size. It has its Williamson's Diamond Mine, and it has attracted considerable expenditure on oil exploration (by Shell), but little else. Yet it is mining which is, historically seen, the most attractive sector for private enterprise in tropical Africa [12].

---

10 The East African investment allowance since 1962 has been 20% which allows 120% of the original investment to be written off for tax purposes, equivalent to a 48% subsidy. This has the undesirable side-effect of favouring capital-intensive techniques.

11 See KESSEL, op. cit. for evidence of over-protection.

12 Oddly enough it may also be for basically geological reasons that Kenya has developed ahead of Tanzania — specifically concerning the physical structure of the natural harbour of Mombasa. See B. S. HOYLE: *The Seaports of East Africa*. Political reasons have been more important only in the sense that more

In the earlier years, as the historical section showed, these factors resulted in a capital inflow which was only a trickle. In the 1961–1964 period, political complications were added. But from 1965 onwards the capital account has been distinctly better. Three reasons are proposed to account for this.

- The energetic search for project formulation by the NDC.
- A sufficiently extensive array of project promotions by NDC and Central Government to achieve a Rosenstein-Rodan-type of breakthrough with new Hirschman-type linkages.
- The emergence of the Treasury as an effective developmental force (around 1964) capable of presenting the case for official foreign capital participation quite effectively, and supervising its terms with increasing acumen.

All these three points have been documented in the historical section, so it is not necessary to evidence them here.

Public Capital Account

The development of the public capital account was indicated in Table 11 and is further clarified below. A full description of the behaviour of external public debt will not be possible until certain research, now under way in the Treasury, is completed. The desiderata are identified [13] as:

- Separating the externally held public-issued bonds from the domestic holdings. (This was done experimentally for mid-1966). This is a problem arising from the British accounting system.
- Doing the same exercise, on Zanzibar Government stocks.
- Recording the behaviour of external borrowing by parastatals, and subsidiaries of parastatals.
- Recording the behaviour of external debt of the East African Community and its Corporations, which is a joint obligation of the three East African States.

These are serious desiderata, but on the other hand the Government-to-Government loans, and loans from official international sources, being of a contractual nature and mostly tied to specific projects, can be well analysed, and these form the bulk of the debt [14].

---

favourable political circumstances might have outweighed the disadvantage of natural endowment.

13 By the Treasury, in successive *Budget Surveys,* and by the author.
14 There is still some unclarity. Successive Budget Surveys do not give the same totals for the same year; the 1968 issue disagrees with the Appropriation Accounts as to whether the Kilimanjaro Hotel Equipment loan is from a company (GUS Export) or a Government (Israel). The author has simply used his best judgement.

In addition to the peripheral areas referred to above, the Central Government public debt falls into several parts, namely:

- Funded Debt. These are public-issued stocks, partly held in Tanzania and partly elsewhere (mainly U.K.), for which a sinking fund must be regularly built up. The figures are best given gross, disregarding the sinking fund, since the sinking funds are not necessarily external assets. However, this overstates the external debt [15].

- Loans from various Governments, and from the International Development Association — mostly project-tied.

- Special loans from the U.K. Government for payment of compensation and commutation of pension to former British civil servants whose service in this country was cut short by the independent Government of the

Table 126. *Central Government Debt*
(Millions of Shs.)

Outstanding in	1964	1965	1966	1967	1968
Funded Debt					
1. Guaranteed Loan 1952/72	(10.0)	(10.0)	(10.0)	(10.0)	(8.6)
2. Govt. Stocks, various, up to 1987	(355.0)	(368.4)	(453.2)	(530.1)	(566.9)
3. Total	(365.0)	(378.4)	(463.2)	(540.1)	(575.5)
A. *of which:* external debt	?	?	192.9	?	?
B. Unfunded Debt, External					
1. U.K. Exchequer Loans	65.4	63.9	62.3	60.6	52.0
2. Other U.K. loans	2.1	12.5	24.9	32.0	27.8
3. Loans, other Governments	30.3	61.9	90.0	163.5	182.1
4. IDA and Internat. Wheat Board	3.3	16.2	36.6	74.4	112.5
5. Special loans					
a) Commuted Pensions	37.0	47.0	54.0	55.4	47.5
b) Compensations	65.0	85.4	104.8	120.0	102.9
6. Private loans					
a) Contractor Finance	15.9	16.1	12.1	8.1	3.5
b) Other	71.8	64.2	54.3	43.6	36.9
7. Total unfunded	(290.8)	(367.2)	(439.0)	(557.6)	(565.2)
C. *Total External*	?	?	631.9	?	?

Sources: Background to the Budget 1967/68 and 1968/69; Appropriation Accounts 1966/67. The Lint and Seed Marketing Board Loan 1974 (£1 mn.) is excluded. The dates of each year are: 31st March for 1968; 30th June, others.

---

15 Not only are externally-held sinking funds overlooked, but the interest and capital gains earned from them are also overlooked.

214

Republic. These loans must be regarded as a special category since they are the subject of dispute.

- Loans from the unofficial sources, e.g. manufacturers of equipment, banks, etc.

This Central Government external debt will be summarised (Table 126) and then examined in detail.

The Funded Debt consists of bonds, some floated in the London market, some issued in Dar es Salaam. The following table shows how interest rates have risen.

Table 127. *Funded Debt Instruments Ranked by Issue Date: Interest Rates*

Instrument	Rate of Interest [a] %
1. Guaranteed Loan 1952/72	4
2. Inscribed Stock 1970/73	$3^1/_2$
3. Inscribed Stock 1967/72	$4^1/_4$
4. Inscribed Stock 1978/82	$5^3/_4$
5. Tanganyika Registered Stock 1975/79	$5^1/_2$
6. Tanganyika Registered Stock 1980/83	$6^1/_4$
7. Tanganyika Registered Stock 1967/68 and 1981/84	$6^1/_2$
8. Tanganyika Registered Stock 1969	$6^1/_2$
9. Tanganyika Registered Stock 1975/78	$6^1/_2$
10. United Republic of Tang. & Zanzibar Registered Stock 1970/71	$6^3/_4$
11. United Republic of Tanzania Registered Stock 1970/71 . . .	$6^1/_2$
12. United Republic of Tanzania Registered Stock 1983/85 . . .	$6^3/_4$
13. United Republic of Tanzania Registered Stock 1974/76 . . .	$6^1/_2$
14. United Republic of Tanzania Registered Stock 1980/81 . . .	$6^3/_4$

[a] Payable half-yearly; dates differ. Stocks were not necessarily issued at par.

Source: Appropriation Accounts, 1966–1967.

The hardening of terms is quite clear when one compares for instance, Inscribed Stock 1970/73 at $3^1/_2$% with the subsequent issue of Registered Stock 1970/71 at $6^1/_2$%. Nevertheless, the outstanding debt has increased between June, 1964 and March, 1968 by Shs. 211.9 mn. or 12% per annum. Most of the increase has been taken up by residents of Tanzania including the Bank of Tanzania and the National Provident Fund.

The unfunded debt shows the following characteristics:

- It doubled between 1964 and 1968 (approximately)
- Several new lenders came to the assistance of Tanzania.
- British funds fell as a proportion of the local.
- Interest charges fell as softer loans were attracted.
- Contractor and other private finance diminished both relatively and absolutely.

Table 128 shows the various official sources of funds, intergovernmental and international, excluding the special U.K. loans for pensions and compensations.

Table 128. *Unfunded International and Other Official Loans*
(Millions of Shillings)

Outstanding in	1964	1965	1966	1967	1968
1. British Exchequer 6%	27.6	26.9	26.2	25.4	21.8
2. British Exchequer 6¹/₂%	37.8	37.0	36.1	35.2	30.2
3. Commonwealth Assistance (U.K.) (Tanganyika Credit)	2.1	6.5	10.9	15.0	13.2
4. Commonwealth Assistance (U.K.) (Nyumba ya Mungu project)	–	6.0	14.0	17.0	14.6
5. U.S.A.I.D. (various projects)	13.3	38.8	60.9	72.8	88.9
6. Kreditanstalt (agriculture)	16.6	22.8	24.7	29.6	29.0
7. Israel (irrigation)	0.4	0.3	0.8	0.4	0.2
8. Yugoslavia (transportation)	–	–	2.0	1.3	0.9
9. Sweden (various)	–	–	1.6	5.2	8.1
10. China (sterling loan)	–	–	–	40.0	40.0
11. China (other)	–	–	–	3.4	3.4
12. Zambia (road)	–	–	–	10.0	10.0
13. Canada (town planning)	–	–	–	0.7	1.2
14. U.S.S.R. (commodity credit)	–	–	–	0.1	0.4
15. International Wheat Board (commodity credit)	–	–	–	3.8	6.2
16. International Development Association (various)	3.3	16.2	36.6	70,6	106.3
Total	101.1	154.5	213.8	330.5	374.4

Source: Appropriation Accounts, 1966–1967.

The interest charges vary as follows. The dearest is the Israeli irrigation loan which is at 1% above U.K. Bank Rate (minimum 5%).

The second dearest source is the U.K. In addition to the two Exchequer loans at 6% and 6¹/₂%, there are the two "Commonwealth Assistance" schemes, one of which is at ¹/₄% above U.K. Treasury Bill Rate, the other is at 6³/₄%.

Apart from these two countries (which on the 1968 figures had supplied 32% of the outstanding official debt), all other countries give Tanzania loans on soft terms, ranging from 3¹/₂% to interest-free. The dearest tranche is Shs. 11,4 mn. of the U.S.A.I.D. money which comes at 3¹/₂%; this is followed by the West German and Yugoslav money at 3%. The U.S.S.R. commodity credit is at 2¹/₂% and the Swedish loans are at 2%. For U.S.A.

and I.D.A. funds, between $3/4\%$ and $1^1/4\%$ is at present paid; the Zambia road loan is at 1%; Chinese and Canadian funds are free of interest (and with generous grace-periods)[16].

Soft loans outstanding in 1968 amounted to 79% of the total unfunded debt (1964: 33%). The outstanding unfunded debt on hard terms actually diminished absolutely since 1967.

The interest payable in 1966/67 on the unfunded debt of Table 128 outstanding at mid-1966 worked out at 3.7% overall. Taking the unfunded debt, still excluding the special loans, together with the estimated external holdings of funded debt, the average interest rate might be in the neighbourhood of 4% at that date. Since then new debts at a higher rate of interest have arisen in respect of nationalisations, which will tend to offset the general fall in the average rate.

Finally, the special loans. This is a complicated subject which is described at length, though not exhaustively, in the Budget Speech of 1968. Under the Public Officers Agreement made with the U.K. as part of the Independence settlement, the Tanganyika Government assumed liability in respect of expatriate civil servants for (1) compensation for loss of office, and (2) commutation payments in lieu of pension rights. The amounts involved clearly would depend on the timing of the dismissals, the last of which was in 1968.

For (1), the U.K. agreed to meet half the cost and to extend a credit line of up to £6 million for the remainder. This was exhausted by a final drawing in 1966/67. It is repayable, with a grace period of 7 years, in 19 equal instalments, in respect of each drawing.

For (2), the U.K. gave a credit line of up to £3 million, at an interest rate of $1/4\%$ above U.K. Treasury Bill rate, i.e. between $5^1/2\%$ and 7% according to the dates of drawing, again in equal annuities over 19 years for each drawing with 7 years' grace. This credit line was almost exhausted in 1966/67, and in 1967/68 the Tanzania Government became liable for budgetary outgoings in respect of civil servants whose jobs were Africanised in that year[17].

Immediately before the 1967/68 financial year the Tanzanian Government informed the U.K. Government that it regarded these arrangements as unfair, and requested the U.K. Government to assume the liabilities in respect of the *Colonial* service, i.e. service up to the date of Tanganyika independence. It added that it was willing to pay for those services which it had decided it required, i.e. service after independence. After certain offers and counter-

---

16 Of course these are only the nominal interest rates. Effective rates tend to be higher due to tying provisions. USAID equipment delivered to the University at a nominal rate of 2% was found to have an effective rate of 14%.

17 Those who retired normally, and therefore receive normal pensions, were already a normal charge on the recurrent Budget of Tanzania, and are accepted as such.

offers, related in the 1968 Budget Speech, negotiations broke down, and the Tanzania Government unilaterally repudiated the contentious part of the liability, thereby reducing the outstanding debt to £2,233,200, as compared to the £7½ million at which it had stood at the end of March, 1968 (see Table 126, 5a and 5b).

The U.K. response was to cut off further possibilities of aid, but otherwise appears to have accepted this position.

The present overall position appears to be that the gross external public long-term debt amounts to about Shs. 1,1 billion. Without the abrogation of part of the Special Loans, and the sterling devaluation of 1967, this would have been about Shs. 1,3 billion. In addition there are contingent liabilities of about Shs. 1,8 billion, but these are already included in the private capital account, where they are direct liabilities.

Table 129. *External Public Debt, Recent Estimates*

	Shs. mn.	Date of estimate	
Central Government			
Funded	192.9	June, 1966	(A)
Unfunded	565.2	March, 1968	(B)
Parastatal borrowing	130	April, 1968	(A)
Compensation commitments	225	July, 1968	(A)
less: already paid	−20	April, 1968	(A)
Total	1,093		
Contingent Liabilities			
East African Community	$1/3 \times 2100 = 700$	April, 1968	(A)
Guarantees and confirmations	326	June, 1967	(B)
Joint guarantees	$1/3 \times 2411 = 803$	June, 1967	(B)
Total	1,829		
Abrogations and Windfalls			
U.K. Special Funds	150.3	March, 1968	(A)
less new balance	−44.4	June, 1968	(C)
Sterling Devaluation	75	Nov. 1967	(A)
Total	180.9		

Sources: • *Background to the Budget 1967/68* and *1968/69.* (A)
       • *Appropriation Accounts, 1966/67.* (B)
       • Budget Speech, 1968. (C)
Further details may be found in Appendix II.

IX. MONETARY MOVEMENTS, RESERVES AND PERIMETER DEFENCES

1. Monetary Movements

It is convenient to begin this section by an examination of the transactions which fall into the description of "monetary movements" or "change in reserves".

Table 130. *Monetary Movements, July 1965–Dec. 1966*
(Millions of Shillings)

	1965 Jul.—Dec.	1966 Jan.—June	1966 Jul.—Dec.	Year
1. Bank of Tanzania foreign exchange reserves, rise (+) or fall (—) due to regular transactions	N.A.	+ 5.9	+46.0	+51.9
2. East African Currency Board remittances, *net* to Tanzania (+) or from Tanzania (—)	+46.2	+123.4	N.A.	+123.4
3. Government Agency accounts, swing in favour (+) or against (—) Tanzania	—13.4	+20.7	+ 7.2	+27.9
4. Consolidated Fund investments, rise (+) or fall (—)	—46.0	— 0.1	N.A.	— 0.1
5. Monetary institutions (other than Bank of Tanzania and Currency Board) external net balances, rise (+) or fall (—)	—30.9	+32.6	—10.6	+20.0
6. East African Currency Board Surplus released to Tanzania				
for I.M.F. account	+ 7.7	+ 7.7	0.0	+ 7.7
for A.D.B. account	+ 9.2	+ 9.2	0.0	+ 9.2
7. East African currency, postal and handpayments net (estimated)	—30.0	—30.0	—14.2	—44.2
Overall	—57.2	+169.4	+28.4	+195.8

N.A. = Not Applicable.
Source: Bank of Tanzania: *Economic Report, July–Dec. 1966.*

In Table 130, what is of interest, is not so much the figures, which may not be accurate, but the classification of entries. These are to be understood as follows:

- Bank of Tanzania foreign exchange reserves, change due to regular transactions. This item is compiled directly from the Central Bank's accounts, being the net of foreign exchange bought from or sold to (a) commercial banks and (b) Government. It is equal to the change in foreign assets held with central banks abroad *due to regular transactions;* irregular transactions (excluded) consist of foreign assets *taken over* in the setting up of the Bank of Tanzania; interest, appreciation and depreciation on foreign assets; and proceeds of the currency conversion[1].
- Prior to the first operations of the Central Bank in mid-June, 1966, the EACB served as a central monetary authority; its purchase/sales of sterling in dealings with the commercial banks and the Treasury[2] are shown here. After June, 1966 there is no further entry; sales of sterling to the Central Bank are excluded since they do not reflect any balance of payments transaction "above the line".
- Government Agents are the Crown Agents in London and Bombay; transactions through the Bombay office are in fact negligible. The London account is permitted to oscillate around zero; when necessary, the Bank of Tanzania replenishes it on behalf of the Tanzania Government (in terms of Table 130, a minus entry in 1. and a plus entry in 3.; note that the signs in this table are the reverse of the conventional notation whereby an improvement in the balance of payments shows a minus sign in the monetary movements account).

  Since the formation of the State Trading Corporation which has its own overseas agents it will be possible to include the new agents in this table, but it would be more logical to show it in a separate part of the official capital account (above the line).
- Consolidated Fund Investments were foreign securities (other than sinking funds) held by the Treasury before the Central Bank was established. As Table 130 shows, Shs. 46,1 mn. of these were liquidated in 1965/66, before the remainder (and the proceeds) were handed over to the Central Bank. This liquidation would normally appear in the long-term official capital account, not under monetary movements; it was included in this table because the table was designed to show the overall balance of payments in the most realistic way. Since these assets (whether or not liquidated) have now been incorporated into the reserves of the Central Bank, no more entries will be made. Any further liquidation would be

---

1 If these special transactions are included, item (1) becomes almost equal to the change in Bank of Tanzania external assets, since its external liabilities were negligible over the period in question.

2 The EACB annual report shows different figures because Treasury is omitted.

merely a change in the structure of foreign exchange reserves; any change in the *total* would be included in item 1. of Table 130.

- Changes in the external position of other monetary institutions covers the commercial banks and the Post Office Savings Banks. This item is quite conventional except that the foreign assets of commercial banks include sterling bills, discounted at the request of exporters. If this item were not included here, a new item would have to be inserted elsewhere, as the EASD tabulations do no contain it at all. It is not very significant but it is a useful invasion of the largely unknown territory of changes in the terms of payment.
- EACB surpluses released to Tanzania are the sums paid by EACB to the IMF and the African Development Bank as Tanzania's subscriptions. They came out of EACB's profits accrued over past years. It was decided to treat them as a contribution to reserves as of the time when they were made available rather than as of the earlier years when they were gradually earned by EACB and accruing as a contingent asset (not yet disposable or liquid). However, it was not thought proper to attribute them to any period shorter than the full financial year during which they were released; hence they are attributed equally over the first two columns of Table 130.
- The last item is based on estimation. During the period to which Table 130 refers, a process of currency redemption was in progress (and still is). The old East African notes and coins were being called in through the banking system and replaced by Tanzania with national currency. The EACB credits the Bank of Tanzania with sterling at par for all the old currency which is collected and destroyed.

So long as some EACB currency remains in circulation the possibility exists of settling debts by physical movement of EACB currency across the borders, to or from Kenya or Uganda. This is clearly a monetary movement, either adding to or depleting the country's convertible reserves, and it is therefore necessary to allow for it in the balance of payments tabulations. The EASD tabulations omitted it because no estimate was available of such payments; but the 1966 Annual Report of the Currency Board contained an estimate, for the first time, namely an outflow of Shs. 60 mn. for the financial year 1965/66. This was part of a flow-of-funds matrix developed recently by the Nairobi statisticians. In Table 130 this figure is shown, arbitrarily split into two 6-monthly periods of Shs. 30 mn. each.

This item must decrease over time as the EACB currency is withdrawn. The pattern of withdrawals over time can be estimated on the basis of data of previous currency conversions [3].

This is the basis for the estimate of Shs. 14.2 mn. in the July-December,

---

3 See EACB: *Annual Report, 1966.*

1966 column; about Shs. 2 mn. may be expected for the first half of 1967 and negligible figures thereafter (the curve is asymptotic).

The figures of Table 130 are the first ever produced for the overall balance of payments on a financial basis in Tanzania [4].

Reserves

Table 131 shows the movement of the Bank of Tanzania's external assets, the relation of which to the foregoing was explained in footnote 1.

Table 131. *Bank of Tanzania Net External Assets*
(Millions of Shillings)

	1966	1967	1968
End of:			
January	–	420.4	435.6 [a]
February	–	434.6	478.9 [a]
March	–	434.4	490.2 [a]
April	–	427.8	505.0 [a]
May	–	428.0	506.4 [a]
June	160.1	420.7	490.4 [a]
July	231.7	389.5	431.6 [a]
August	290.6	387.2	420.9 [a]
September	319.3	376.6	442.2 [a]
October	335.4	378.9	448.2 [a]
November	359.8	362.0 [a]	462.0 [a]
December	389.7	397.7 [a]	512.5 [a]

[a] After loss of 35.8 due to sterling devaluation.

Source: Bank of Tanzania, monthly statement of liabilities and assets.

Table 131 shows:

- the same pattern of a stronger balance of payments in the first half of the calendar year as was shown in Table 130;
- there has been no monthly drop in reserves larger than Shs. 31,2 mn. (so far), other than the controlled drop of Shs. 58 mn. in Juli 1968 which was connected with planned official compensation payments.

While there is no way of knowing daily fluctuations from published data, the above suggests that it would be safe to hold as little as Shs. 50 mn., and probably considerably less, of the reserves in the form of demand deposits, and probably even less in the December-May period. With reserves of Shs. 500 mn. an investment of Shs. 450 mn. at (say) 5% would bring in

---

4 This is more accurate than totalling the elements "above the line", and can be produced more quickly; monthly figures are also easily obtainable. The method was developed by the author with the assistance of the accountants of the institutions concerned, whose hardworking co-operation is here acknowledged with gratitude.

222

Shs. 22.5 mn. which is sufficient to make a very noticable impact on the balance of payments indeed. This compares with the yield of Shs. 19.9 mn. earned in the time of the Currency Board (1965). It is to be presumed, however, that the foreign assets are not merely

- demand deposits and
- foreign Government securities,
- but cover a more complete spectrum of liquidities including Treasury Bills and possibly time deposits of various kinds. It is also to be presumed that the portfolio is actively "managed" so as to benefit from capital gains in securities markets.

Table 132 shows external assets of a conditional nature, held in the name of the Treasury (and therefore additional to those of Table 131) as at mid-1967.

Table 132. *Tanzania's Subscriptions to International Financial Organisations as at June, 30th, 1967*

1. *International Monetary Fund:* Part subscription
   Gold equivalent to $2,244,200 paid in 1962;
   gold equivalent to $1,750,000 paid in 1966;
   T.Shillings equivalent to $70,000 paid in 1966;
   total equivalent to $4,064,200   or *Shs. 29.1 mn.*

2. *International Bank for Reconstruction and Development:*
   Part subscription: 333 shares of $100,000 each of which
   $1,000 was paid up, plus T.Shillings payment of
   Shs. 214,060;
   total equivalent to $3,629,683   or *Shs. 25.9 mn.*[a]

3. *International Finance Corporation:*
   subscription to 184 shares fully paid at $1,000 (1962/63),
   total $184,000   or *Shs. 1.3 mn.*

4. *International Development Association:*
   part subscription, $ 168,330   or *Shs. 1.2 mn.*

5. *African Development Bank:*
   part subscription towards 315 shares of $10,000; 70% paid,
   at $2,205,000   or *Shs. 15.75 mn.*

6. Total in Shillings   =   *73.25 million*[b]

---

[a] Nominal value of shares is of course much higher.
[b] Since mid-1967, a subscription to the East African Development Bank has presumably been paid, but no information on this has been published.
Source: Appropriation Accounts, 1966–1967, with minor amendments.

Of these, the only portion which may be considered as drawable immediately, as of right, without difficulties or problems is the IMF gold tranche, which is $3,994,200, equivalent to Shs. 28.5 mn. To date no drawing from the IMF has been made, nor has any stand-by credit facility been requested.

The remaining Shs. 44.75 mn. are illiquid assets, the use of which is not foreseen.

2. Short-term Private Capital Movements

Short-term private capital movements, including leads and lags in the terms of payments for merchandise, are, as remarked earlier, a largely uncharted area. Of the advanced economies, only two (West Germany and Japan) have thought it advisable to invest sufficient resources in balance of payments research to produce reasonably good statistics of short-term private capital on a monthly basis. If it is not done on a monthly basis, it is scarcely worth doing at all, since "hot money" requires rapid correctives. In Japan particularly, where the whole banking liquidity has for some years relied heavily on the short-term money markets of the world, good monthly statistics of short-term private capital movements are essential. Short-term forecasting is also active. Tanzania however does not have a bill market, nor does it rely on Euro-dollars. Shifts in interest rate differentials between Tanzania and outside countries are not believed to have any significant impact on the balance of payments, hitherto. Moreover, the cost of such research is considerable. Since a shift in the average payment period of only 2 days would represent an inflow or outflow of over Shs. 25 mn., the degree of accuracy necessary to achieve useful results would be very high indeed[5].

On the other hand it is argued in an earlier section of this book that swings in payments, particularly on the import side, are likely to increase in importance; and some *indicators* (rather than comprehensive statistics) would be relatively easy to construct, especially with the help of the State Trading Corporation and the National Bank of Commerce.

Apart from the swing due to changes in the methods of financing (see Appendix VII) a certain swing is possible in the balance of so-called "inter-company accounts". This is discussed in Appendix IV.

Another important source of fluctuation is inter-bank accounts. Changes which may occur in the National Bank of Commerce's balances with banks abroad, other than those due to customers' transactions, are:

- Change in the NBC's view of the minimum balance needed with a particular bank or in a particular country as a working balance.
- Desire to hold a balance in excess of a normal working balance in order

---

5 At the time of writing these words (end-July, 1968) the latest customs returns available from Mombasa cover the month of January!

224

to promote better relations with a particular bank or as a reward for services already received.

- Change in the number of foreign banks with which balances are held.
- Making of an arrangement (facility) to overdraw an account with a foreign bank.
- Opening a Tanzania shilling account (loro account) in the books of the NBC in the name of a foreign bank.
- Facility to overdraw a loro account.
- Placing part of the balance of an account on a time-deposit basis.

The first three of these may be regarded as changes involved in the early months of the NBC's existence when its arrangements "settle down" on the basis of its newly-established international reputation, but the last four may occur at any future time.

The opening of a loro account is particularly advantageous for Tanzania. Not only does the NBC receive a lump sum of foreign exchange when selling the Tanzania shillings needed for the opening balance, but a proportion of future regular transactions will be routed through the new account, thus reducing the foreign exchange needed in the foreign (nostro) account as a working balance[6].

In order to establish a loro account with the NBC, a foreign bank must have confidence both in the efficiency and probity of the NBC and in the parity of the Tanzania shilling relative to its own currency. In general this places the national banks of developing countries at a disadvantage, but Tanzania is relatively fortunate in these respects and a substantial loro business has

---

6 Prior to nationalisation the practice varied between different banks. As an example the Standard Bank's City Drive Branch (the largest in the country) had the following arrangements:
- House accounts in 16 foreign currencies which could be either debit or credit balances (payments made via London).
- Direct nostro accounts with two foreign banks (credit balances).
- House accounts in Kenya and Uganda shillings (credit balances), together with
- Loro accounts in Tanzania shillings (debit balances) in the name of the leading Standard branch of both Kenya and Uganda.

The interesting point is that the 16 foreign currency house accounts could be either in the red or in the black. An overdrawn nostro account would therefore appear in the EASD balance of payments data (and banking data) as a balance due to a bank abroad as though it were a loro account. This is normally the case with balance of payments statistics. Yet there is an important difference: a loro account (like a credit nostro balance) can continue indefinitely, whereas an overdrawn nostro will require settlement unless special arrangements are made. The house accounts system of the Standard Bank did permit *individual* debit balances to run on but only if the *sum* of the house accounts was approximately in balance. The NBC has to make special arrangements if it wishes to overdraw on nostro account, and then interest is charged, so such overdrawings are not desirable.

been quickly built up. At the end of June, 1967, loro balances totalled Shs. 2 mn., as against Shs. 90 mn. of nostro balances. But at November 1st of the same year, loro balances totalled Shs. 17 mn. as against Shs. 64 mn. nostro. Thus a saving of Shs. 15 mn. was effected in five months of work by the Foreign Manager[7]. Furthermore, over the same period, arrangements were made for foreign overdraft facilities worth over Shs. 100 mn., the presence of which (even unutilised) makes it possible to bring working balances closer to the zero mark[8]. Since November, 1967, further progress has presumably been made, but it is to be doubted whether Tanzania, as a developing country, can ever achieve the parity of nostro and loro accounts which would be desirable. The reserve currencies, of course, are on the other side of the picture. It may be added that the holders of loro accounts tend to be other developing countries.

3. Perimeter Defences

The perimeter defences of the Tanzania shilling may now be summarised as follows.
1. Inter-company accounts
2. NBC nostro credit balances
3. NBC overdraft facilities
4. NBC loro accounts
5. Central bank reserves
6. IMF gold tranche

The first of these is unknown, but 2.–6. are under constant surveillance. At the end of October, 1967 items 2, 3, 5 and 6 totalled over Shs. 570 mn. This position is clearly a strong one.

What is less satisfactory is the weakness of corrective instruments which can be brought into action when it is seen that the balance of payments is worsening.

As described in the historical section, large parts of the import bill are no longer compressible, as they used to be before Independence. This is a general judgement irrespective of whether monetary, fiscal or direct controls are used. It may be added that these controls are themselves weak and uncertain in their operation. With the absence of developed money markets,

---

7 Source: NBC, Report and Accounts, 7th Feb.–30th June, 1967.

8 Such balances earn no interest; foreign exchange sold to the Bank of Tanzania can be invested in securities. Theoretically the NBC could invest in foreign securities too, but this would be less efficient as a double margin of liquidity would be required.

and with bank credit determined, as it is, primarily by considerations of collateral security, there is no effective monetary policy in Tanzania. Fiscal policies are more effective, but (a) they have to be harmonised with those of Kenya and Uganda — which implies a certain rigidity, and (b) import tariffs are already so high that industries tend to be over-protected, with inflationary consequences. It is not likely that an all-round raising of tariffs would be contemplated. For the same reason direct import controls are more likely to be relaxed than to be stiffened. Another approach, that of wage restraint, is already in powerful operation, but any intensification of wage restraint would be more likely to be determined by political or man-power considerations than by the balance of payments.

There remains the possibility of reducing or postponing imports of capital goods (insofar as they are not fully financed by foreign credit on sufficiently favourable terms). Unfortunately the institutional mechanism for discriminating between wanted and unwanted capital goods, and imposing the restraint upon the NDC or other importer concerned, is not yet sufficiently developed. Nor would it be easy to strike a balance of inconvenience between private and public sector importers of capital goods.

Basically, therefore, the position is that Tanzania relies on foreign official loans and grants to sustain a development programme which proceeds as fast as projects can be mounted. The Bank of Tanzania does not act as a brake. So long as the reserves are so strong, it might be difficult for the Bank to assume such a rôle, but if the experience of other countries is any guide, it will be obliged to do so eventually, and even at the present stage some firmer criteria based on foreign exchange effects ought, in the view of the present writer, to be imposed upon projects as they are formulated. (A fuller discussion of this appears in Appendix VIII). So long as exports are largely autonomous, imports are largely incompressible, foreign assistance (as was shown earlier) tends to fluctuate perversely, and terms of trade are worsening, it becomes a matter of importance, *no matter how large the reserves appear to be*, to examine critically the balance of payments effects of the whole industrial policy and to make both limiting criteria (for long-term planning) and contingency plans (for corrective instruments in the shorter-term).

Again we come back to institutional problems which are themselves an aspect of underdevelopment; but this is not discouraging, since the development of economic institutions over time has been a major theme, and an optimistic motif, of this present book.

X. ECONOMIC RELATIONS WITH KENYA

The superiority of Kenya over Tanzania in terms of GDP, industry, and trade balance is often attributed to the cooler climate of Kenya which is said to make that country more attractive to Europeans and therefore to European capital investment. In fact, the distribution of Europeans in East Africa does not conform at all closely to climatic zone. The southern highlands of Tanzania, for instance, have been relatively neglected, though their superior climate has been well known to Europeans at least since the Colonial Lexicon of 1920[1]. In Kenya, probably the greatest force making for the superiority has been the port of Mombasa, which owes its advantages to geological rather than climatic factors. If we take as best for agriculture that land which is above 3,000 ft over sea level and has an annual rainfall of over 30 inches in 4 years out of 5, we find that Mombasa is over 150 miles from such land, while Dar es Salaam has it closer at hand, in the Southern Highlands. Most of that land is however in Uganda, which for historical-political reasons has been served by the Mombasa port. Most of the remainder is in Western Tanzania which on the whole is not served at all, so far as long-distance transportation is concerned. Smaller areas are in the Southern Highlands of Tanzania and the Highlands of Kenya, of which only the latter is served by rail (to Mombasa). The building of the Uganda-Kenya railway is thus of prime significance. ELIOT's misgivings on this point were indeed unfounded[2].

The other factor is the geology of the port of Mombasa. Mombasa actually has two harbours, the Old Harbour, still used by dhows and retaining essentially its medieval form, and the Kilindini Harbour, capable of taking modern vessels. According to the recent study by HOYLE[3]:

"The fact that Mombasa has been a seaport of significance in both medieval and modern times is largely attributable to her possession of not one harbour but two, contrasted in area, depth and capacity, a condition of site which has enabled the port to adapt itself successfully to functional and navigational changes."

Mombasa can take ships of up to 65,000 tons, having an entrance channel

---

1 Deutsches Koloniallexikon, Leipzig, 1920.
2 ELIOT: op. cit.
3 B. S. HOYLE: *The Seaports of East Africa*, Nairobi, 1967.

with a minimum depth of 13 fathoms (78 feet). Dar es Salaam has a minimum of 19 feet (30 feet at high tide); Mtwara, 32 feet; Tanga, 19.25 feet (for lighterage only); Zanzibar, about 18 feet (mostly lighterage). Analysing defects of these ports with reference to their oceanic location, their water site, their land location and their land site, HOYLE finds that Tanga is defective in two of these respects, Dar es Salaam and Mtwara in one, and Mombasa in none.

The leading commodity exported through Mombasa is coffee, which is collected first in Kampala, Nairobi and Moshi (in that order of rank by volume). The huge cotton crop of Uganda is also exported via Mombasa; very little Kenya cotton is exported. Mombasa also handles some sisal from northern Tanzania. Not only is Mombasa the only port which has significant hinterlands in other countries, but it is also, according to HOYLE, the most favoured port in terms of the geographical overlapping of its various export commodity hinterlands.

These factors go to explain the concentration in Kenya of services associated with trade: wholesale entrepôts, insurance, banking, technical after-sales services, etc. They are not necessarily indigenous to Kenya — normally not, in fact — but operate out of Kenya so far as Tanzania is concerned. Tanzania's balance of payments therefore shows a considerable import of services from Kenya including payment for a considerable margin of value added for goods imported through Mombasa and bulk-broken in either Mombasa or Nairobi. This margin has been a bone of contention between the two countries for three decades; in 1965 it was valued at Shs. 72 mn.[4] Such a situation tends to be self-perpetuating until nationalisation is resorted to.

The hypothesis is advanced here that the Kenya economy had by the First World War reached a level of *potential* superiority over that of Tanganyika, but that this affected Tanganyika in a cumulative, negative way only after the economies had been brought into close contact with one another by the Customs Union which was introduced shortly after the expulsion of Germany from Tanganyika. The free interchange of local products started in 1923 and that of imported products started in 1927, the latter being the more important from the point of view of our hypothesis.

It seems likely that, in terms of manufacturing capacity, Kenya was not significantly ahead of Tanganyika at the period when this took place. Thus, in the first five years of the trade statistics (1920–24) Tanganyika's exports to Kenya-Uganda (a single entity for statistical purposes) were recorded as £2.4 million while the corresponding imports were only £2.1 million. These figures are, however, not very reliable. The first reasonably accurate set of figures on inter-East African trade in local produce relate to the early

4 EASD and Central Statistical Bureau, Dar es Salaam.

Table 133. *Interterritorial Trade (Local Produce), 1931–1933*

| | Kenya | | Uganda | | Tanganyika | |
	Imports £	Exports	Imports £	Exports	Imports £	Exports
1931	159,259	178,013	118,697	173,404	145,419	71,958
1932	165,663	157,839	113,265	152,859	139,101	107,331
1933	150,581	153,148	141,088	148,945	153,882	143,458

Source: Memorandum presented to the Governors' Conference, May, 1934. These figures do not agree with Tanganyika's trade reports which show generally higher figures but a similar picture as regards the balance. For the German period, BRODE makes a case that Tanganyika had a stronger economy than Kenya; see Appendix V.

'thirties and show Tanganyika in that deficitary position which she has been in ever since.

The cumulative process which, on our hypothesis, led to the present position, began to operate therefore in the 1920's though its material basis was of earlier origin. The most important events during the twenties were the 1923 and 1927 customs arrangements. The free trade in local produce was probably not detrimental to Tanzania in itself; it stimulated the export of rice and ghee to Kenya-Uganda. By 1933 these two items, the Hirschman-linkages of which are relatively limited, amounted to about half of Tanganyika's exports to Kenya-Uganda. The free import of Kenya produce involved some loss of customs revenue, on the other hand, and possibly some loss of foreign exchange (since Kenya produce might be bought instead of cheaper but dutiable outside produce)[5], particularly if Kenya were developing a range of high-cost, tariff-protected industries exporting to the Tanganyika market. Such a range apparently did not exist at the time and was not a source of anxiety to the Tanganyika authorities, but was to develop later. There was in fact no Tanganyika resistance to the free trade in local produce.

The resistance was against free trade in imported produce with its corollary, the (approximately) common external tariff.

According to PEDLER, Tanganyika's Customs and Excise manager[6], Kenya

---

5 This loss has been investigated in relation to the recent period by several writers, but its calculation in respect of these early years does not appear to be possible. The relevant literature is: the RAISMAN Report (see footnote 11); Dharam GHAI's "Territorial Distribution of the Benefits and Costs of the East African Common Market" in *East African Economic Review,* June, 1964; Arthur HAZLEWOOD: "The East African Common Market: Importance and Effects", *Bulletin* of the Oxford University Institute of Economics and Statistics, February, 1966, and Robert N. WOOD: "The East African Common Market: a Reassessment", *idem,* No. 4 of 1966. See also footnotes 6 and 13.

6 F. J. PEDLER: *Customs Arrangements with Kenya and Uganda,* 1934.

230

pressed hard for this from the 1922 conference of Comptrollers of Customs onwards.

"The new (proposed external) tariff was really entirely a Kenya proposal. Its purpose was partly to secure more revenue, and this aspect was stressed. It appears however from the report of the Kenya Tariff Committee, 1929, and from correspondence which passed in 1930, that the 1922 tariff was definitely drawn up as a protectionist instrument for Kenya products. There is no evidence that the Government of Tanganyika was aware of this at the time."

In November, 1922, Sir Robert Coryndon, Governor of Kenya, visited Sir Horace Byatt, Governor of Tanganyika, in Dar es Salaam and an agreement was made for the free interchange of both local and imported goods. Byatt was obviously under great pressure since the new Kenya tariff had stopped the export of ghee and rice, stocks of which were accumulating at Mwanza, and Kenya was able to make the duty-free acceptance of these perishable goods conditional upon the whole package deal. After this problem had been disposed of, Byatt found a technicality on which to revoke his commitment to free interchange of imported goods, giving reasons which re-opened the entire controversy. In particular he said that Mombasa would not always remain the entrepôt of the East African coast. Das es Salaam was likely to develop into a port of no less trade importance and he could not adopt any scheme which would in any way hinder or delay such development [7]. Thus Byatt was striking at the entrepôt trade of Kenya, which by this time had taken over Zanzibar's rôle vis-à-vis Tanganyika, but with the added growth of the various commercial and financial services relating to trade, the adverse balance of payments effects of which have been commented on in this book. He was not concerned, it seems, about the overprotection of Kenya's manufacturing industry; but given the new high Kenya tariff, and the aforesaid balance of payments effects, Kenya's future preponderance in manufacturing was implicit in the tariff proposals like a Trojan Horse.

In 1924 the Treasurer and the Comptroller of Customs in Tanganyika officially "advised against a customs union on the grounds that it would make this country a commercial satellite of Kenya, and subordinate Tanganyika to Kenya influences" [8]. In reply, the British Secretary of State for the Colonies directed that the institution of a complete customs union should no longer be delayed. Byatt's resistance was thus overruled and the customs union agreement was eventually brought into force on 1st August, 1927.

Kenya's service exports were given a further artificial boost during the Second World War, when the British Government started a War Risks

---

7 PEDLER: *op. cit.*
8 PEDLER: *op. cit.*

Insurance Scheme to cover losses of stocks of merchandise[9] through enemy action. This was introduced first for Kenya and Uganda. It was later introduced for Tanganyika but with higher premia; Zanzibar decided not to participate at all because of the high premia and the technical provisions which did not suit local conditions[10]. These circumstances gave merchants an incentive to stock their wares in Kenya rather than Tanganyika, and so to use Mombasa rather than Tanganyikan ports. The extent of this effect is not, however, known.

Such were the historical origins of the cumulative process which economic theory leads us to expect between two areas, one more advanced than the other, engaged in mutual trade. Geological, climatic, historical and political factors were involved, giving rise to an array of *de facto* comparative costs, on which the economic process was based. Within the economic process, the importation from Kenya of services related to trade has been singled out as having key importance. To see it as an important matter for action by the national authorities, however, we have to jump from Byatt's work in the 1920's, to the Raisman Report of 1961, the Treaty for East African Co-operation of 1966, and the Arusha Declaration of 1967. We may also briefly mention the abortive Kampala Agreement of 1964.

By 1964 the cumulative process of imbalance had reached a point which is shown by the following tables.

Table 134. *Inter-East African Trade, 1962–1964*
(Millions of Shs.)

	Exports from Tanzania to:		Imports of Tanzania from:	
	Kenya	Uganda	Kenya	Uganda
1962	56	9	207	35
1963	62	10	216	42
1964	87	20	271	49

Source: E. A. Customs & Excise Dept. Zanzibar included in Tanzania.

Table 135. *Manufacturing and Services as percentage of GDP*

	1962 %	1963 %	1964 %
Tanzania	38	37	40
Uganda	38	37	37
Kenya	57	57	58

Source: GDP originating in sectors other than agriculture, livestock, hunting, fishing, forestry, mining and quarrying as percentage of GDP, at current factor cost. Calculated from data in Budget Surveys of the three countries.

9 Major commodities other than cotton.
10 They did not suit Tanganyika either but the Bill was forced through regardless. See Legislative Council Proceedings, 1942.

Table 136. *Percentage Share of Each Country in East African Manufacturing and Services*

	1962 %	1963 %	1964 %
Tanzania	29	28	29
Uganda	21	22	22
Kenya	50	50	49

Source: See Table 135.

These figures show a high degree of imbalance but with signs of stabilisation; they refer to the period when the redistributive proposals of the RAISMAN Report[11] were in operation. The principal innovation here was the Distributable Pool.

This was a fund into which each country paid 40% of tax revenues derived from the profits of companies engaged in manufacturing and finance, plus 6% of customs and excise revenues. Half of the proceeds were used to finance various Common Services, such as the Meteorological Department, and the other half distributed equally between the three countries. The net redistributive effect would of course depend on the location of expenditures by the Common Services concerned[12].

This was a palliative measure, and a definite improvement. How far it fell short of a complete remedy may be realised when it is calculated that in order to equalise the value of manufacturing and service output in the three countries, a capital transfer from Kenya equal to about one year's total Kenya product would be required[13].

In 1964 the three Heads of Government met in Nairobi and decided to take more energetic measures to redress the trade balances. An emergency committee was set up in Kampala, and produced proposals known as the Kampala Agreement. This involved the *direction of industry* in favour of Tanzania and Uganda, by negotiation with companies and by licensing. However, it was not ratified by Kenya, and industries were promoted in Kenya which were supposed to be reserved for Uganda or Tanzania; the Agreement became a dead letter[14].

11 East Africa: *Report of the Economic and Fiscal Commission*, Colonial Office. 8 Cmnd. 1279, Feb. 1961.
12 In 1965 these were about 50% in Kenya, 17% in Uganda, 18% in Tanzania and 15% elsewhere.
13 Calculation in M. J. H. YAFFEY: "The Treaty for East African Co-operation: an economic commentary", published in *Private Enterprise and the Corporate Form in East Africa,* by P. A. THOMAS (editor), Nairobi, 1968.
14 One of the disputes concerned Tanzania's interest in setting up her own monetary system, with a separate Central Bank and separate currency. In retrospect, these moves (in 1966) may be seen to be essential in the control over commercial banking, one of the services formerly centred in Nairobi.

In the Treaty for East African Co-operation, direction of industry was formally abandoned by Tanzania together with the Distributable Pool, in exchange for

- a direct attack on the trade imbalances by means of temporary customs duties (transfer taxes), with accompanying small fiscal benefits;
- biased promotion of industry through an East African Development Bank; and
- relocation of the headquarters of certain Common Services, with corresponding changes in their expenditure patterns.

The Treaty has been analysed in detail elsewhere[15]; to summarise, it is expected to have a substantial once-for-all redistributive effect in favour of Tanzania in 1968–70, and a smaller continuing redistributive effect depending partly on the vigorous management of the Development Bank, but it has little or no power to attract new industry to Tanzania, and Kenya remains the most attractive location for new industries on the whole.

The Arusha Declaration of 1967 called for the nationalising of, inter alia, banking, insurance, and major import-export trade; this has been followed by film distribution. All these affect Kenya, which exported or re-exported these services to Tanzania to a considerable extent[16]. The Kenya Government has reacted, so far as is known, with sympathy, and has no doubt even been moved to consider the possibilities of emulation, as has the Government of Zambia.

This should be encouraging to the economist, for if this were not so, Tanzania would be forced into a series of embarrassing choices between her national interests and her regard for the future of regional and Pan-African co-operation, and the future for the latter would be less bright. But it is perhaps too early to assess the prospects for peaceful coexistence within East Africa of Tanzania's socialism and Kenya's very different chosen path. This may be clarified in the next few years. As Mr. JAMAL presciently said in 1964[17]:

"In the next 10 years ... the realities both at home and abroad will have become clearer. The relationship between economic systems, political systems and social systems will have been better understood in the context of each state's own circumstances. The ability to express the country's own genius will have been fortified by the numbers of trained and skilled personnel which will have come out of universities and other institutions."

---

15 See footnote 13; parts of that material have been incorporated into this book (see the section on Imports).

16 The transport-route problem has also been attacked by the stipulation that imports subject to specific licensing must now be imported via Tanzanian ports.

17 Hon. A. H. JAMAL (now Minister for Finance, Tanzania): *The Critical Phase of Emergent African States,* Nairobi, 1965. (Lecture given in Common Course at Dar es Salaam University College, October 20th, 1964).

XI. PERSPECTIVES FOR THE FUTURE

In balance of payments analysis, one is always concerned with looking ahead. Is a crisis impending? What is the early warning system? How effective would correctives be? Or to be more optimistic: how fast a rate of growth can be maintained without a crisis? Can the pitfalls of external debt be avoided? How far can Tanzania reduce its dependency on the goodwill of richer nations?

Attempts have been made to calculate the balance of payments projections for years ahead by econometric methods; there is Professor CLARK's model[1], recently up-dated by the World Bank, and that of Mr. and Mrs. DAHL[2]. Some econometric elements were also employed in a projection made by myself[3] in 1966.

The assumptions of such procedures are the following:

- All variables are precisely determined. This ignores the advances made in price theory by CHAMBERLIN, SWEEZY, *et al.*

- They are determined by a limited number of other variables. The degree of simplification is usually admitted.

- The determinants are themselves quantifiable economic variables. No attempt is made to introduce political or sociological factors, whether quantifiable or otherwise. These are shown merely as changes in magnitude of economic variables such as the savings ratio, birth rate, etc.

- Relationships between variables are established by statistical study of earlier years. Even though in the earlier years these relationships or coefficients were very unstable they are assumed to be stable or to change in a fixed manner for the future years.

- Changes in the world environment are assumed either not to take place or to take place in the form of, simply, a change in the commodity terms of trade. This disregards the historical evidence.

- The pattern of causal relationships is assumed not to change, even over a period of great length and constitutional upheaval.

---

1 Paul G. CLARK: *Development Planning in East Africa.*
2 In: FAALAND and DAHL: *The Economy of Tanzania.*
3 M. J. H. YAFFEY: *Tanzania's Balance of Payments Projections, 1966–1971*, ERB Restricted Paper, 1966.

Such a forecast, in view of the kind of analysis made in the previous chapters, would be unthinkable. The importance of the institutional or so-called "non-economic" factors has been revealed.

In the merchandise trade account, we have stressed the importance of marketing channels which are undergoing change. A total transformation of the services account has taken place following the Arusha Declaration. The capital account is under strong political pressure, and is not all open to prediction on any economic basis. The balance struck by all of these factors will determine Central Bank policy and thus further affect the merchandise trade. Under these circumstances any prediction must be dismissed as charlatanry. The most that can be done (as is scrupulously explained by DAHL) is to combine a number of heroic assumptions and finish up with a "bench-mark" which may be of value to planners [4].

Lest this should be taken as an attack on econometric forecasting in general, it should be pointed out that Tanzania is rather a special case because of

- its internally disaggregated economy,
- its rapid institutional changes,
- its scarce high-level manpower, and
- its openness.

These remarks would *not* apply to econometric forecasting, say, in the United States.

It will be appropriate, therefore, to discuss some of the main determinants without attempting to calculate the fine balance resulting from them.

The starting point must be the state itself, its administrative capability, and its policies.

As an instrument of encouraging agricultural exports, the state has in the past been weak. It has failed to cope with quality problems in coffee, cashew, and hides. It has occasionally backed the wrong horse (aromatic tobacco). It has failed to impose cultivation discipline (cotton, coffee) or where it has been imposed the cultivators have lost interest in the crops (West Lake). Its marketing institutions have imposed some dangerously high markups (cashew, groundnuts). Its village settlements have been less successful than the spontaneous schemes. Its export taxation policy has been one of trial and error. The agricultural extension officers are said to spend no more than $1^1/_2$ hours per day on the field. *Yet the export tonnage doubled between 1962 and 1967.* Independence has had a tremendous psychological effect in releasing latent energy in the rural sector. Insofar as this energy has been taken out of the realm of *laisser-faire* and subjected to planning and control by a multiplicity of experimental institutions run by extremely ill-

---

4 There is, of course, an element of charlatanry in planning. One goes from bench-mark to bench-mark.

educated persons, it has inevitably been wasted to an extent; and as the years go by, the excitement of building one's own independent land must wane unless it is reinforced by economic results. The early years were however characterised by the consolidation of the *central* government; the most able civil servants, and new graduates, gravitated towards Dar es Salaam. Not until 1969 was a centrifugal flow found to be possible. The raising of the quality of the rural civil service; the replacement of some of the earlier political appointees with better-trained younger men; and the renovation of the Independence spirit by means of a higher degree of local autonomy; these have become both political and economic necessities. The growth rate of exports therefore depends partly on the success of implementing the policy of decentralisation in the civil service.

Disaggregating to the major crops, we can see the crucial importance of Government action at the lower levels. In sisal, the problem is essentially how to compel Brazil to co-operate in a price stabilisation scheme, and if this cannot be done, how to get out of sisal. In cotton, much seems to depend on the success of Regional Commissioners in getting the proper timetable of cultivation tasks followed. In coffee, the wastes due to bad processing by co-operatives are a part of the wider problem of building up a sound co-operative movement. Cashew has been affected by poor management — and so on. All these are fields in which the central Government is working for improvements, gradually overcoming its manpower problems.

In the industrial sphere the problem has been similar: again, there is a high rate of increase in production, but also some difficulty in canalising and controlling the investment to ensure that it accords with national objectives. In this case, however, a further strengthening of the centre may still be required. The problems of project identification and evaluation, moreover, become more acute as the "easy" large items of imports are replaced one by one. As with agriculture, there is a tendency to concentrate increasingly on improving efficiency in existing commodities; but unlike agriculture, industry is faced with labour relations difficulties. Government has legislated to curtail the growth rate of urban incomes, which in itself saves foreign exchange on the import side, but the resulting dissatisfaction creates problems of reduced effort-intensity which is liable to have a negative effect on the export side. Of course, this is bound up with the behaviour of prices. The extension of the price-control system, in spite of its administrative (and inherent) difficulties and dangers, may well prove to be vital for the preservation of the present incomes policy. This in turn could be easily upset by a rise in import prices, such as could be caused by price-inflation abroad, freight rate increases, or devaluation of the Tanzanian shilling. All three of these possibilities are tendencies which are consistently promoted by interested parties, and as consistently (until now) resisted by the East African authorities, but the line is weakly held, especially on freight rates.

Commercial policy is the third main area of Government influence. The cornerstone is of course the East African Community, with its Treaty for East African Co-operation.

It is significant that in recent years Tanzania's trade with Kenya and Uganda has actually fallen, both import and export. This is due to import substitution. The transfer taxes will exert a further depressive influence on this trade. One would expect new incomes to be generated by the relocation and decentralisation of the Headquarters of the jointly-owned enterprises and services, but at the time of writing (after about $2^1/_2$ years of the Treaty) no noticeable progress has been made in that direction.

As yet the Treaty has separated, rather than brought together, its member states because the transfer taxes have come into operation before the income-generating measures. It does not appear to be making East Africa more attractive to foreign capital, as was earlier hoped. Probably some measures will be devised to revitalise the Community.

Meantime this Treaty maintains the common external tariff, which entails a certain rigidity; the result is that import *licensing* has become the main instrument of commercial policy. It is only by licences that it is possible to make importation of goods from certain countries conditional on the sale of surplus coffee or other agricultural products to those countries. This kind of "parallel trading" is increasingly the central concern of official commercial policy, following the large coffee crops of 1965 and 1966.

This is of course new to Tanzania. In other countries where it is a regular practice — e.g. Poland — machinery has been established to handle it; through a network of trade missions, prices can be compared, quotas established. Tanzania has yet to establish a system of world-wide price-comparison and so has no means of assessing any offer except by comparison with prices currently being paid to existing suppliers. These are in general *catalogue prices*. There is clearly great scope for applying pressure on the import price index by institutional changes, as and when the necessary manpower becomes available. Such pressure could usefully be applied irrespective of whether commercial policy happens to be dominated at any moment by a surplus of coffee.

In the light of these many unknowns, it is difficult to predict the course of the trade balance. Exports may be expected to rise, let us say, by over 6% per annum *given* good weather and a solution to the problems of at least two of the three major crops. Imports of consumer goods will probably stagnate; even with very satisfactory export proceeds it is doubtful whether consumer imports can be allowed to rise at more than $4^1/_2\%$ per annum in money terms.

An extrapolation of import trends gives a very unsatisfactory picture:

Table 137. *Import Value Extrapolations* [a], *1975*
(Shs. mn.)

Category	1965—1967 average	Growth rate %	1975 result	% of Tanganyika total 1965—1967	1975
Consumer	508	*1.7*	675	37	17
Intermediate	251	*14.5*	851	16	21
Transport	178	*18.0*	790	11	20
Capital	463	*13.5*	1,447	29	36
Miscellaneous	36	*11.0*	92	2	2
Total:					
Tanganyika	1,508	*11.0*	3,855	100	100
Zanzibar	65	*11.0*	166	(+4)	(+4)
Tanzania	1,573	*11.0*	4,021	104	104

[a] Projections at 1962–1967 growth rate from 1963–1967 (average) base, except items in brackets.

An import bill of Shs. 4 billion for 1975 would be much too large. An extrapolation of exports on the 1965–67 base gives:

Table 138. *Export Value Projections, 1975*
(Shs. mn.)

	Growth rate %	1975 exports
Optimistic [a]:	*8.1*	3,429
	8	3,402
	7	3,127
Moderate:	*6.5*	2,998
	6	2,874
Pessimistic:	*5*	2,639

[a] The "optimistic" growth rate of 8.1% is obtained by taking the actual volume growth rate of 1962–1967 (8.6%) and subtracting the average annual fall in the export price index of developing countries in the decade ending 1967 (0.5%). This is a typical "bench-mark".

Putting together these extrapolations we have:

Table 139. *Trade Balance, 1962–1967 and 1975 Extrapolation*
(Shs. bn.)

	1962	1963	1964	1965	1966	1967	1975 Opt.	Mod.	Pess.
Exports	1.2	1.4	1.6	1.5	1.9	1.8	3.4	3.0	2.6
Imports	1.1	1.1	1.3	1.4	1.7	1.6	4.0	4.0	4.0
Balance	+0.1	+0.3	+0.3	+0.1	+0.2	+0.2	—0.6	—1.0	—1.4

The permissible trade deficit must depend on the service, transfer and capital accounts.

These have been discussed in previous chapters and we refer especially to Chapter 6 in which the foreign exchange savings arising from nationalising certain service enterprises have been pointed out[5]. Banking and insurance alone should show a saving of over Shs. 30 mn. As regards the extension of existing activities, tourism is expected to bring in an additional Shs. 200 mn. or so by the end of the Second Five-Year Plan. Then another important source of savings is the diversion of imports and exports from the Kenya port of Mombasa to Tanzanian ports.

Official donations and capital inflows to Tanzania have also been rising steeply; offset, however, in certain years by private outflows, which are volatile in large amounts.

This will depend perhaps most of all on the reactions of overseas investors to the socialist policies pursued in Tanzania. Let us merely say, however, that the funds available to finance a trade deficit should be substantially more, by 1975, than they were in 1967:

Table 140. *Foreign Exchange Available to Finance 1975 Imports*
(Shs. mn.)

Funds available other than export proceeds, additional to 1967 funds (Shs. mn.) Export growth rates %	500	450	400	350	300	250	200
8.1	3928	3879	3828	3778	3728	3678	3628
8	3900	3850	3800	3750	3700	3650	3600
7½	3761	3711	3661	3611	3561	3511	3461
7	3627	3577	3527	3477	3427	3377	3327
6½	3498	3448	3398	3348	3298	3248	3198
6	3374	3324	3274	3224	3174	3124	3074
5½	3054	3004	2954	2904	2854	2804	2754
5	2939	2889	2839	2789	2739	2689	2639

(lines are at Shs. 500 mn. intervals)

Let us now consider how the funds scheduled in Table 140 will be spent on different categories of imports.

Firstly, there is almost certainly a need for a *rising* flow of consumer imports, in real terms. This is not only a *political* need; it is needed because of the state of affairs in domestic manufacturing. Domestic industry is on the whole over-protected; a phase of attention to productivity and "Sanierung" is very probably required. Accordingly a growth rate of consumer imports of 2.5%

5 On the basis of approximate calculations for an incremental capital-output ratio.

in real terms (less than the population growth rate) is proposed as a suitable target figure. To this we must add at least 2% for price rises; in the decade ending 1967 the f.o.b. price index of goods exported by the U.K. rose 23%, by West Germany 14.3%, by Holland 6%, and by Japan 17%. Accordingly we must expect an increase of consumer imports in value terms of (at least) 4.5% p.a., which raises the 1975 level from 675 to 861 mn. Shs.; but this is essentially a *policy* variable.

Transport equipment, which between 1962 and 1967 grew at 18.0%, may be broken down into cars and other equipment. Cars may be held down, by fiscal or other methods, to the 1967 level of Shs. 27 mn. The remainder has grown at 17.9% partly because of the Zambia operation. How this will be affected by the railway and by the need to develop the internal economy is impossible to say, but it certainly seems unlikely that the 1975 figure need be much higher than the exceptionally high figures of recent years. Prior to the Zambia operations the growth rate was 12.6% which seems about right for the expansion of the internal market; the earlier figures projected on that basis give a value of Shs. 316 mn. for 1975, and also indicate that the present "exceptional" imports are levelling off at around Shs. 70 mn. p.a. For 1975, therefore, 316 (normal) + 100 (exceptional) + 27 (cars) are proposed, a total of Shs. 443 mn., which compares with Shs. 790 mn. in the mechanical extrapolation.

It seems odd that, while capital goods imports have risen at 13.5%, intermediate goods imports have risen at 14.5%. Part of this increase has been oil imports, which have risen fast. We may assume these in future to grow at no more than the rate of increase of transport equipment (9.8%) to reach a figure of Shs. 294 mn. by 1975. The remainder have risen at 16.4% which is extremely high by comparison with the 13.5% growth rate of capital goods imports, indicating bad investments relying excessively on imported raw materials. For the future it will be absolutely necessary to exercise vigilance over this point, and to develop domestic linkages instead. Assuming the non-oil intermediate input growth rate can be firmly held down to the capital goods growth rate we can take these two items together, as a further policy variable.

The following table shows the import bill resulting from various combinations of policy as regards the importation of capital and consumer goods. Once again the lines drawn through the table are at intervals of Shs. 500 mn., and each of these intervals corresponds to a similar interval in Table 140 above, indicating compatibility of assumptions.

It will be noticed that the top interval in Table 141 with imports of over Shs. 4 bn., is totally missing from the range of practical (and optimistic) possibilities shown in Table 140.

It will also be noticed that the interval boundaries in Table 140 are almost horizontal, which indicates that for the purposes of this exercise it does not

Table 141. *1975 Import Value Projections* [a]
(Shs. mn.)

Growth rate for capital goods %	Growth rate for consumer goods					
	5½%	4½%	3½%	2½%	1½%	½%
16				4019	3954	3894
15	4061	3979	3902	3832	2767	3707
14	3889	3807	3731	3660	3595	3535
13	3729	3646	3570	3500	3435	3375
12	3580	3480	3422	3351	3286	3226
11	3441	3359	3282	3212	3147	3087
10	3312	3229	3154	3083	3018	2958
9	3192	3110	3034	2963	2898	2838
8	3080	2997	2922	2851	2786	2726

[a] All growth rates are from a 1965–1967 average base.

make a great deal of difference what happens to the non-merchandise surplus. We can therefore concentrate on the three more crucial variables: the export growth rate, which is *in part* a policy variable; the consumer imports growth rate, which is (as mentioned above) determined in part by political necessity; and the capital goods imports growth rate, which in spite of its overriding importance in the long-run, has to be a dependent variable because it is the only one which it is always possible to treat as a residual.

The result is summarised in Table 142.

Table 142. *Feasible Growth Rates for Capital Goods Imports*
(% per annum, compound)

Export growth rates %	Growth rate for consumer goods					
	5½%	4½%	3½%	2½%	1½%	½%
8.1	13–14	13–15	13–15	14–15	14–16	15–16
8	13–14	13–15	13–15	13–15	14–15	15–16
7½	12–13	12–14	12–14	12–14	13–15	13–15
7	10–12	11–13	11–13	12–14	12–14	12–14
6½	9–11	9–12	10–12	11–13	11–13	11–13
6	8–10	9–11	9–11	10–12	10–12	11–13
5½	– 8	– 8	8– 9	8–10	8–10	8–11
5			– 8	8– 9	8– 9	8–10

The area bounded by the dotted line represents a number of possibilities all of which are consistent with maintaining approximately the 1962–67 growth rate for capital goods imports. It will be noticed that if this is to be continued with a high growth rate of consumer goods (5^1/$_2$%), a very optimistic assumption about export growth (8%) must be made. Even the "moderate" (6^1/$_2$%) assumption is incompatible with maintaining the 1962–67 growth rate of capital goods imports over a very wide range of possible behaviour patterns for consumer goods imports, from over 5^1/$_2$% p.a. growth to no growth at all.

The actual rate of growth of consumer goods imports from 1962–67 has been 1.7% per annum. Although the expatriate market makes up possibly one-third of the market, and is diminishing in numbers, the rapid rise of expatriates' per capita incomes and the supposedly high marginal propensity to import of the Tanzanian two-thirds indicate that the demand will grow despite the exodus of expatriates. Recently, rises in import duties have choked off the demand, and textiles in particular were affected by a downward adjustment of inventories in 1967. Consequently consumer goods imports actually dropped 19% between 1966 and 1967. Between 1962 and 1966 the rate of growth was 7.5%, however. The figure proposed as a target is 4.5% which the present writer regards as, realistically, about the lowest attainable in the context of planned economic expansion with GDP growing at about 6.7%.

Table 142 indicates that if this figure is accepted together with a moderate expectation of export growth, a painful choice has to be made between incurring heavy external debt burdens and reducing the rate of growth of capital goods imports to under 12%. The policy of long-run self-reliance indicates the latter strategy.

A growth rate for capital goods imports of 10%–12% as compared with the actual rate of 13.5% achieved in 1962–67 does not mean a slow pace of development. It should not be inconsistent[6] with a growth rate of 6.7% for GDP, which was the target in the First Five-Year Development Plan, nor with a certain rise in the capital goods' share of imports.

This kind of non-predictive reckoning leads to the conclusion that the situation is likely to become, not a desperate foreign exchange crisis, but one in which the available resources will be tightly stretched to meet the political demands upon them: demands for current consumption (of imported consumer goods) and for future consumption (by the use of imported capital goods). The crucial factors are those twin unpredictables, the agricultural export performance and the political situation; and these are of course linked, since good political leadership has an impact on the rural labour-input (inter alia).

It would appear that given a fair measure of success in this area, the course on which Tanzania is embarked is a viable one and no heavy injections of foreign finance will be required.

---

6 See also M. J. H. YAFFEY: *The Effect of Nationalisation on Current External Payments*, ERB Paper 69.2., Dar es Salaam, 1969.

APPENDIX I

Tanzania Mainland: Summary Balance of Payments, 1961–1966

Current Account Transactions

	Gross Receipts (credits) Shs. mn.					
	1961	1962	1963	1964	1965	1966 (prov.)
A. Goods and Services						
1. Merchandise Transactions	1,063	1,059	1,304	1,499	1,398	1,761
2. Non-Monetary Gold Movements	25	25	26	23	23	14
3. a) Freight etc. on International Shipments	3	3	5	6	8	10
b) Insurance on International Shipments	2	2	3	3	3	4
4. Other Transportation	27	33	43	51	61	75
5. Foreign Travel	31	40	47	47	54	62
6. International Investment Income	36	38	38	46	46	41
7. Government Transactions n.e.i.						
a) Military	14	3	3	3	4	2
b) Other	13	20	28	31	32	38
8. Other Services	8	10	10	12	15	16
Total Goods and Services	1,222	1,233	1,507	1,721	1,644	2,023
B. Transfer Payments						
9. Private Transfer Payments	48	46	51	52	53	45
10. Government Transfer Payments	97	141	110	96	110	72
Total Transfer Payments	145	187	161	148	163	117
A + B all Goods, Services, and Transfers	1,367	1,420	1,668	1,869	1,807	2,140

Current Account Transactions

	Gross Payments (debits) Shs. mn.					
	1961	1962	1963	1964	1965	1966 (prov.)
A. Goods and Services						
1. Merchandise Transactions	1,053	1,094	1,123	1,253	1,373	1,722
2. Non-Monetary Gold Movements	–	–	–	–	1	1
3. a) Freight etc. on International Shipments	4	3	3	3	3	3
b) Insurance on International Shipments	1	1	1	2	2	2
4. Other Transportation	40	41	52	49	50	56
5. Foreign Travel	47	51	45	41	42	29
6. International Investment Income	99	112	163	139	133	160
7. Government Transactions n.e.i.						
a) Military	–	–	–	–	–	1
b) Other	6	10	13	16	21	20
8. Other Services	37	42	39	38	39	39
Total Goods and Services	1,287	1,354	1,439	1,541	1,664	2,033
B. Transfer Payments						
9. Private Transfer Payments	55	65	56	58	56	46
10. Government Transfer Payments	41	59	68	75	80	86
Total Transfer Payments	96	124	124	133	136	132
A + B all Goods, Services, and Transfers	1,383	1,478	1,563	1,674	1,800	2,165

Current Account Transactions

	1961	1962	Net Credits Shs. mn. 1963	1964	1965	1966 (prov.)
A. Goods and Services						
1. Merchandise Transactions	10	Dr[a]35	181	246	25	39
2. Non-Monetary Gold Movements	25	25	25	23	22	13
3. a) Freight etc. on International Shipments	Dr1	–	2	3	5	7
b) Insurance on International Shipments	1	1	1	1	2	2
4. Other Transportation	Dr13	Dr8	Dr10	2	11	18
5. Foreign Travel	Dr16	Dr10	2	7	12	34
6. International Investment Income	Dr63	Dr74	Dr125	Dr93	Dr87	Dr121
7. Government Transactions n.e.i.						
a) Military	14	3	3	3	4	1
b) Other	7	10	15	15	11	18
8. Other Services	Dr28	Dr32	Dr29	Dr26	Dr24	Dr29
Total Goods and Services	Dr64	Dr120	63	181	Dr19	Dr18
B. Transfer Payments						
9. Private Transfer Payments	Dr7	Dr19	Dr5	Dr6	Dr3	Dr1
10. Government Transfer Payments	55	81	41	22	31	Dr14
Total Transfer Payments	48	62	36	16	28	Dr15
A + B all Goods, Services, and Transfers	Dr16	Dr58	99	197	8	Dr33

[a] Dr = debit

Capital Account and Monetary Movements

	Liabilities (Net increase or credit) Shs. mn.					
	1961	1962	1963	1964	1965	1966 (prov.)
C. *Capital Movements*						
11. a) Private Long Term	50	58	155	79	103	136
b) Government Enterprises Long Term	45	Dr4	Dr5	8	Dr1	79
12. a) Private Short Term	–	–	8	14	10	2
b) Government Enterprises Short Term	–	–	–	6	Dr6	–
13. Local Government	–	–	–	–	–	–
14. Central Government						
a) Long Term	59	43	54	88	82	87
b) Short Term	30	26	Dr15	–	2	Dr25
15. Central Monetary Institutions:						
a) E.A.C.B. & Bank of Tanzania	–	–	–	–	–	–
b) Accounts with I.M.F.	–	–	–	–	–	–
16. Other Monetary Institutions:						
a) The Commercial Banks	–	–	–	–	–	Dr91
b) Post Office Savings Bank	–	–	–	–	–	–
Total Capital	184	123	197	195	190	188

	Assets (Net increase or debit) Shs. mn.					
	1961	1962	1963	1964	1965	1966 (prov.)
C. *Capital Movements*						
11. a) Private Long Term	74	86	97	184	124	8
b) Government Enter- prises Long Term	5	6	4	13	27	Cr7
12. a) Private Short Term	2	Cr[a]11	Cr13	34	30	16
b) Government Enter- prises Short Term	25	Cr20	Cr3	Cr3	1	1
13. Local Government	Cr2	9	Cr2	–	–	–
14. Central Government						
a) Long Term	5	9	7	2	Cr37	19
b) Short Term	–	20	21	–	2	Cr6
15. Central Monetary Institutions:						
a) E.A.C.B. & Bank of Tanzania	Cr37	–	30	Cr9	25	147
b) Accounts with I.M.F.	–	18	–	–	–	13
16. Other Monetary Institutions:						
a) The Commercial Banks	97	8	29	Cr81	Cr52	Cr65
b) Post Office Savings Bank	Cr3	Cr1	1	–	–	Cr22
Total Capital	166	124	171	140	120	104

[a] Cr = credit

Capital Account and Monetary Movements

			Net Credit Shs. mn.			
	1961	1962	1963	1964	1965	1966 (prov.)
C. *Capital Movements*						
11. a) Private Long Term	Dr24	Dr28	57	Dr105	Dr21	128
b) Government Enterprises Long Term	40	Dr10	Dr8	Dr5	Dr28	86
12. a) Private Short Term	Dr2	12	22	Dr20	Dr20	Dr14
b) Government Enterprises Short Term	Dr25	20	3	10	Dr8	Dr1
13. Local Government	2	Dr9	2	–	–	–
14. Central Government						
a) Long Term	54	34	47	86	118	67
b) Short Term	30	6	Dr36	–	–	Dr18
15. Central Monetary Institutions:						
a) E.A.C.B. & Bank of Tanzania	37	–	Dr30	9	Dr25	Dr146
b) Accounts with I.M.F.	–	Dr18	–	–	–	Dr12
16. Other Monetary Institutions:						
a) The Commercial Banks	Dr97	Dr8	Dr29	81	52	Dr25
b) Post Office Savings Bank	3	1	Dr1	–	–	22
Total Capital	18	Dr0	28	56	68	87

General Summary of Net Credits

			Shs. mn.			
	1961	1962	1963	1964	1965	1966 (prov.)
Merchandise and Gold	35	Dr10	206	269	47	53
Services	Dr99	Dr110	Dr138	Dr88	Dr67	Dr71
Transfers	48	62	36	15	28	Dr15
Capital and Monetary Movements	18	Dr1	28	55	68	86
Net Errors and Omissions	Dr2	59	Dr132	Dr251	Dr76	Dr53

Source: Communications by East African Statistical Department, Nairobi; data in thousands of pounds converted to millions of shillings at par. Items may not add to total shown because of decimal rounding.

APPENDIX II

External Debt Servicing

Some further light is shed on the capital account by the following statement:

"External public debt servicing in 1967/68 was of the order of 5⁰/₀ of total foreign exchange earnings. While this is a relatively low figure, projections suggest that if net external borrowing by the public sector, including parastatals, were to average Shs. 200 mn. annually, it would tend to rise each year by approximately 0.5⁰/₀ of foreign earnings, unless very favourable loan terms or very high rates of export growth were achieved." (*Background to the Budget*, 1968/69.)

This may be illustrated numerically by using rough estimates derived from the data already presented in the capital account section.

First we estimate interest payments as follows:

					Shs. mn.
Funded debt	Shs. 192.9 mn. (in 1965) at	5⁰/₀	=	9.6
Unfunded debt	Shs. 565.2 mn. (in 1967) at	3.7⁰/₀	=	20.9
Parastatal debt	Shs. 130 mn. (in 1968) at	6⁰/₀	=	3.4
				33.9

(EASD data show above actuals in 1965 at 37.3) For 1968 total, say . . . 40.0
Compensation for nationalisation, starting 1969. Shs. 205 mn. × 6¹/₂⁰/₀ . . 13.0

53.0

Second we estimate the total implied external debt servicing:

Total foreign exchange earnings, 1968 official estimate = Shs. 2,122.5 mn. 5⁰/₀ of this is Shs. 106 mn. Assuming earnings grow at 6⁰/₀ per year, and percentage needed for debt servicing rises at 0.5⁰/₀ per year, we have:

Year	Earnings	Debt Service	⁰/₀
1968	2,122.5	106	5
1969	2,249.8	124	5¹/₂
1970	2,384.8	143	6
1971	2,527.9	164	6¹/₂

In 1968 the estimated outstanding, excluding nationalisation compensation, was Shs. 1,093 mn., and the interest charge about Shs. 40 mn. Taking the assumptions of a Shs. 200 mn. net annual increase and a constant average interest rate, we have:

Year	Outstanding	Interest	Compensation Interest	Total Interest
1968	1,093	40	–	40
1969	1,293	47	13	60
1970	1,493	54	13	67
1971	1,693	61	13	74

Deducting these interest payments from the projected debt servicing we arrive at projected redemption:

Year	Debt Service	Interest Element	Repayment of Principal
1968	106	40	66
1969	124	60	64
1970	143	67	76
1971	164	74	90

APPENDIX III

Example of an Exclusive Agency Agreement

AN AGREEMENT made this first day of February One Thousand Nine Hundred and Fifty Eight, between B.S.A. Cycles Ltd., whose registered office is situated at Coventry Road, Sheldon, Birmingham 26, England (hereinafter called "the Manufacturer") of the one part, and Messrs. Smith Mackenzie & Co. of P.O. Box 30090, Nairobi, Kenya (hereinunder called "the Distributor") of the other part, WHEREBY IT IS MUTUALLY AGREED AS FOLLOWS:

1. This agreement shall remain in force from the 1st January, 1958 until the 31st January, 1961, and if the same is continued thereafter, then it shall continue subject to three months' notice of cancellation in writing on either side.

2. The Manufacturer concedes to the Distributor during the period of this agreement the sole right of selling B.S.A. and New Hudson branded Bicycles and spare parts thereof, in the East African territories namely, KENYA, UGANDA, TANGANYIKA and ZANZIBAR, and undertakes that he will not supply same to any firm in that territory except to the Distributor while the Distributor undertakes to order and pay for a quantity of Bicycles not less than a figure to be subsequently agreed with the Manufacturer as being a reasonable annual target, or such less quantity as the Manufacturer can supply.

Provided always and it is hereby agreed, that nothing herein contained shall prevent the Manufacturer from supplying direct Bicycles or other goods into the territory hereinbefore mentioned, to Government Departments, Crown Agents for the Colonies or other official organisations.

3. The Manufacturer agrees to make available to the Distributor B.S.A. or New Hudson models equivalent to their counterparts marketed under the Raleigh or other trade marks of Raleigh Industries Ltd. and the Distributor undertakes not to sell any of these models at a lower cash price than that ruling at the time for its equivalent model in the Raleigh range.

4. The Distributor undertakes to take delivery of the number of Bicycles they may require in approximately equal monthly lots divided over the period of duration of this agreement and will give detailed specifications for the same at least four months before the date at which the first delivery is to be effected. The Manufacturer shall keep to these delivery dates ar far as possible but he shall not be liable in damages or otherwise for any delay whatsoever. It is, however, provided that if delay is excessive, the Distributor shall have the option of cancelling the quantity of Bicycles so delayed. The Distributor further agrees that he will keep a representative stock of the Manufacturer's bicycles during the period of this agreement.

5. The Standard specification of the bicycles shall be as per catalogue but the Manufacturer reserves the right to make alterations at any time. The guarantee of

the Manufacturer as to quality is limited to that stated in the Manufacturer's current catalogue.

6. The Distributor undertakes to maintain suitable premises, including Show Rooms and Service Stations; to keep an adequate stock of spare parts to service the Manufacturer's bicycles throughout his territory defined and to employ a full time Representative who will be solely concerned with actively promoting sales of B.S.A. and New Hudson bicycles and spare parts throughout the whole of his Territory.

7. The Distributor shall not directly or indirectly sell the Manufacturer's bicycles and bicycle parts to buyers resident outside his territory defined.

8. The Distributor agrees to disburse on advertising in the East African territories a minimum sum of 3/– per machine imported by him into the territories during the course of the first calendar year. In respect of the second and third year of this agreement the figure will be subject to agreement at a later date.

9. The present prices and conditions upon which the Manufacturer agrees to supply goods under this agreement to the Distributor as per schedule, which the Distributor hereby acknowledges he has received, but the Manufacturer hereby reserves the right to alter or amend these prices at any time, without notice.

10. The Distributor undertakes during the period of this agreement not to sell any Bicycles other than B.S.A., New Hudson or other products of Raleigh Industries, Ltd., without first having obtained the written consent of the Manufacturer to do so, such consent not to be unreasonably withheld.

11. In case of non-fulfilment by the Distributor, or any of the conditions of this agreement, or if a receiving order be made against the Distributor, or in case the Distributor being a Limited Company, shall go into liquidation (except for the purpose of reconstruction or amalgamation) or have a Receiver of any of its assets appointed, the Manufacturer has the right either to suspend deliveries or to cancel the agreement immediately, by giving notice to the Distributor in writing at any time.

12. The Manufacturer shall refer to the Distributor any Trade and Retail enquiries received from his Territory.

13. The terms of payment are as follows:

> Net cash against documents in London,
> through Messrs. Gray, Dawes & Co. Ltd.,
> 122 Leadenhall Street, London, E.C. 3.

14. It is hereby agreed by and between the parties hereto that this agreement shall be construed according to the laws of England and that any dispute which may arise shall be settled by referring same to the jurisdiction of the English law and its courts.

15. The Distributor is not authorised to transport any business, give any warranty, make any representation or incur any liability on behalf of the Manufacturer.

AS WITNESS the hands of the parties hereto, the date and year first above written.

Witness to the signature of

For and on behalf of
SMITH MACKENZIE & CO. LTD.
Director.

Witness to the signature of

For and on behalf of
B.S.A. CYCLES LIMITED
Sales Director.

252

APPENDIX IV

Authorised Inter-Company Accounts (External)

Certain companies are authorised by the Exchange Controller to operate running accounts with companies outside the Scheduled Territories. Accounts with companies in Kenya/Uganda are permitted with neither formality nor scrutiny.

The major companies involved have been sisal estates, oil companies, and shipping agencies. The oil companies run up debts for imports (together with small invisibles and transfers) and settle quarterly or at even longer intervals; the debit balance may exceed Shs. 5 mn., so that more prompt settlement would be of some significance. Shipping agents collect occasional freight charges and passenger fares, for which they debit themselves together with small invisibles and transfers, deducting their commissions; settlement is generally quarterly and can be in significant sums. One company for which information is available paid to various shipping lines in mid-September, 1966 Shs. 620,000 and still had Shs. 308,000 of liabilities at the end of that month; a shift, for example, to monthly settlements would therefore probably involve a short-term outflow of some millions of shillings taking all the shipping agencies together.

This is clearly a field in which more research could profitably be undertaken.

The sisal companies are now so effectively under Government control (for the most part) that their terms of payment ought not to be a source of concern.

APPENDIX V

Relations Between German and British East Africa

1903–1909

(quoted in H. BRODE: *British and German East Africa*, English edition, London, 1911)

Total Value (in Sterling) of Direct Trade between German East Africa and British East Africa

Year	Total Import to British East Africa	Imported from German East Africa	Per Cent of Total Import	Total Export of British East Africa	Exported to German East Africa	Per Cent of Total Export	Grand Total of Trade between German East Africa and British East Africa
1903	436,947	–	–	159,815	1,065	0.6	1,065
1904	518,143	10,585	2.7	234,664	503	0.2	11,088
1905	672,360	10,971	1.6	332,839	2,305	0.7	13,276
1906	753,647	10,824	1.4	440,705	2,981	0.6	13,805
1907	799,717	8,070	1.1	515,052	2,875	0.5	10,945
1908	797,158	10,488	1.3	436,313	2,982	0.7	13,470
1909	775,246	17,079	2.2	590,057	4,532	0.8	21,611

Value (in Marks) of Import and Export into and from German East Africa in Transit through British East Africa

	1904	1905	1906	1907	1908	1909	1910 (from January to June)
Import							
Moshi	122,681	169,534	247,114	191,041	290,998	432,401	178,176
Schirati	116,780	93,585	123,574	93,130	46,135	77,695	40,635
Muansa	602,850	1,125,423	2,390,154	2,480,996	1,741,294	1,859,811	1,504,729
Bukoba	501,239	509,266	754,386	770,427	465,461	1,090,349	645,476
Total	1,343,550	1,897,808	3,515,228	3,535,594	2,543,888	3,460,256	2,369,016
Grand total of import	14,338,888	17,655,350	25,152,851	23,806,369	25,152,851	33,941,700	–
Per cent	*9*	*11*	*14*	*15*	*10*	*10.2*	–
Export							
Moshi	182,450	149,018	163,497	132,456	119,040	175,857	94,338
Schirati	88,338	150,958	184,643	195,263	94,767	174,677	91,082
Muansa	423,246	1,353,326	1,957,959	2,407,965	1,389,174	1,694,444	1,318,567
Bukoba	434,925	511,834	762,189	721,870	439,501	956,953	613,374
Total	1,128,959	2,165,136	3,068,288	3,457,554	2,042,482	3,001,931	2,117,361
Grand total of export	8,950,565	9,949,661	10,994,712	12,500,179	10,873,856	13,119,500	–
Per cent	*13*	*22*	*28*	*28*	*19*	*22.9*	–

Value (in Sterling) of Transit Goods Imported into British East Africa

1903	18,400
1904	57,067
1905	131,751
1906	172,216
1907	189,647
1908	157,020
1909	228,002

Value (in Sterling) of Goods Exported from German East Africa
in Transit through British East Africa

1903	6,107
1904	43,270
1905	93,179
1906	138,030
1907	174,661
1908	102,119
1909	167,000

According to British statistics.

Gross Receipts of Uganda Railway from German Lake Ports Traffic, 1904–1910

	Passengers Rs	Goods Rs	Total Rs
1 Feb. 1904 – 31 Mar. 1904	387	13,998	14,385
1 Apr. 1904 – 31 Mar. 1905	17,529	200,871	218,400
1 Apr. 1905 – 31 Mar. 1906	51,597	438,449	490,046
1 Apr. 1906 – 31 Mar. 1907	41,950	210,093	252,043
1 Apr. 1907 – 31 Mar. 1908	76,061	563,858	639,919
1 Apr. 1908 – 31 Mar. 1909	n. a.	553,748	n. a.
1 Apr. 1909 – 31 Mar. 1910	58,356	662,203	720,559

APPENDIX VI

Schematic Evolution of Trade

It may be useful to view the development of Tanzania's external trade relations schematically, and to compare this schema with a standard or normative schema. A normative schema has been provided by Ignacy SACHS, using the following notation (we have modified it very slightly):

M = machines and equipment;

R = raw materials both mineral and agricultural, also fuel and power, and transport;

C = consumer goods including C_N (necessities) and C_L (luxuries).

255

The subscripts t and m indicate production by traditional and modern sectors respectively.

In Stage 1 the economy is backward and stagnant; exports are raw materials (traditional) and/or consumer luxuries (beverages). In Stage 2 machinery is imported. In Stage 3 these machines produce new raw materials for export (Rm) and require new imported inputs (Rm). To feed urban workers, food (C_{Nm}) may have to be imported. In Stage 4 machines to produce machines ($M \rightarrow M$) begin to be imported. Stage 5 is a developed economy suffering from a degree of dualism and absence of machinery exports. Stage 6 is a balanced economy with all types of imports and exports. Ignacy Sachs adds:

> "Needless to say, this schema provides a mere illustration of the likely direction of changes, and the concrete paths followed by different countries obviously do not conform to a uniform pattern."

We may compare this standard pattern to the actual evolution in the case of Tanzania on the basis of the evidence presented in Chapter 2. Schematically this appears to have been as follows. To Sachs's notation we add transport (T) and services (S), and consumer luxuries which *become* necessities, particularly textiles (C^*).

Schema of Evolution of Tanzania's Foreign Trade

Stage	Period	Production	Exports	Imports
1.	–1890	$C_{Nt} + R_t + T_t$	R_t	$C_{Lm} + C^*_m$
	German control			
2.	1890–1914	$C_{Nt} + R_t + T_t$ plus T_m (railways, roads, marine) and some S (banks, shops)	R_t plus R_m	$C_{Lm} + C^*_m$ plus $M (\rightarrow C, \rightarrow R_m, \rightarrow T_m)$ $+ C_{Nm}$(rise) $+ R_m$ $+$ some S
3.	(1914–1918)	(same $+ C_{Lm}$)	(none)	(none)
	British control			
4.	1918–1939	same as Period 2	Same as Period 2	Reduced M; more C_{Lm} (expatriates); otherwise as Period 2.
	War-time controls			
5.	1939–1951	same	same	M restricted sharply; C^*_m (textiles, food) restricted; jute (R) restricted; S increasing (Govt. activities); otherwise as Period 4.
	Devaluation; Korean War			
6.	1951–1961	same	same	same with more T and more M, R, and C_{Lm}

256

Stage	Period	Production	Exports	Imports
	Independence			
7.	1961–1966	same plus C_{Lm} and C^*_m	same plus C_{Lm} (very small)	continuation of trend of Period 6, with more S also
	Arusha Declaration			
8.	1967–	same and more S, i.e. now lacking only M, and more S and R_m for balance; C_L inhibited by incomes policy	same and some S, i.e. now lacking only M, with pre- ponderance still of R_t	C_L (stagnant); C_N (stagnant); R rising (esp. fuels); S sharply reduced; M and T rising further.

The main differences between the present position and the balance of SACHS's final stage are:

- Lack of a machine-producing sector, which will always be inhibited by the small-ness of the country;
- Continuation of traditional sector;
- Exports are still chiefly R;
- Continuing net import of services;
- Export of C_L continues to be very small.

The non-normal switches in the pattern and departures from the Sachs model are clearly due to political events, which the model, naturally, could not take into account. The model moreover assumes no Government intervention. Nevertheless, the secular forces can be seen at work, even if sometimes in the guise of a fortuitous disturbance.

APPENDIX VII

Methods of Paying for Tanzania's Imports

The letter of credit is a form of payment which is generally used, at the exporter's insistence, when he ascribes a weak credit-rating to the importer. Since the countries of East Africa are poor and underdeveloped, one might suppose that East African importers would in the main fall into this category and be obliged to open letters of credit. However, such is not the case. A recent survey in Uganda showed that only 10% of imports were paid for under letters of credit; for Kenya and Tanzania no statistics are available but the proportion is believed to be a minority. The principal cases where letters of credit are required appear to be:

- imports from the U.S.A., which in general ascribes a low credit-rating to East Africa at the present time;

- imports from Japan, which normally insists on letters of credit for balance of payments reasons; and
- revolving documentary credits placed in favour of London confirming houses (more about these, below).

In general the letter of credit follows standard international practice. The importer requests the National Bank of Commerce ("the issuing bank") to request a foreign bank to open a documentary credit in favour of the exporter whereby he will receive immediate payment in his own currency on presentation of shipping documents (or, in the case of Kenya, Uganda, Zambia: overland freight documents) evidencing the dispatch of the articles ordered.

The wording of the credit, which must ensure without being impossibly detailed that the articles were dispatched *as ordered,* is a skilled task, the difficulty of which undoubtedly makes letters of credit unpopular in Tanzania where skills are scarce.

The foreign bank notifies the National Bank of Commerce that it has paid out under the credit and (normally) reimbursed itself by debiting the account of the N.B.C. on the same date. The latter bank reimburses itself by debiting the account of its customer, the importer. The importer then has to wait for the arrival, unloading, inspection, transportation and sale of the goods before he is placed in funds himself. Various forms of finance are available from the N.B.C. to provide accommodation to the importer; the simplest is the "overdraft facility" which carries interest at 7–9% according to the status of the borrower.

In cases where the credit rating of the borrower is poor, the Bank may fear that his account will not be sufficiently in funds to bear the debit when the use of the letter of credit is notified. In such cases, a sum is debited to the account at the time of opening the letter of credit — usually between 10% and 25% of the value of the letter of credit. This is placed in a separate (frozen) account. If the exporter is slow in taking up the credit, this "margin requirement" can mean considerable extra cost.

The most common form of payment for imports is not the letter of credit but the bill for collection. The exporter in this case sends the shipping documents through his own bank to the National Bank of Commerce requesting the latter to collect payment from its customer and make the remittance. This bill may be payable "on sight" in which case the importer will have to take an overdraft or other form of finance from the N.B.C. as described above; or it may be a usance bill, payable (typically) 90 days after sight, in which case the exporter is supplying the finance (no doubt by arrangement with his own bank) at a cost included in the invoice price of the goods.

A hybrid form of bill for collection, possibly peculiar to East Africa, is the bill which is worded for payment "on sight" but which is understood to allow the importer time to await the arrival of the goods and inspect them before payment is made. This is in effect a usance bill, with tenor varying up to 90 days or even more. This originated in pre-War days when there was virtually no airmail postal service. The bills would arrive by sea at the same time as the goods. They now arrive by air before the goods but the same terms of payment are extended and the same wording has lingered on in the documents [1].

In cases where the exporter provides (or arranges) credit, he will if possible insure against the risk of default through one of the state agencies which exist for that

---

1 It is excusable because to make the bill payable on arrival would contravene mercantile legislation which requires payment at a "fixed or ascertainable future time". The payment is therefore requested immediately but a variable grace period is added.

purpose in several countries. This is likely to add upwards of $1^1/2^0/0$ to the invoice price of the goods[2]. Should no such arrangements exist in the exporter's country, the exporter himself or his bank may bear the risk and then it is reasonable to suppose that the implicit risk-premium included in the invoice price will be even higher[3]. Alternatively a confirming house can be used.

It is common in East Africa for the importer to make use of an overseas "confirming house" particularly in London. Some of these houses are companies affiliated to important expatriate importers in East Africa. Some smaller houses are offshoots of East African citizen importers. Others again are independent. Most are affiliated to a merchant bank.

The procedure most frequently operated is as follows. The importer has the "agency" or "franchise" for the products of a particular manufacturer. He makes out an order (probably each month) and sends it to his confirming house. The latter passes it on to the manufacturer and follows it up with telephone calls to ensure speedy delivery, notifying the importer of the ship on which the goods are to be placed. On shipment the confirming house pays the manufacturer and raises either a sight draft or a usance draft against the importer. If foreign finance is required a usance draft will be raised and lodged with the co-operating bank. It may be sent at maturity to the National Bank of Commerce, or it may be paid under a revolving letter of credit.

The revolving letter of credit is an instrument frequently used in trade between Britain and her colonies or former colonies. The British exporter has the advantage of having a claim upon a *bank* in the importer's country as well as upon the importer himself; frequently it is a British bank, though no longer so in Tanzania. The importer has the advantage that he need not open a separate letter of credit for each order with scrupulously correct wording in each case; he leaves the paper-work almost entirely to the confirming house. Also the drawing of usuance bills under the letter of credit provides him with a source of finance in addition to his local sources, and it is one which he would not get if the confirming house, to whom he is well known, did not support the application to the bank concerned.

It is fairly clear that the confirming house does very little *work;* it is merely a post-office. But it provides access to a new source of finance for the importer, and one which moreover is usually cheaper than is available in the developing countries where interest rates are typically high. It is particularly attractive for the small-scale importer, whose local borrowing-power is severely limited, and who finds it difficult to muster the skills needed to open independent letters of credit, and whose purchases are so sporadic that knowledge of delivery dates is important.

SYRETT, in *Finance of Oversea Trade* (London, 1964) writes:

> "The practice of ordering through indenters[4] is much more common in trade between the United Kingdom and the Dominions and Colonies than it is in (British) trade with other markets; this is for reasons associated with the economic development of the Empire, which, though interesting, cannot be considered germane to the present study."

---

2 There is, however, a long-term downward trend in the cost of official export credit insurance cover.

3 Since the spreading of risk is not so great, and the information used for assessing risk is not so abundant. The official export credit insurance schemes tend to be nonprofit-making, moreover.

4 Indenting houses, i.e. confirming houses. Working on closed indents is the most common practice. A closed indent is an order which specifies the manufacturer's name; intelligent buying is thereby ruled out.

What these houses in fact appear to be doing is taking the margin between the cost of borrowing in the U.K. and the cost of borrowing in developing countries; as is well known, the latter tends to be high. In exchange they perform some clerical work, but in the case of closed indents (where no market research is required because the manufacturer is named by the importer) this is nominal. At the present time, interest rates in the U.K. are exceptionally high and it is interesting to note that as those rates haven risen, confirmation margins have narrowed from the $5-7^{1}/_{2}\%$ mentioned by SYRETT (1964) to $2^{1}/_{2}-3\%$ which is normally paid by East African importers. Sometimes even lower figures ($1^{3}/_{4}-2\%$) are now being quoted in bulk lines, and can be applied to non-bulk lines by good negotiation. Whether the commissions will rise again when U.K. interest rates are normalised remains to be seen. The interesting point is that the cost of the work of the confirming houses must be no more than $2^{1}/_{2}\%$, and if the function could be transferred to countries with lower interest charges such as the U.S.A., Switzerland, etc., with the commissions held down (through ownership and control by the importers), the cost of the imports would be significantly reduced. The vaunted standing of the confirming houses ("the exporter relies on their good name") is not essential since they pay the exporter spot cash.

Let us now compare the costs of the various forms of payment. We will assume two importers, "B" and "W" whose credit-rating is best and worst respectively. We will assume that finance is required for three months, and the rates applicable for borrowing are 9% in the U.K., 6% in Holland (these two representing a range of realistic possibilities) and in East Africa 7% for "B" and 10% for "W". We will take the confirming house commission as $2^{1}/_{2}\%$; export credit insurance cover as $1^{1}/_{2}\%$ per transaction; banks' opening commissions on documentary credits as $1/_{4}\%$ and collection commissions $1/_{8}\%$; other commissions and charges are ignored. It is assumed at first that the importer does not purchase foreign exchange on a forward basis.

The various forms of payment compared here are:

1. foreign finance arranged by a confirming house by the discounting of 90-day bills (abbreviated CONF 90-days);

2. documentary acceptance credits, i.e. letters of credit which call for the acceptance of 90-day bills by the issuing bank so that they can be discounted by another foreign bank, or the same one (abbreviated D/A BILLS);

3. usance bills for collection, credit being provided by the manufacturer (abbreviated 90-DAY COLLS);

4. the East African "sight draft" payable after arrival of goods on a collection basis; assuming 90-day effective credit, this is the same as 3. above (abbreviated ARRIVALS);

5. documentary letters of credit providing for sight drafts to be raised against the importer and paid by the N.B.C. on an "advances" basis [5] (abbreviated D/P BILLS); and

6. credit provided by the N.B.C. against the security of 90-day bills drawn in sterling by a London confirming house against the importer (abbreviated SBAA meaning sterling bills advanced against).

---

5 The margin requirement imposed by the bank is assumed to add $1/_{4}\%$ to the importer's costs; this figure is arrived at by taking a 25% margin over 1 month (turnover every three months) at 9%. This is not applicable to "B".

Alternative Payment Methods: Cost to Importer

		Imports from U.K.		Imports from Holland	
		"B" %	"W" %	"B" %	"W" %
Foreign Finance	1. Conf. 90-Days	4.875	4.875	3.875	3.875
	2. D/A Bills	4.000	n. av.	3.250	n. av.
	3. 90-Day Colls	3.875	n. av.	3.125	n. av.
	4. Arrivals	3.875	n. av.	3.125	n. av.
Local Finance	5. D/P Bills	2.000	2.750	2.000	2.750
	6. SBAA	4.250	5.000	4.250	5.000

n. av. = not available

It can be seen from this that for the importer with the weakest credit-rating ("W"), option 5. is the cheapest, viz. letters of credit relying on local finance. This is open to the objections already mentioned, which leaves option 1. next in order of preference. This explains the widespread use of confirming houses. Option 6. is an additional method which may be resorted to where the need for additional finance is very pressing, especially in dealing with U.K. goods, for which option 6. is not much dearer than option 1.

For the importer with the best credit-rating ("B"), it appears that local finance (option 5) is somewhat cheaper than foreign finance especially if the latter is very expensive, but also where the foreign borrowing costs are not unusually high (e.g. Holland). Given also the objections already mentioned against opening letters of credit, the preference for foreign finance as in options 3. and 4. is however understandable, especially 4. which is the most advantageous.

These details explain the traditional pattern of forms of payment in East Africa.

Since December 11th, 1967, the East African banks have permitted importers to buy foreign exchange on a forward basis at a premium of 2% per annum. Assuming that it becomes normal practice to use this facility, importers who are receiving credit from abroad (options 1, 2, 3, and 4) will have to add $1/2\%$ to their costs. The comparison now becomes:

Cost to Importer, with Forward Cover, of Alternative Payment Methods

		Imports from U.K.		Imports from Holland	
		"B" %	"W" %	"B" %	"W" %
Foreign Finance	1. Conf. 90-Days	5.375	5.375	4.375	4.375
	2. D/A Bills	4.500	n. av.	3.750	n. av.
	3. 90-Day Colls	4.375	n. av.	3.625	n. av.
	4. Arrivals	4.375	n. av.	3.625	n. av.
Local Finance	5. D/P Bills	2.000	2.750	2.000	2.750
	6. SBAA	4.250	5.000	4.250	5.000

This makes some difference. The weak importer "W" may now find it cheaper to have his confirming house bills discounted locally rather than in a centre with very high rates like London. The stronger firm "B" may find it desirable to open letters of credit with local finance (option 5) despite the unpleasant paper-work involved, rather than pay after 90 days on a collections basis with a differential of up to 2.375% in London.

Those importers who believe that the high rates in Europe have come to stay, at least for a few years, will therefore tend to try to make arrangements for more local finance. This shift must, of course, affect the balance of payments adversely.

It is not likely, however, that importers are highly mobile in this respect. Many will continue to use foreign finance because the nature of their business causes them to use all possible sources to the utmost. Others will disregard the cost of foreign finance and credit insurance because it is implicit in the invoice price, which tends to go up periodically anyway without adverse effects on profits. It is not customary for the financing and insurance charge to be expressly disclosed in the consumer goods trade [6] since importers automatically take whatever credit is allowed to them. The tightness of money in East Africa has prevented the emergence of any habits among borrowers of choosing carefully the cheapest source of credit. But now, with unprecedently dear money in the U.K. and rising rates elsewhere, the calculation will begin to be a normal part of business life. It may not be long before borrowers' responses are sufficiently alert to cause noticeable shifts across the balance of payments. In that event, the powers of the central banks to vary interest rates and/or the premium on forward exchange cover will probably have to be invoked.

APPENDIX VIII

Criteria for Consideration of Import-Substituting Projects

1. Net Value Added per Unit of Capital Employed

"Value added" for this purpose is adjusted upwards where the price of domestic inputs is expected to increase, or where the new demand for such inputs is likely to transform methods of production in such a manner as to release additional resources (either of same inputs or of their factors of production) for ready absorption into existing uses; *minus* any curtailment of alternative products insofar as these are not in surplus.

2. Foreign Exchange Effect

Though several different formulae may be used for calculating the foreign exchange effect, two considerations are particularly important: a) import-content coefficient of initial outlay; b) pay-off period in terms of foreign exchange of the whole project. Where the project will never pay off in terms of foreign exchange (owing to high initial import costs, rapid wear-out of equipment, large remittance of profit overseas, large depreciation to be offset against taxes on remittable profit, etc.) it will not normally be accepted. Where the payoff period is over five years, it is unlikely to be considered satisfactory from a balance of payments point of view.

It should be noted that in making this calculation the additional demand for imports generated by additional incomes and the multiplier effect is not taken into account, on the grounds that while such a calculation would be in order for a single project,

---

6 In such cases the use of foreign finance will add to the customs duty if the latter is ad valorem. No attempt has been made to allow for the effects of this in the tables.

it is not in order for a whole programme, the effect of which should be to reduce the marginal propensity to import. This does not appear very satisfactory since the marginal propensity to import will not be reduced to zero but will remain significant for the foreseeable future. It is further argued that if this element were to be included in the calculation virtually no projects would appear to be viable, and I believe this is partly true; unless and until a large number of consumer-good manufacturing industries based on local inputs with adequate domestic transport systems and adequate domestic demand are developed, the marginal propensity to spend income on imported goods is likely to remain high (which is in turn an impediment to local industrial development if the full balance of payments criterion is rigorously applied) but this import demand can in the meantime be rendered less damaging by selectively increasing the customs duties.

3. Employment Generated per Unit of Capital

It should be borne in mind that the induction of population into wage-employment has been extremely slow [1].

Numbers employed in Tanzania, 1963–1967

	Total employment number	Index: 1962 = 100
1963	340,344	85.7
1964	351,257	88.5
1965	333,755	84.1
1966	336,497	84.8
1967	346,398	87.3

Source: Background to the Budget, 1967–1968.

4. Generation of Rural Incomes

The desire to increase the per capita income of the rural sector has been strengthened by the Arusha Declaration. In recent years the real income of the rural sector has stagnated, while that of the urban areas has increased significantly.

5. Profit per Unit of Capital Employed

Profit is reckoned, so far as possible, on a national accounts basis rather than on a commercial basis.

There is no explicit criterion as regards efficiency nor as regards the adequacy of market demand, nor as regards optimum plant size. These criteria are subsumed under 1. and 5.

In obtaining the data necessary to apply these criteria a good deal of subjective judgement has to be used. Moreover, since (owing to the manpower shortage already mentioned) it is not normal for several actually competing projects to be presented for appraisal simultaneously, the ideal procedure of *ranking* projects is replaced by one of appraising each project in the light of a guess as to what competing alternatives might appear *later*. For these reasons no formal application of the criteria

---

1 There was a substantial decline on the sisal estates especially after 1964.

can be expected; nor are the criteria expressed with sufficient precision to permit of mathematical weighting to be given to each. Finally, it should be mentioned that ministries vary in the importance they attach to different criteria, and although the general policy is a Cabinet directive, this still leaves some room for friendly disputation between ministries in the initial stages when subjective impressions of the nonmeasurable data-elements are being worked out. This system may in fact have an advantage over a more orderly system in that it encourages the full exploration of all aspects of a project.

Bibliography

The following compilation of works having a bearing on Tanzania's balance of payments has been divided into two parts. The first part consists of all types of publication, in alphabetical order by author. The second part consists of official publications by the Governments of, successively, German East Africa, Zanzibar Protectorate, Tanganyika Territory, Republic of Tanganyika, United Republic of Tanganyika and Zanzibar, and the United Republic of Tanzania. These are arranged by subject.

ANDERSEN, O. M. and KIMBLE, H.: *The Control of Retail Prices in Tanzania.* National Price Control Advisory Board. Board Paper 13/67. Dar es Salaam, 1967. Mimeo.

ARKADIE, B. VAN: "Gross Domestic Product Estimates for East Africa", in: *Economic & Statistical Review,* 9, 1963.

—: "Import Substitution and Export Promotion as Aids to Industrialisation in East Africa", in: *East African Economic Review,* December, 1964.

—: *The Structure of the Economies of East Africa,* East African Institute of Social Research, Kampala, 1964. Mimeo.

— and NDEGWA, P.: "Future Trade, Balance of Payments and Aid Requirements of East Africa", in: *East African Economic Review,* I, New Series, 2, 1965.

ARRIGHI, G.: "International Corporations, Labour Aristocracies and Economic Development in Tropical Africa", in: HOROWITZ (ed.): *The Corporations and the Cold War,* London, 1968.

BADGER, D. G.: *Report on the Balance of Payments of Uganda.* Entebbe, 1965.

BANK OF TANZANIA: *Economic Report,* six-monthly; March, 1967, onwards.

—: *Statements of Assets and Liabilities,* monthly.

—: *Exchange Control Ordinance,* Dar es Salaam, 1967.

BARTLETT, C. A.: *Statistics on the Zanzibar Protectorate, 1895–1935.* London.

BECK, A. D.: "The Kilombero Valley of South Central Tanganyika", in: *East Africa Geographical Review,* 2. April, 1964.

BELLAMY, J.: *The Cotton Industry of Tanganyika,* Dar es Salaam, Tanganyika Standard, 1963.

BESEN, S. M.: "An Empirical Analysis of Commercial Bank Lending Behaviour", in: *Yale Economic Essays,* Fall, 1965.

BLUMENTHAL, E.: *The Present Monetary System and its Future,* Report to the Government of Tanganyika, Dar es Salaam, 1963.

BRODE, H.: *British and German East Africa,* London, Edward Arnold, 1911.

BROWNING, P. R.: "Banking and Money in East Africa", in: *East African Economic Review,* July, 1954.

—: "A Note on the Balance of Payments of East Africa, 1946–1953", in: *East African Economic Review,* 2. July, 1955.

BURKE, F. G.: *Tanganyika Pre-Planning,* Syracuse University, 1965.

CAMERON, D.: *My Tanganyika Service, and some Nigeria,* London, 1939.

CARTER, A. G. T.: "The Balance of Payments of East Africa, 1956–1961", in: *East African Economic Review*, 10 (2), Dec. 1963.

—: "The Development of the Hard Fibre Industry", in: *East African Economic & Statistical Review*, March, 1966.

CHARLE, E.: "The Concept of Neo-Colonialism and its Relation to Rural Economic Systems", in: *Social & Economic Studies* (Jamaica), December, 1966.

CLARK, P. G.: *Development Planning in East Africa*, Nairobi, 1965.

—: "Towards more Comprehensive Planning in East Africa", in: *East African Economic Review*, 10 (2), December, 1963.

CLARK, R.: *Economic Considerations in determining Coffee Policies in East Africa.* Mimeo. Nairobi, 1967.

CO-OPERATIVE SUPPLY ASSOCIATION OF TANGANYIKA: *Progress Report*, Dar es Salaam, Sept., 1964. Mimeo.

CORDEN, W. M.: *Recent Development in the Theory of International Trade*, Princetown University, 1965.

—: "The Structure of a Tariff System and the Effective Protection Role", in: *The Journal of Political Economy*, Vol. LXXIV, No. 3, June, 1966.

CRAIG, J.: "An East African Import Price Index, 1954–1963, calculated from Supplying Countries' Export Indices", in: *East African Economic Review*, June, 1966.

CROFTON, R. H.: *Statistics of the Zanzibar Protectorate, 1893–1920*, London, Eastern Press, 1921.

DAHL, H. E.: *The Economy of Tanzania*, Christian-Michelsen Institute, Bergen, 1967.

DOUGLAS, D. W.: "Structure and Advice – the case of Kenya", in: *American Journal of Economic Sociology*, XXIV, 4, 1965.

DUE, J. F.: "The Reform of East African Taxation", in: *East African Economic Review*, Dec., 1964.

EAST AFRICAN AIRWAYS: *Annual Report*, Nairobi, E.A.A.

EAST AFRICAN COMMON SERVICES ORGANISATION: *Annual Report*, 1964, Nairobi, EACSO, 1965.

—: East African Customs & Excise Tariffs, 1967.

—: *Estimates and Expenditure of the East African Common Services Organisation for the year 1964/65.* Nairobi.

—: *Report of the East African Metric Commission*, Nairobi, 1967.

EAST AFRICAN CURRENCY BOARD: *Annual Reports, 1921–1967*.

EAST AFRICAN CUSTOMS & EXCISE: *Annual Trade Report of Kenya, Uganda and Tanganyika, 1949–1967*.

EAST AFRICAN HIGH COMMISSION: *Report for the Period 1st July, 1961 to 30th June, 1962*, Nairobi, EACSO, 1962.

EAST AFRICAN INSTITUTE OF SOCIAL & CULTURAL AFFAIRS: *Problems of Economic Development in East Africa*, ten papers (Nairobi), 1965.

EAST AFRICAN POSTS & TELECOMMUNICATIONS: *Annual Reports*, Nairobi.

EAST AFRICAN RAILWAYS & HARBOURS: *Annual Reports*, Nairobi.

EAST AFRICAN STATISTICAL DEPARTMENT: *East African Economic and Statistical Bulletin* (quarterly), 1948–1961; *Economic and Statistical Review, 1962*.

—: *The Balance of Payments of East Africa, 1959, 1960 and 1961*, Nairobi, EACSO, 1963.

—: "Notes on Economic Development in East Africa", in: *Economic & Statistical Bulletin*, No. 1, 1968.

—: "Household Budget Survey of Africans living in Dar es Salaam 1956/57", in: *Economic & Statistical Bulletin*, No. 39, March, 1958.

—: *East African Insurance Statistics* (Annual) 1963, 64, 65, 66.

266

EAST AFRICAN STATISTICAL DEPARTMENT: "Notes on Insurance in East Africa, 1947–1951", in: *Quarterly Economic & Statistical Bulletin*, Sept., 1953.

—: "Notes on Insurance in East Africa, 1947–1957", in: *Quarterly Economic & Statistical Bulletin*, Dec., 1958.

—: "Some Notes on Tanganyika's Development from 1947–1952", in: *Quarterly Economic & Statistical Bulletin*, No. 19, March, 1953.

—: "The Tanganyika European Family Budget Survey, 1951–52", in: *East African Economic & Statistical Bulletin*, No. 16, 1952.

—: *East African Trade Indices: Revised External Trade Indicies 1954–1961 with Commentary*, Nairobi, 1963.

—: "A Short Exposition of the Revised Indices of the External Trade of East Africa", in: *Quarterly Economic & Statistical Bulletin*, Dec., 1959.

—: "Summary and Guide to some of the main provisions in the Treaty for East African Co-operation", in: *Economic & Statistical Review*, No. 22/23, March/June, 1967.

—: *The Territorial Incidence of the EACSO General Fund Services, 1960–65*, Nairobi, 1966. Mimeo.

ECONOMIST INTELLIGENCE UNIT: *Ocean Shipping and Freight Rates and Developing Countries*, 1964.

EHRLICH, C.: "Some Aspects of Economic Policy in Tanganyika, 1945–1960", in: *Journal of Modern African Studies*, II, 2, 1964.

ELIOT, C.: *The East African Protectorate*, London, 1905.

ELKAN, W.: "The East African Trade in Wood Carving", in: *Africa*, October, 1958.

FAALAND, J. and DAHL, H. E.: *The Economy of Tanzania*, Bergen, 1967; *The Economy of Kenya*, Bergen, 1967; *The Economy of Uganda*, Bergen, 1967.

FOOD AND AGRICULTURE ORGANISATION: *FAO Commodity Review*, Rome. Annual.

—: *Present Wood Consumption and Future Requirements in Tanganyika*, Rome, FAO, 1962.

—: *Report of the First Session of the Study Group on Hard Fibres to the Committee on Commodity Problems*, CCP 67/5 (CCP:HF 66/14), Sept., 1966.

—: *Report of Meeting of Sisal and Henequen Producers, Rome, 10–13 July, 1967*, CCP:HF 67/6, July, 1967.

—: *Report of the Second Session* (etc. as above), CCP: 67/27 (CCP:HF 67/14), Sept., 1967.

—: *Study Group on Hard Fibres, Consultative Sub-Committee. First Session, Rome, 23–26 Jan., 1968 Report.* CCP:HF 68/9 (CCP:HF/SC 68/4), Jan., 1968.

—: *Study Group on Hard Fibres, Consultative Sub-Committee. Second Session, Rome, 25–28 June, 1968 Report.* CCP:HF 69/6 (CCP:HF/SC 68/9), June, 1968.

FRANK, C. R.: "The Production and Distribution of Sugar in East Africa", in: *East African Economic Review*, Dec., 1963.

FUGGLES-COUCHMAN, N. R.: *Agricultural Change in Tanganyika, 1945–1960.* Food Research Institute Publication, Stanford, 1964.

GALE, G. W.: "Food Balance Sheets for the African Populations of East Africa", in: *East African Medical Journal*, 37, May, 1960.

GASKIN, M.: "Monetary Flexibility in Dependent Economies", in: *East African Economic Review*, June, 1965.

GHAI, D. P. (ed.): *Portrait of a Minority: Asians in East Africa*, Nairobi, 1965. Second edition forthcoming.

—: "Territorial Distribution of Benefits and Costs of the East African Common Market", in: *East African Economic Review*, 11 (1), June, 1964.

GRAMLEY, L. E.: "Deposit Instability at Individual Banks", in: *Essays on Commercial Banking* (Kansas City, 1962).

GREEN, R. H.: "Economic Union in East Africa: Principles, Prices and Proceeds", in: *East African Institute of Social Research* (EDRP 353) 1965. Mimeo.

— and SEIDMAN, A.: *Unity or Poverty? The Economics of Pan-Africanism.* London, 1968.

GRIMM: *Der wirthschaftliche Werth von Deutsch Ostafrika.* Berlin, 1886.

GROES, N.: *The Possibilities of Monetary Policy in Tanzania,* ERB-Paper 66/2, Dar es Salaam, 1966. Mimeo.

GUILLEBAUD, C. W.: An Economic Survey of the Tea Industry of Tanganyika. *Tanganyika Standard,* Dar es Salaam, 1963.

—: *An Economic Survey of the Sisal Industry of Tanganyika,* 2nd edn. Tanganyika Sisal Growers' Association, 1958. 3rd edn., 1966.

GUTMANN, P. M.: "External Financing and the Rate of Economic Growth", in: American Economic Review, Sept. 1967.

HADDON-CAVE, C. P.: "Real Growth of the East African Territories, 1954–1960", in: *East African Economic Review,* June, 1961.

HANCE, W. A. and VAN DONGEN, I. S.: "Dar es Salaam: the Port and its Tributory Area", in: *Annals of the Association of American Geographers,* Dec., 1958.

HARLOW, V. and CHILVER, E. M.: *History of East Africa,* Vol. II. Oxford, 1965.

HAWKINS, H. C. G.: *Wholesale and Retail Trade in Tanganyika,* New York, Washington, London, 1965.

HAZLEWOOD, A.: *Rail and Road in East Africa.* Oxford, 1964.

—: "The East African Common Market: Importance and Effects", in: *Bulletin of Oxford University Institute of Economics & Statistics,* XXVII, 1, 1966.

—: "The Territorial Incidence of the East African Common Services", in: *Bulletin of Oxford University Institute of Economics & Statistics,* XXVII, 3, 1965.

HELLEINER, G. K.: *Agricultural Export Pricing Strategy in Tanzania,* ERB Paper 66/6, Dar es Salaam, 1966. Mimeo.

—: *Benefits and Costs of an East African EEC Trade Agreement,* ERB (Restricted) Paper 66/1, Dar es Salaam, 1966. Mimeo.

—: *The Measurement of Aggregative Economic Performance in East Africa,* ERB Paper 67/13, Dar es Salaam, 1967. Mimeo.

—: *Rationalisation in the Tanzania Sisal Industry,* ERB (Restricted) Paper 68/2, Dar es Salaam, 1968. Mimeo.

—: *Trade, Aid and Nation-Building in Tanzania,* ERB Paper 67/3, Dar es Salaam, 1967. Mimeo.

—: *Transfer Taxes, Tariffs and the East African Common Market,* ERB Paper 67/16, Dar es Salaam, 1967. Mimeo.

HICKS, U. K.: "The Revenue Implications of the Uganda and Tanzania Plans", in: *Journal of Development Studies,* II.3, 1966.

HILL, J. F. R. and MOFFET, J. P.: *Tanganyika: A Review of its Resources and their Development.* Government of Tanganyika, 1955.

HILL, M. F.: *Permanent Way (Kenya und Uganda Railway),* Nairobi, 1950.

—: *Permanent Way (Tanganyika Railways),* Nairobi, 1960.

HILLARD, R. J.: "The Cement Industry of East Africa", in: *East African Economic Review,* Dec., 1959.

HIMMELFARB, D.: *The Technology of Cordage Fibres and Ropes.* New York, 1957.

HOLLINGSWORTH, W.: *Zanzibar under the Foreign Office, 1890–1913,* London, 1953.

HOROBIN, P. W.: "Insurance Investment in East Africa", in: *East African Economic & Statistical Review,* Dec., 1961.

HOWE, C. W. and KARANI, H.: "A Projection Model for the Kenya Economy: a study in development planning and comparative economic structures", in: *East African Economic Review,* I New Series, 2, 1965.

268

HOYLE, B. S.: *The Seaports of East Africa*, Nairobi, 1967.

ILIFFE, J.: *Tanganyika under German Rule*, Nairobi, 1968.

INGHAM, K.: *A History of East Africa*, London, 1962.

INSTITUTE OF PUBLIC ADMINISTRATION: *Problems of Foreign Aid* (Conference Report), Dar es Salaam, 1964.

INTERNATIONAL BANK FOR RECONSTRUCTION AND DEVELOPMENT: *The Economic Development of Tanganyika*, Baltimore, 1961.

INTERNATIONAL MONETARY FUND: *Balance of Payments Manual*, 1961, New York.

INTERNATIONAL MONETARY FUND/INTERNATIONAL BANK FOR RECONSTRUCTION AND DEVELOPMENT: *Direction of Trade*, Monthly.

JAMAL, A. H.: *The Critical Phase of Emergent African States*, Nairobi, 1965.

JANTZEN, G.: *Ostafrika in der Deutsch-Englischen Politik 1884–1890*. Hamburg, 1934.

JOHNSON, H. G.: *Economic Policies towards Less Developed Countries*, Washington and London, 1967.

—: "The Theory of Tariff Structure, with special reference to World Trade and Development", in: *Trade and Development*, Etudes et Travaux de l'Institut Universitaire de Hautes Etudes Internationales, No. 4.

KARMILOFF, G.: "Regional Plan Implementation: Tanzania's Experiment", in: *East African Economic Review*, 1, 2, June, 1965.

KASAMBALA, J. S.: *Policy Statement to the Budget Session of the National Assembly*, by Hon. J. S. KASAMBALA, Minister for Commerce & Co-operatives, June, 1964, Dar es Salaam.

KENNEDY, T. A.: "An Estimate of Uganda's Balance of Payments, 1949/1957", in: *East African Economic Review*, July, 1959.

—, ORD, H. W. and WALKER, D.: "On the Calculation and Interpretation of National Accounting Material in East Africa", in: *African Studies in Income and Wealth*, SAMUELS, L. H. (ed.), London, 1963.

KESSEL, D.: *Effective Protection of Industry in Tanzania*, ERB Paper 67/8, Dar es Salaam, 1967. Mimeo.

KNIPERS, C.: *Tourism in Tanganyika*, Dar es Salaam, 1963.

KOLONIAL-ABTEILUNG DES AUSWÄRTIGEN AMTS: *Deutsches Kolonialblatt* (annual) 1890–1914, Berlin. *Beilage zum Deutschen Kolonialblatt* (annual).

Koloniale Zeitschrift, Fortnightly, Berlin, 1899 onwards.

KOLONIAL-WIRTSCHAFTLICHES KOMITEE: *Verhandlungen der Baumwollbau-Kommission* (irregular), Berlin.

—: *Verhandlungen der Ölrohstoff-Kommission* (irregular), Berlin.

KREININ, M. E.: "Price vs. Tariff Elasticities in International Trade — a suggested reconciliation", in: *Journal of Political Economy*, June, 1966.

KRISHNA, K. G. V.: "Some Economic Aspects of an East African Federation", in: *East African Economic Review*, 8 (2), Dec. 1961.

LAMADE, W.: *The Role of Marketing Boards in Tanzania*, ERB Paper 67/1, Dar es Salaam, 1967. Mimeo.

LANGER, W. L.: *The Diplomacy of Imperialism, 1890–1902*, 2nd edn., New York, 1960.

LESLIE, J. A. K.: *A Survey of Dar es Salaam*, London, New York, Nairobi, 1963.

LEYS, C. and ROBSON, P. (ed.): *Federation in East Africa*, London, 1965.

LINT & SEED MARKET BOARD: *Annual Reports*, Govt. Printer, Dar es Salaam.

LISTOWEL, J.: *The Making of Tanganyika*, London, 1965.

LITTLE, A. D.: *Tanganyika Industrial Development*, Dar es Salaam, 1961.

LIVINGSTONE, I.: "The Economic Development of Tanganyika: The World Bank Review", in: *East African Economic Review*, 8, 1, June, 1961.

Lofchie, M. F.: *Zanzibar: Background to Revolution,* Princeton, 1965.

Loynes, J. B.: "From Currency Board to Central Bank", in: *East African Economic Review,* December, 1960.

Lugard, F. D.: *The Rise of our East African Empire,* London, 1893.

Lury, D. A.: "Trade Statistics of the Countries of East Africa, 1945–1964", in: *East African Economic & Statistical Review,* March, 1965.

Macharia, D.: "The Role of Railway Transportation in the Economic Development of East Africa", Syracuse University, 1966.

Maitra, P.: "Import Substitution Potential in East Africa", in: *East Africa Institute of Social Research,* Nairobi, 1967.

Marlin, P. von: *The Impact of External Economic Relations on the Economic Development of East Africa,* Munich, 1966, Ifo-Institut. Mimeo.

Massell, B. F.: *East African Economic Union: an evaluation and some implications for policy.* The Rand Corporation, Santa Monica, 1963.

—: "Industrialisation and Economic Union in Greater East Africa", in: *East African Economic Review,* 9.2, Dec., 1962.

—: "Trade between East Africa and Neighbouring Countries", in: *East African Economic & Statistical Review,* Sept., 1962.

McDermott, P. L.: *British East Africa,* 2nd edn., London, 1895.

McDonald, D. R.: *Enemy Property in Tanganyika,* Cape Town, 1946.

McKinlay, A. C. M.: "The Coalfields and the Coal Resources of Tanzania", in: *Geological Survey Bulletin,* No. 38, Dar es Salaam, 1965.

McWilliam, M. D.: "Is there a Case for an East African Central Bank?", in: *East African Economic Review,* Jan., 1959.

Mead, D. C.: "Monetary Analysis in an Underdeveloped Economy: a case study of three East African territories." *Yale Economic Essays,* Spring, 1963.

Meier, G. M.: *International Trade and Development,* New York, 1964.

Meyer, H. (ed.): *Das Deutsche Kolonialreich,* Leipzig, Vienna, 1909.

Michaely, M.: *Concentration in International Trade,* Amsterdam, 1962.

Mikesell, R. F.: *Public Foreign Capital for Private Enterprise in Developing Countries,* Princetown, 1966.

Morgan, D. J.: *British Private Investment in East Africa,* London, 1965.

National Development Corporation: *Annual Report & Accounts,* annual, Dar es Salaam.

Ndwegwa, P.: *The Common Market and Development in East Africa,* Nairobi, 1965.

—: "Preferential Trade Arrangements among Developing Countries", in: *East African Economic Review,* Dec., 1960.

Newlyn, W. T.: "Gains and Losses in the East African Common Market", in: *East African Institute of Social Research* (EDRP 79), Kampala, 1965. Mimeo.

—: "Monetary Systems and Integration", in: *East African Economic Review,* June, 1964.

—: "Take-Off considered in an African Setting", *Yorkshire Bulletin of Economic & Social Research,* XIII, 1, 1961.

Newman, P.: "Foreign Investment and Economic Growth: the case of East Africa, 1963–70", in: *East African Economic Review,* Dec., 1964.

Nye, J. S.: "East African Economic Integration", in: *Journal of Modern African Studies,* I, 4, 1963.

O'Connor, A. M.: "New Rail Construction and Pattern of Economic Development in East Africa", in: *Transactions of the Institute of British Geographers,* 36, 1965.

OFFICER, L. W.: "The Effect of Monopoly in Commodity Markets upon the Foreign Exchange Market", in: *Quarterly Journal of Economics*, Harvard University, Cambridge, Mass., May, 1966.

OLIVER, R., and MATHEW, G.: Vol. I. *History of East Africa*, Oxford, 1965.

ORD, H. W.: "An Outline of East Africa's Balance of Payments, 1953–55", in: *East African Economic Review*, 3, Jan., 1957.

—: "Social Accounting and Inter-Territorial Transactions in East Africa", in: *East African Economic Review*, Dec., 1962.

—: "A Study of Capital Formation in East Africa, 1946–1958", *East African Institute of Social Research*, Kampala, 1962. Mimeo.

PAASCHE, H.: *Deutsch-Ostafrika*, Wirtschaftliche Studien, Berlin, 1906.

PATEL, H. D. and RIORDAN, E. B.: "Making the most of Sisal Exports: an analysis of prices paid to Tanganyika and Uganda", Rural Development Project Paper No. 22, Makerere, 1962, and *East African Rural Development*, Vol. I, No. 1, 1968.

PEACOCK, A. T. and DOSSER, D. G. M.: *The National Income of Tanganyika, 1952–1954*, London (HMSO Col. Res. Stud. No. 26), 1958.

PEDLER, F. J.: *Customs Arrangements with Kenya and Uganda*, 1934.

PETERS, C.: *Die Gründung von Deutsch-Ostafrika*, Berlin, 1906.

PÖSSINGER, H.: *The Possibilities and Limitations of Smallholding Sisal in East Africa*, Munich, Dec., 1965, Ifo-Institute, mimeo.

PRATT, C. A.: *Projection Lamp Supply Service*, Institute of Education, Dar es Salaam, 1967. Mimeo.

PRIOR, J.: *Voyage along the East Coast of Africa*, London, 1819.

RAMM-ERICSON, N.: "The Price Movements in East Africa's Exports", in: *East African Economic & Statistical Review*, June, 1964.

REDDAWAY, W. B.: *Effects of U.K. Direct Investment Overseas*, Cambridge, U.K., 1967.

REICHSAMT DES INNERN: "Deutsch-Ostafrika als Ein- und Ausfuhrmarkt", in: *Berichte über Handel und Industrie*, Band XIII, Heft 10, Berlin, 18. Jan. 1910.

RESNICK, J. R.: "Labour Force Survey of Tanzania", *East African Institute of Social Research*, Kampala, 1966. Mimeo.

RESNICK, I. N. (ed.): *Tanzania: Revolution by Education*, Arusha, 1968.

RICHARDS, P. J.: "Shipping Problems of Underdeveloped Countries", in: *Bulletin of Oxford Institute of Economics & Statistics*, August, 1967.

ROAD RESEARCH LABORATORY, U. K. Ministry of Transport: *Vehicle Operating Costs on Bituminous, Gravel and Earth Roads in East and Central Africa*, London, HMSO., 1967.

ROBINSON, B. D.: "Arabica Coffee Production in Tanganyika", in: *Tanganyika Coffee News*, II, 9, 1962.

ROBINSON, N. J.: *The History of Smith Mackenzie & Co.*

ROE, A. R.: *Commercial Bank Borrowing and Central Bank Control*, ERB Paper 66/5, Dar es Salaam, 1966. Mimeo.

—: *The Impact of the East African Treaty on the Distribution of EACSO Benefits*, ERB Paper 67/15, Dar es Salaam, 1967. Mimeo.

ROOT, F. R.: *Strategic Planning for Export Marketing*, Copenhagen, 1964.

ROSBERG, C. G. and SEGAL, A.: *An East African Federation*, New York Carnegie Endowment for International Peace, 1963, International Conciliation, No. 543.

ROWE, J. W. F.: *The World's Coffee*, London (HMSO), 1963.

RUSSELL, E. W. (ed.): *The Natural Resources of East Africa*, Nairobi, 1962.

RUTHENBERG, H.: *Agricultural Development in Tanganyika*, Springer-Verlag, Berlin, Heidelberg, New York, 1964 (Ifo-Institut).

SACHS, I.: "The Significance of the Foreign Trade Sector and the Strategy of Foreign Trade Planning", in: *U.N., Planning the External Sector: Techniques, Problems and Policies* (Turkey), 1965, ST/TAO/SER. C/91.

SCHNEE, H. (ed.): *Deutsches Kolonial-Lexikon*, Leipzig, 1920.

SCHNITTGER, L.: *Besteuerung und wirtschaftliche Entwicklung in Ostafrika*, Springer-Verlag, Berlin, Heidelberg, New York, 1966 (Ifo-Institut).

SELSJORD, M.: "Recent Development in Commercial Banking in East Africa: a statistical analysis", in: *East African Economic & Statistical Review*, Sept., 1966.

SELWYN, P. and WATSON, T. Y.: *Report on the Economic Development of the Zanzibar Protectorate*, Zanzibar, 1962.

SINGH, D. C.: "A Study of Motor Vehicle Insurance in East Africa, 1950–64", in: *East African Economic & Statistical Review*, No. 17, Dec., 1965.

SISAL GROWERS ASSOCIATION OF TANGANYIKA AND KENYA: *Hard Fibres*, quarterly, London, June, 1951 onwards.

SLESINGER, R. E.: "Some Comments on International Inequality as related to International Trade for Emerging Nations", in: *Industrial Economics Journal*, July/Sept., 1966.

STAPLEDON, R. de S.: "East Africa in 1979", in: *East African Economic Review*, I (2), Jan., 1955.

STEWART, I. G. and ORD, H. W. (eds): *African Primary Products and International Trade*, Edinburgh, 1965.

STOUTJESDIJK, E. J.: "Prospective Demand for Manufactures in East Africa: a survey", *East African Institute of Social Research* (EDRP 96), Kampala, 1966. Mimeo.

STURMEY: *Ocean Freight Rates and Economic Research*, Geneva, 1966.

TALBOT-PHIBBS, J. A.: *Report on a Survey of Inter-Territorial Trade between Tanganyika and Northern Rhodesia and Nyasaland*, Dar es Salaam, 1954.

Tanga Post and East Coast Advertiser, Weekly, Sept. 6th, 1919–June 25th, 1921.

TOBIAS, G.: *High-level Manpower Requirements and Resources in Tanganyika, 1962–67*, Government Paper No. 2 of 1963, Dar es Salaam, 1963.

UGANDA GOVERNMENT: *Report on the Balance of Payments of Uganda*, by Dr. D. G. BADGER, Entebbe, 1965. Mimeo.

UNITED AFRICA PRESS LTD.: *Industry in Africa*, 5th edn., 1966–1967.

UNITED KINGDOM, Colonial Office: *East Africa: Report of the Economic and Fiscal Commission*, Cmd. 1279, London, 1961.

UNITED NATIONS CONFERENCE ON TRADE AND DEVELOPMENT: *Establishment or Expansion of Merchant Marines in Developing Countries*, TD/26/Supp. 1, 20th Nov., 1967 (New Delhi).

UNITED NATIONS ECONOMIC COMMISSION FOR AFRICA: *African Timber Trends: preliminary report on Western Africa and Equatorial East Africa*. Prepared in collaboration with FAO, Jan., 1964.

—: *Development of Steel Industry in East and Central Africa*, Oct./Nov., 1965, E/CN. 14/INR/87/Add 2.

—: *Investment Laws and Regulations in Africa*, E/CN. 14/INR/28/Rev. 2, New York, 1965.

—: "Trade in East Africa", in: *Economic Bulletin for Africa*, Vol. III, No. 1, Jan., 1962.

UNITED NATIONS TECHNICAL ASSISTANCE MISSION: *The Economic Implications of East African Federation: Report by a U.N. Technical Assistance Mission to the Government of Tanganyika*, Addis Ababa, 1962.

UNITED NATIONS, TRUSTEESHIP COUNCIL: *Report of the U.N. Visiting Mission to Tanganyika*, Dar es Salaam, 1949 (Report of 1948).

United Nations, Trusteeship Council: *Report on Tanganyika,* New York, 1958 (Report of 1957).

United States Department of Agriculture, Economic Research Service: *The Agricultural Economy of Tanganyika,* by Carey B. Singleton, Washington, 1964.

United States Department of State: *Resumé, Conclusions and Proposals on the AID In-House Tanzania Agriculture Reconnaissance Team.* Unclassified mimeo from Dar es Salaam office, November, 1967, ref. EGA/ID/CDF/DP, Washington, 1967.

Usambara Post, Weekly, 1905–1911, Tanga.

Van Arkadie: See Arkadie, van.

Van de Laar, A. J. M.: *Perspective on the Parastatals: NDC,* ERB (Restricted) Paper 68/5, Dar es Salaam, 1968. Mimeo.

Vanek, J.: "Protection Tarifaire des Industries Naissantes", in: *Revue Economique,* Paris, Nov., 1966.

Wagner, J.: *Deutsch-Ostafrika,* Berlin, 1886.

Walker, D.: "Tanganyika's National Income", in: *East African Economic Review,* Jan., 1959.

Weekly News (Tanganyika), 1928–1966, Later: *Tanzania Weekly News,* Nakuru (Kenya).

Weindling, L.: *Long Vegetables Fibres,* Columbia, New York, 1947.

West, R. L.: "An Estimated Balance of Payments for Kenya, 1923–1939", in: *East African Economic Review,* 3. July, 1956.

Westergaard, P.: *Cashew Nuts: the Quality Problem,* ERB Paper 68/8, Dar es Salaam, 1968. Mimeo.

Wood, A.: *The Groundnut Affair,* London, 1950.

Wood, R. N.: "The East African Common Market: a reassessment", in: *East African Economic Review,* No. 4 of 1966.

Woolf, L.: *Empire and Commerce in Africa,* New York, 1920.

Yaffey, M. J. H.: *Balance of Payments Management,* ERB Paper 66/1, Dar es Salaam, 1966. Mimeo.

—: *Bank Liquidity after Nationalisation,* ERB (Restricted) Paper 67/1, Dar es Salaam, 1967. Mimeo.

—: *Foreign Exchange Loss through Banking Operations: the Case of Tanzania,* ERB (Restricted) Paper 67/3, Dar es Salaam, 1967. Mimeo.

—: *Tanzania's Balance of Payments 1966–71,* ERB (Restricted) Paper 66/2, Dar es Salaam, 1966. Mimeo.

—: "The Treaty for East African Co-operation: an economic commentary", in: *Private Enterprise and the Corporate Form in East Africa.* Thomas P. A. (ed.), Nairobi, 1968.

Zanzibar and Pemba Clove Growers' Association: *The Aims and Objects of the Clove Grower's Association and the Services it renders to the Clove Trade and Agriculture,* Zanzibar, 1951/52.

Zanzibar Trade and Tourist Committee: *A Guide to Zanzibar.*
1st edn., 1932;
2nd edn., 1939;
3rd edn., 1949.

Zeitschrift für Kolonialpolitik, Kolonialrecht und Kolonialwirtschaft, Berlin, Monthly, 1898.

GOVERNMENT:

A. GERMAN PERIOD

KAISERLICHES GOUVERNEMENT VON DEUTSCH-OSTAFRIKA: *Berichte über Land- und Forstwirtschaft in Deutsch-Ostafrika*, irregular, Heidelberg, 1902–1906.

REICHS-KOLONIALAMT: *Die deutschen Schutzgebiete in Afrika und der Südsee*, annual, 1909/10–1912/13.

B. PRESIDENTIAL PAPERS

NYERERE, J. K.: McDougall Memorial Lecture, F.A.O. "A World Plan is Essential", President of the Republic of Tanzania, 15th November, 1963, Dar es Salaam, Information Division, 1963.

TANZANIA GOVERNMENT (no department specified) GOVERNMENT PAPER No. 3, 1967: *Report to the Government of the United Republic of Tanzania on Wages, Incomes and Prices Policy* (report by the International Labour Office).

—, GOVERNMENT PAPER No. 4: *Wages, Incomes, Rural Development, Investment and Price Policy,* Dar es Salaam, 1967.

NYERERE, J. K., President of the United Republic of Tanzania: "Socialism and Rural Development", Dar es Salaam, September, 1967, *Government Printer.*

C. AGRICULTURE

TANGANYIKA AGRICULTURAL CORPORATION: *Report and Accounts for 1963/65*, Dar es Salaam, Central Statistical Bureau, The Treasury, 1965.

TANGANYIKA: *Annual Report of the Land Bank of Tanganyika,* Dar es Salaam, Government Printer, 1950–1961.

TANGANYIKA AGRICULTURAL CREDIT AGENCY: *Report of the Governing Board for the year ending 31st Dec. 1962.*

TANGANYIKA: Veterinary Debt: *Role of Livestock in the Subsistence and Cash Economy of Tanganyika,* 1962. Mimeo.

TANZANIA: National Agricultural Products Board, *Halmashauri ya Taifa Isimamiayo Mazao,* 1964, Dar es Salaam, 1964.

—: National Agricultural Products Board Official Handbook, Dar es Salaam, 1965 (?).

—: Ministry of Agriculture, Forests & Wildlife, *Monthly Market Report,* Dar es Salaam.

TANGANYIKA: Ministry of Lands, Forestry & Wildlife, *Tanganyika's Timber Resources,* Dar es Salaam, 1962.

—: Ministry of Agriculture, Forest Division, *Annual Report, 1964.*

—: Ministry of Lands, Forests & Wildlife, Lands Division, *Annual Report, 1963, 1964.*

D. CENTRAL STATISTICAL BUREAU

UNITED REPUBLIC OF TANGANYIKA & ZANZIBAR, CENTRAL STATISTICAL BUREAU: The National Accounts of Tanganyika 1960–1962, Dar es Salaam, 1964.

—: *Census of Industrial Production in Tanganyika 1961,* Dar es Salaam, 1964.

TANGANYIKA, CENTRAL STATISTICAL BUREAU: *Household Rural Surveys in Tanganyika: Pilot Surveys in Bagamoyo, June, 1961,* Dar es Salaam, 1962.

—: *Village Economic Surveys: Morogoro and Bagamoyo 1961/62,* Dar es Salaam, 1963.

—: *Census of Large-Scale Commercial Farming in Tanganyika, 1962,* Dar es Salaam, 1963.

274

United Republic of Tanzania, Central Statistical Bureau: *Census of Large-Scale Farming, October, 1964*, Dar es Salaam, 1965.

—: *Family Budget Survey of Middle Grade African Civil Servants, 1963*, Dar es Salaam, 1964.

Tanzania, Central Statistical Bureau: *Employment and Earnings in Tanganyika*, Dar es Salaam, annual.

Tanganyika, Central Statistical Bureau: *Family Budget Survey of Lower Paid African Workers in Dar es Salaam, April, 1965*, Dar es Salaam, 1965.

—: *Household Budget Survey of Wage-Earners in Dar es Salaam 1965*, Dar es Salaam, 1967.

United Republic of Tanzania, Central Statistical Bureau: *Survey of Industries, 1965*, Dar es Salaam, 1967.

Tanzania, Central Statistical Bureau: *Monthly Statistical Bulletin, Statistical Abstracts* (annual), 1964, 1965.

E. COMMERCE & INDUSTRIES

Tanganyika, Ministry of Commerce & Industry: *Commerce and Industry in Tanganyika*, Dar es Salaam, 1961.

Economist Intelligence Unit on behalf of Tanganyika Government: *Investment Opportunities in Tanganyika*, London (no date given).

Tanzania, Ministry of Commerce & Industries (Industrial Studies & Development Centre): *A Short Guide to Investors*, Dar es Salaam, 1967.

—. Ministry of Industries, Mineral Resources & Power: *Annual Report of the Mines Division*.

F. PLANNING

Tanganyika: *Development Plan for Tanganyika 1961/62–1963/64*, Dar es Salaam, 1962.

United Republic of Tanganyika & Zanzibar: *Five Year Plan for Economic and Social Development 1st July, 1964–30th June, 1969*, Vols I and II (Tanganyika), Dar es Salaam, 1964.

Tanzania, Manpower Planning Unit: *Survey of the High Level Manpower Requirements and Resources for the Five Year Development Plan 1964/65 to 1968/69*, Dar es Salaam, 1965.

Tanzania, Ministry of Economic Affairs & Development Planning: *First Year Progress Report on the implementation of the Five Year Development Plan (Public Sector), 1st July, 1964–30th June, 1965*, Dar es Salaam, 1965.

—, National Assembly: *Periodic Progress Report on the implementation of the Five Year Development Plan*, Dar es Salaam, 1965.

—, Ministry of Information & Tourism: *A Stride Forward*, speech by the Minister for Economic Affairs & Development Planning (The Hon. P. Bomani) to the National Assembly, June 14th, 1966, Dar es Salaam.

G. TREATIES

Tanzania: *Treaties, Agreements, etc. 1964*, United Republic of Tanganyika & Zanzibar, Kampala Agreement, Dar es Salaam, Information Services, 1964.

—: *Treaty Series*, Vol. 1, 1965; Vol. II, 1967.

—: *Treaties, etc. 1967*, Treaty for East African Co-operation, signed in Kampala, Uganda, on 6th June, 1967, Nairobi, printed on behalf of the EACSO by the Government Printer, 1967.

H. TREASURY AND CUSTOMS

TANGANYIKA TERRITORY: *Trade Report* (Annual), 1921–1948.

TANGANYIKA/TANZANIA: Treasury, *The Appropriation Accounts, Revenue Statements, etc.* (title subject to change), annual, 1921–1967.

TANZANIA TREASURY: *Background to the Budget: An Economic Survey* (annual).

—: *Systems of Taxation in Tanzania*, by J. R. MODI, Dar es Salaam, 1965.

TANZANIA: National Assembly, Speech by the Hon. the Minister for Finance, introducing the estimates of revenue and expenditure to the National Assembly, 1961, Dar es Salaam.

I. ZANZIBAR

ZANZIBAR PROTECTORATE: *Zanzibar Blue Book*, Annual, 1914–1947.

—: *Report on the Accounts of the Zanzibar Protectorate* (Annual), 1953–1958.

—: *Annual Report on the Accounts of the Zanzibar Protectorate* (Annual), 1959–1960.

—: *Estimates of Revenue and Expenditure*, 1949–1960.

—: *Report and Recommendations on the present position and future prospects of agriculture in the Zanzibar Protectorate*, Zanzibar, 1959.

—: *The Pattern of Income, Expenditure, and Consumption of Unskilled Workers in Zanzibar*, Zanzibar, 1962.

J. MISCELLANEOUS

TANGANYIKA TERRITORY: *Blue Book* (Annual), 1921–1948.

TANGANYIKA: *Proceedings of the Legislative Council, 1926–1961; Parliamentary Debates (Hansard)* and *National Assembly Debates (Hansard), 1961–1965; Majadiliano ya Bunge (Hansard)*, 1965.

TANGANYIKA TERRITORY (later Tanzania): Geological Survey Dept, *Bulletins* (irregular), 1932 (?), Numbered 1–38. Also *Memoirs*, Nos. 1 and 2, and Short Papers 1–30.

TANGANYIKA: Survey of the Geology of Tanganyika, Part IV: *Economic Geology* by J. F. HARRIS, Dar es Salaam, 1961.

UNITED REPUBLIC OF TANZANIA: *Gazette, Acts Supplement*, Dar es Salaam.

—: *Gazette Extraordinary*, XLVIII, 50, B, 1st December, 1967, General Notice No. 2441, "Open General Licence and Imports Licensing Procedure".

TANZANIA: Transport Licensing Authority, *Annual Report*.

TANGANYIKA: *Report of the Tanganyika Salaries Commission (Adu Report)*, 1961, Vol. 2, Dar es Salaam.

INDEX

African Development Bank 223
Agency agreements —
  effect of, on supply elasticities 65
  example of 251–2
  in export trade 187
  in import trade 27, 133
  typical provisions of 149
Agriculture —
  as proportion of exports 20, 101
  as proportion of GDP 19
  state encouragement to 236–7
Amani Agricultural Research Institute 46
Anato 120
APM (average propensity to import)
  see Propensity to import
Arusha Declaration 33, 99n, 100, 209,
  234
Asbestos 126–7, 130

Bank of Tanzania —
  as brake on economy 227
  external assets of 35, 36, 222
  founded 35
Bankruptcies —
  of German investments 44
  see also Risk differential
Beeswax 120, 121
Bentonite 127
Biased relationship with rich countries
  36–40
Bicycles 140, 251–2
Brand names —
  in exports 131
  in imports 147
  in tinned milk 147–152
Business confidence —
  differing by sector 205
  erroneous 98
  historical factors affecting 37
  importance of 25
  see also Risk differential

Capital, long-term 203–223
  see also Loans, external Planning
Cashew nuts 77, 81, 87, 88
  market study 116–119
Cassava 120
Cassiterite, see tin
Castor seed 121
Cattle 131
Cement 127
China, People's Republic of 93, 128,
  133, 193, 201
Cloves —
  demand for 42, 120
  introduced in Zanzibar 42
  secular price rise of 47
  unskilled labour sufficient for 49
Coal 127
Coffee —
  market study 89, 111–6
  price 81
  production 87
Colonial Development Corporation 127
Commonwealth Preference 132n
Communications 165n, 190
  see also Transportation
Comparative advantage 130
Consolidated Fund Investments 219–220
Consumer choice 148
Consumer rationality, see brand names
Contractor finance 215
COSATA (Co-operative Supply Asso-
  ciation of Tanganyika) 123, 144–5
Cotton —
  export of 77, 81, 87, 88n, 89
  market study 108–111
Council for Mutual Economic Assistance
  (CMEA) 133
Credit Creation, effect of absence of 41,
  54, 74–5
Crown Agents —
  as purchasing agents 23
  borrowing from 67

277

Studies within the African Research Programme
of the
Ifo-Institut für Wirtschaftsforschung, Munich

Published:

a) in the series "Afrika-Studien"

(No. 1–18 by Springer-Verlag, Berlin – Heidelberg – New York; No. 19 ff. by Weltforum-Verlag, Munich)

No. 1 **Development Banks and Companies in Tropical Africa**
By Naseem Ahmad and Ernst Becher, 1964, 86 pages, in German

No. 2 **Agricultural Development in Tanganyika**
By Hans Ruthenberg, 1964, 212 pages, in English

No. 3 **National Accounting Systems in Tropical Africa**
By Rolf Güsten and Helmut Helmschrott, 1965, 69 pages, in German

No. 4 **Contributions to Internal Migration
and Population Development in Liberia**
By Hans W. Jürgens, 1965, 104 pages, in German

No. 5 **The Annotated Bibliography of Social Research in East Africa
1954—1963**
By Angela von Molnos, 1965, 304 pages, in German

No. 6 **The Political and Economic Role of the Asian Minority
in East Africa**
By Indira Rothermund, 1965, 75 pages, in German

No. 7 **Land Tenure Reform in Kenya**
By Hanfried Fliedner, 1965, 136 pages, in German

No. 8 **Taxation and Economic Development in East Africa**
By Lübbe Schnittger, 1966, 216 pages, in German

No. 9 **Problems of Economic Growth and Planning:
The Sudan Example**
By Rolf Güsten, 1966, 74 pages, in English

No. 10 **African Agricultural Production Development Policy
in Kenya 1952—1965**
By Hans Ruthenberg, 1966, 180 pages, in English

No. 40   Economic Statistics in Developing Countries: the Example of
Uganda
By Hanns Hieber, 1969, 244 pages, in German

No. 41   Problems of Land-Locked Countries: Uganda
By W. Fischer, 1969, 274 pages, in German

No. 42   Investigations into Health and Nutrition in East Africa
By H. Kraut/H.-D. Cremer (eds.), 1969, 342 pages, in English

No. 43   The African as Industrial Worker in East Africa
By O. Neuloh a. o., 1969, 440 pages, in German

No. 44   Rice Cultivation in West Africa — A Presentation of the Economic and Geographical Differences of Cultivation Methods
By B. Mohr, 1969, 163 pages, in German

No. 45   Structure and Growth of the East African Textile and Garments
Industry
By H. Helmschrott, 1969, 130 pages, in German

No. 46   Social Change in Kiteezi (Buganda), a Village within the Sphere
of Influence of the Township of Kampala (Uganda)
By E. C. Klein, 1969, 160 pages, in German

No. 47   Balance of Payment Problems in a Developing Country: Tanzania
By M. Yaffey, 1970, 284 pages, in English

No. 50   Cultural Change and Anxiety Reaction among the Yoruba of
Nigeria
By Staewen/Schönberg, 1970, ca. 430 pages, in German (with an
English Summary)

No. 52   Planning Processes: The East African Case
By R. E. Vente, 1970, 233 pages, in English

To be published shortly in the series "Afrika-Studien":

No. 48   Fodder Plants in the Sahel Zone of Africa
By R. Bartha (in German, English and French)

No. 49   Status and Use of African Lingua Francas
By B. Heine (in English)

No. 51   Studies in Production and Trade in East Africa
By P. Zajadacz and Contributors (in English)

No. 53   Financial Aspects of Development in East Africa
By P. Marlin and Contributors (in English)

No. 54   Administration and Economic Exploitation of German East
Africa before 1914
By D. Bald

286

b) in the African Studies special series "Information and Documentation"

No. 1   Africa-Vademecum (basic data on the economic structure and development of Africa)
Prepared by F. Betz, 1968, 163 pages, in German, with additional headings in English and French

No. 2   Development Banks and Institutions in Africa
By H. Harlander and D. Mezger, 1969, 211 pages, in German

c) as mimeograph (African Research Reports)

Economic Planning and Development Policy in Tropical Africa
By N. Ahmad, E. Becher and E. Harder, 1965, 283 pages, in German (out of print)

The Human Factor in the Development of the Kilombero Valley
By O. Raum, 1965, 56 pages, in English (out of print)

The EEC Market Regulations for Agricultural Products and their Implications for Developing Countries
By H. Klemm and P. v. Marlin (out of print)

The Impact of External Economic Relations on the Economic Development of East Africa
By P. v. Marlin, 1966, 110 pages, in English (out of print)

Crop Cultivation on the Island of Madagascar with Special Reference to Rice Growing
By Alfred H. Rabe, 1965, 346 pages, in German

Economic Research in Tropical Africa. Results of an Informatory Trip to Egypt, Ethiopia, Kenya, Uganda, Tanzania, Malawi, Zambia, Congo (Kinshasa), Nigeria, Ghana and Senegal in April and May 1966
By Hildegard Harlander, 1966, 193 pages, in German

Israeli Aid to Developing Countries with Special Reference to East Africa
By F. Goll, 1967, 189 pages, in German

The Economy of South West Africa (a Study in Economic Geography)
By Axel J. Halbach, 1967, 210 pages, in German (out of print)

Co-operative Farming in Kenya and Tanzania
By Nikolaus Newiger, 1967, 157 pages, in English (out of print)

Game Protection and Game Utilization in Rhodesia and in South Africa
By Wolfgang Erz, 1967, 97 pages, in German (out of print)

Zoological Studies in the Kivu Region (Congo-Kinshasa)
By Fritz Dieterlen and Peter Kunkel, 1967, 138 pages, in German

Recent English Economic Research in East Africa. A Selected Bibliography
By Dorothea Mezger and Eleonore Littich, 1967, 383 pages, in German

The Attitude of Various Tribes of the Republic of Togo, Especially the Ewe on the Plateau de Dayes, towards the Problem of Commissioned Cattle Herding by the Fulbe (Peulh) of West Africa
By Julius O. Müller, 1967, 187 pages, in French

Examination of the Physical Development of Tanzanian Youth
By H. W. Jürgens, 1967, 152 pages, in English

The Chemical and Allied Industries in Kenya
By Hans Reichelt, 1967, 182 pages, in English

Traditional Farming and Land Development in the Kilombero Valley/Tanzania
By Eckhard Baum, 1967, 150 pages, in German

The Organization of Milk Markets in East Africa
By Helmut Klemm, 1967, 164 pages, in German

Botanical Investigations in the Masai Country/Tanzania (an Example from the Semi-Arid Areas of East Africa)
By H. Leippert, 1968, 184 pages, in German

Evaluation of Aerial Photography in East Africa (an Inventory)
By K. Gerresheim, 1968, 225 pages, in German

Manufacturing and Processing Industries in Tanzania
By K. Schädler, 1969, 55 pages, in English

Agricultural Development in Malawi
By H. Dequin, 1969, 248 pages, in English

Development Aid to Africa – with Special Reference to the Countries of East Africa
By K. Erdmann, 1969, 186 pages, in German

Vegetable Cultivation in Tropical Highlands: the Kigezi Example (Uganda)
By F. Scherer, 1969, 227 pages, in English

Science and Development Policy. The Problem of Application of Research Results
By M. Bohnet, 1969, 35 pages, in German

Operational Concepts of the Infrastructure in the Economic Development Process
By H. Amann, 1970, 203 pages, in German

Importance, Volume, Forms and Development Possibilities of Private Saving in East Africa
By G. Hübner, 1970, 343 pages, in German

In preparation:

The Present State of Legislation in East Africa
By G. Spreen

Development Possibilities of the Pig and Poultry Industry in East Africa
By H. Späth

Comparative Investigations into the Efficiency of Utilizable Ruminants in Kenya
By Walter/Dennig

Farm Management Systems in Kenya
By v. Haugwitz/Thorwart

Problems of the Transport Economy in Tanzania with Special Reference to Road Transport
By R. Hofmeier (in English)

The Influence of Urbanization upon the Development of Rural Areas — with Special Reference to Jinja (Uganda) and Its Surroundings
By Gerken/Schubert/Brandt

The Interrelationship between Man, Nature and Economy: the Example of Madagascar
By W. Marquardt

The Implications of Tanzania's Administrative System for Her Economic Development
By K. v. Sperber (in English)

Autonomous Institutions in East African Agricultural Production
By H. Blume (in English)

Applied Research in East Africa and Its Influence on Economic Development
By M. Bohnet and H. Reichelt (in English)

Co-operatives in the Sudan: Their Characteristics, Functions and Suitability in the Socio-Economic Development Process
By M. Bardeleben

Mining and Regional Development in East Africa
By T. Möller

The Economico-Geographical Pattern of East Africa
By K. Engelhard

Iraqw Highland/Tanzania: Resource Analysis of an East African Highland and its Margins
By J. Schultz (in English)

Methods and Problems of Farm Management Surveys in Africa South of the Sahara
By H. Thorwart

The Mau-Mau Movement: Its Socio-Economic and Political Causes and Implications upon British Colonial Policy in Kenya and Africa
By J. Muriuki (in English)

Beef Production in East Africa with Special Reference to Semi-Arid Areas
By K. Meyn (in English)

The Requirements for the Means of Transport in East Africa with a View to the Economic Expansion of these Countries
By H. Milbers

Population Trends and Migration in Malawi with Special Reference to the Central Region of Lake Malawi
By U. Weyl

Population Trends in Kenya and Their Implications for Social Services in Rural and Urban Areas
By M. Meck (in English)

Education's Contribution to Economic Development of a Tropical Agrarian Country — the Example of Tanzania
By H. Desselberger

Agrarian Patterns in Ethiopia and their Implications for Economic Growth
By V. Janssen

Development of Law in Malawi
By F. v. Benda-Beckmann (in German)